The Complete Idiot

Emoticon Table

Here's a list of the most common emoticons you'll see used in online chat.

Symbols to Type	What It Means	Symbols to Type	What It Means
:)	Smiling	;-)	Winking
:-)	Smiling, with a nose	8-)	Wearing glasses
:.)	Small-skewed-button-nosed smiley	B-)	Wearing cool shades
		{(:-)	Wearing a toupee
:->	Ironic or devious smile	I-o	Yawning
:-(	Frowning	I^o	Snoring
:-<	Really sad	X-(	Dead
>:-(	Someone mad or annoyed	C=:-)	I'm a chef
:-c	Bummed out	*<:-){	I'm Santa Claus
:-I	Grim	@>—,—`-	A rose
:-D	Laughing	{{{hugs}}}	Hugs, obviously (can substitute names)
:-o	Shouting		
:-O	Shouting loudly	<g>	A grin (can substitute other actions)
:-p	Sticking out my tongue		
:-*	Puckering for a kiss	[thump]	An action
:-x	My lips are sealed	:::thump:::	Also an action
:-{}	I have a moustache	xxooxxoo	Love (or hugs) & kisses
:-()	Big mouth (when you feel you rambled on)		

Acronym Table

Here's a list of the most common acronyms used in online chat.

Symbols to Type	What It Means	Symbols to Type	What It Means
AKA	Also known as	LOL	Laughing out loud
AFK	Away from keyboard	MOTD	Message of the day
BAK	Back at keyboard	NRN	No response necessary
BRB	Be right back	OTOH	On the other hand
BTW	By the way	PITA	Pain in the a**
CU	See you	PMJI	Pardon my jumping in
CUL	See you later	POV	Point of view
FAQ	Frequently asked question(s)	ROTFL	Rolling on the floor laughing
FWIW	For what it's worth	ROTFLOLPIMP	Rolling on the floor, laughing out loud, peeing in my pants
FYA	For your amusement		
FYI	For your information		
GMTA	Great minds think alike	RSN	Real soon now
GR&D	Grinning, running, and ducking	RTM	Read the manual (or message)
HHOK	Ha ha, only kidding	SIFOTCN	Sitting in front of the computer naked
HHOS	Ha ha, only serious	TIA	Thanks in advance
IAC	In any case	TTFN	Ta ta for now
IMO	In my opinion	TTYL	Talk to you later
IMHO	In my humble opinion	WB	Welcome back
IMNSHO	In my not-so-humble opinion	WTG	Way to go
		WTH	What the h*** (or heck)
IMAO	In my arrogant opinion		
IOW	In other words		

tear here

que

Handy IRC Commands

How about a list of commands for chatting on the IRC channels?

Command to Type	What It Does
/list	Lists all the current IRC channels (to limit the list to channels with 5 or more people on them, type **/list -min 5**)
/who #30plus	Lists the users in the #30plus channel
/nick ChatIdiot	Changes your nickname to ChatIdiot (up to 9 characters)
/join #chatzone	Puts you into the #chatzone channel
/whois Spazz	Locates details about the user nicknamed Spazz
/whowas Spazz	If the user logged off, this command tells you who the user was
/msg Spazz Hi there	Sends a private message (saying "Hi there") to the user named Spazz
/query Spazz	Sends all your next messages to Spazz without having to keep typing /msg Spazz for every line
/ignore Spazz all	Ignores all incoming private messages from Spazz
/ignore Spazz none	Turns the ignore feature off
/kick #chatzone Spazz	Kicks Spazz off the #chatzone channel (this only works if you have channel-operator status)
/leave #chatzone	Leave the #chatzone channel
/quit	Exits all the IRC channels you're on, and leaves IRC
/quit See you later	Exits the IRC channels but leaves a message behind saying "See you later"
/me gets up and does a happy dance	Creates the message "ChatIdiot gets up and does a happy dance"

E-mail Addressing

With all the different commercial services and their connections to the Internet, it's easy to send e-mail to your friends, regardless of which service they're using. But it's a little confusing sometimes, so here's a handy table showing how to e-mail friends on the various commercial services.

Sending E-mail To/From	Steps to Take
To CompuServe	Type the user's ID number from CompuServe in the address, such as **12345.678@compuserve.com** (be sure to change the ID number's comma into a period)
From CompuServe	Use the keyword **GO MAIL** to open the mail area. To send e-mail to a user on another service, you'll have to use the prefix **internet:**. To mail to Elvis Presley at America Online, use the address **internet:epresley@aol.com**
To America Online	Address mail to the user's name: **epresley@aol.com**
From America Online	Type the keyword **INTERNET** to open the Internet mail gateway. Address your e-mail using normal Internet procedure: **epresley@**_service_**.com** (substitute the site you're sending to for _service_.com)
To PRODIGY	Type the user's PRODIGY ID number, such as **123ABCD@prodigy.com**
From PRODIGY	Type the jump word **MAIL MANAGER**, then address your mail like any normal Internet site: **epresley@**_service_**.com** (substitute the site you're sending to for _service_.com)
To GEnie	Type user's name, **epresley@genie.geis.com**
From GEnie	Type the keyword **MAIL**, then address your mail as follows: **epresley@**_service_**.com@inet#** (GEnie uses a different Internet mail address, so don't forget the additional **@inet#**)
To DELPHI	Type user's name, **epresley@delphi.com**
From DELPHI	Type the **GO MAIL** command, then type MAIL at the prompt. Address mail as follows: **internet"epresley@**_service_**.com"** (you gotta have those quotation marks in to make it work)

The Complete IDIOT'S GUIDE TO Sex, Lies, and Online Chat

by Sherry Kinkoph

que

A Division of Macmillan Computer Publishing
A Prentice Hall Macmillan Company
201 W. 103rd Street, Indianapolis, IN 46290 U.S.A.

©1995 by Que® Corporation

All rights reserved. No part of this book shall be reproduced, stored in a retrieval system, or transmitted by any means, electronic, mechanical, photocopying, recording, or otherwise, without written permission from the publisher. No patent liability is assumed with respect to the use of the information contained herein. While every precaution has been taken in the preparation of this book, the publisher and author assume no responsibility for errors or omissions. Neither is any liability assumed for damages resulting from the use of the information contained herein. For information, address Que Corporation, 201 West 103rd Street, Indianapolis, IN 46290.

International Standard Book Number: 1-56761-595-3

Library of Congress Catalog Card Number: 94-073199

98 97 96 95   8 7 6 5 4 3 2 1

Interpretation of the printing code: the rightmost double-digit number is the year of the book's first printing; the rightmost single-digit number is the number of the book's printing. For example, a printing code of 95-1 shows that this copy of the book was printed during the first printing of the book in 1995.

Screen reproductions in this book were created by means of the program Collage Plus from Inner Media, Inc., Hollis, NH.

Printed in the United States of America

To all the wonderful people I've met online: Phydeaux, Tara, CyblRR, MusicWiz, Nodsalot, Fido Dido, JamesD7406, Zapata, Huser, Mizzer, Jang74... and everybody else who ever chatted with me unknowingly.

Publisher
Roland Elgey

Vice President and Publisher
Marie Butler-Knight

Editorial Services Director
Elizabeth Keaffaber

Publishing Manager
Barry Pruett

Managing Editor
Michael Cunningham

Development Editor
Melanie Palasia

Production Editor
Kelly Oliver

Manuscript Editor
Barry Childs-Helton

Book Designer
Barbara Kordesh

Cover Designer
Karen Ruggles

Illustrator
Judd Winick

Indexer
Bront Davis

Production Team
*Angela Calvert, Dan Caparo, Brad Chinn, Kim Cofer,
Dave Eason, Jennifer Eberhardt, David Garratt, Joe Millay,
Erika Millen, Beth Rago, Karen Walsh, Robert Wolf*

Special thanks to Scott Parker for ensuring the technical accuracy of this book.

Contents at a Glance

Part 1: Straight Talk About Chatting — 1

1. The Least You Need to Know About Online Chat — 3
   The top ten reasons for using a modem.

2. What's All the Fuss About? — 7
   Finally, someone (me) tells you what the big deal is about this online chat phenomenon.

3. Online Options: What's the Difference? — 19
   The nitty-gritty details about where online chat can be found.

4. Getting Plugged In — 33
   Tips for how you can get up and running online.

5. Exploring Online Services — 45
   See what the various big online services look like and how to use them.

6. Finding Your Way Onto the Internet — 69
   Get the low-down on the Internet and how to chat on IRC.

7. BBSs: Small Group Chatting — 83
   Discover the joys of using BBSs and where to find some near you.

Part 2: Rules and Regulations — 93

8. A Word About Cybermanners — 95
   Learn all about the intricacies of online etiquette.

9. Getting Emotional with Emoticons — 105
   Find out how to use goofy smiley faces in your own online communications.

10. Deciphering Cryptic Online Codes — 113
    A definitive discussion on using online abbreviations.

Part 3: What's Going On Out There? — 119

11. Sex, Lies, and Other Online Motivations — 121
    See what really motivates people to go online and chat with complete strangers.

12. Pick a Sex, Any Sex — 141
    A first-hand account of what happens in online chat.

13. The World of Intimate Conversations — 153
    Discover the secrets of sending personal messages.

14	Chatting and Kids: Do They Go Together?	163
	See what's going on in the kids' and teens' chat channels.	
15	Chatting for Fun or Profit	175
	Learn how to use online chat to network, and find out ways you can advertise.	
16	Online Dangers	185
	Life-saving details about the ugly side of online chat.	
17	Online Troubleshooting	191
	Tips for what to do when things go wrong.	

Part 4: Confessions of an Online Junkie 201

18	How to Become an Online Addict	203
	Take a look at the addictive side of online chat, including horrible billing experiences.	
19	The Good, the Bad, and the Ugly	211
	Lots of advice for using online chat and avoiding the icky stuff.	
20	Rating Online Chat	219
	Find out who has the best chat and how you can save money online.	
	The Important Extra Stuff	227
	Speak Like a Geek: The Complete Archive	259
	Ye old glossary.	
	Index	263
	Where you look stuff up.	

Contents

Part 1: Straight Talk About Chatting — 1

1 The Least You Need to Know About Online Chat — 3

10. You can chat on BBSs, commercial online services, or on the Internet. 3
9. You have to have some sort of connection to chat. 3
8. When you first start out, it's best to watch what's going on before joining in. 4
7. You'll find a wide variety of subjects discussed online. 4
6. Mind your cyber Ps and Qs. 4
5. If you're going to talk the talk, you've gotta learn the lingo. 4
4. Not everything is as it seems. 5
3. Get a handle on your handle. 5
2. Talk is not always cheap. 5
1. Online chatting is as simple as talking… almost. 6

2 What's All the Fuss About? — 7

What Is Online Chatting? 8
Where Do You Find Online Chatting? 10
How Does Chatting Work? 12
How Much Does It Cost? 14
Who Exactly Participates in This Online Chatting? 15
So What's the Big Attraction About Online Chatting? 16

3 Online Options: What's the Difference? — 19

Online Services: The Big Players 20
   What Do They Offer? 20
   Who Runs These Services? 21
   So, How Would I Use a Service? 22
To Be or Not to BBS? 22
   Who Runs These BBSs? 23
   The Many Faces of BBSs 24
   How Do I Get Onto a BBS? 24

Internet: The Open Road on the
  Information Highway 25
    What's So Confusing About It? 25
  Online Options: Pros and Cons 27
  Gee, You've Got a Nice-Looking GUI 28

4 Getting Plugged In 33

  How Do I Start Talking—Fast? 34
    Modem Mayhem 34
    The Mind-Boggling World of Communications
      Software 36
  How Do I Sign Up and Sign On? 37
    Commercial Services: All It Takes Is a Credit Card 37
    The BBS Way: Fiddle with Your Software Settings 38
    Internet Sign-Up: Every Which Way But Loose 38
    When Do They Send a Bill? 39
  Get a Handle on Your Handle 40
    Handle History 40
    Where Do You Use Handles Online? 41
    What Handle Should I Use? 41

5 Exploring Online Services 45

  CompuServe 46
    How Do I Get Online with CompuServe? 47
    Logging Onto CompuServe 48
    Getting CIM 49
    Chatting with the CB Simulator 50
    How Much Is This Costing Me? 52
  America Online 52
    Logging Onto AOL 54
    Take Me to the Chatting Rooms 55
    Check, Please! 57
  PRODIGY 57
    Logging On with PRODIGY 58
    Welcome to Chat 59
    And the Grand Total Is? 61
  GEnie 61
    Summoning the GEnie 63
    Logging Onto GEnie 64

Chatting with GEnie 64
  Send Me a Bill 65
The Other Guys 65
  DELPHI 66
  ImagiNation Network 66
  eWorld 67

6 Finding Your Way Onto the Internet 69

How to Look for an On-Ramp 70
  Let's Go Over Those Internet Connections Again 72
Going Online with the Internet 75
  What Happens Next? 76
IRC 77
  Chatting the UNIX Way 77
  GUI Chatting on IRC 78
Other Chat Areas 79
  Just Plain talk 79
  How About YTalk? 80
  Windows Talking 80
  The Dirt on MUDs 80

7 BBSs: Small Group Chatting 83

How to Find a Chatty BBS 84
  Look Ma, No Software 85
  Who You Gonna Call? 86
How Do I Log On? 88
  Jumping Through Membership Hoops 89
  Finding Your Way to the Chat Area 90

Part 2: Rules and Regulations 93

8 A Word About Cybermanners 95

Minding Your Manners in Cyberspace 96
  The Rule-Makers 96
  You Are Not Alone 97
The Rules of the Road 98
  The Guidelines 98
  Online Etiquette Tips 99
  Newbie Help in Times of Trouble 102
When Cybermanners Go Bad 103

The Complete Idiot's Guide to Sex, Lies, and Online Chat

9 Getting Emotional with Emoticons — 105
What's with the Weird Symbols? — 106
The Smiley Table — 107
How Do I Use Them? — 108
Other Online Actions — 110

10 Deciphering Cryptic Online Codes — 113
What's with the Weird Words? — 114
The Acronym Table — 115
How Do I Use Them? — 117

Part 3: What's Going On Out There? — 119

11 Sex, Lies, and Other Online Motivations — 121
What Really IS Going On Out There? — 122
Just Shootin' the Breeze — 122
Winning Friends and Influencing People — 124
Don't Mind Me, I'm Just Browsing — 126
Get a Hobby — 127
Sending Out an S.O.S. — 128
Flirting — 129
Looking for Love — 130
Then There's Cybersex — 131
Living an Online Lie — 134
Flaming for Fun — 137
Group Discussions — 138
Putting It All in Perspective — 138

12 Pick a Sex, Any Sex — 141
Is Gender Even an Issue Online? — 142
Setting Up Your Profile — 142
Logging On as a Male — 144
Logging On as a Female — 147
Try the Genderless Approach — 151
In Conclusion — 152

13 The World of Intimate Conversations — 153

Is There Somewhere We Can Be Alone Together? 154
   What Do People Put in Private Messages? 156
Using the Private Message Feature 158
   Private Messaging on IRC 158
   Instant Messages on the Commercial Services 160
   BBS Private Message Sending 161
You Can Always Send E-Mail 161

14 Chatting and Kids: Do They Go Together? — 163

Should Kids Chat? 164
   Sorting the Kids from the Adults 165
   What's It Like Talking to Kids? 166
Kid Chat: What Is It? 167
   What Goes On on a Kids' Channel? 167
   What Are the Teens Up To? 170
Safegard Your Kids 171
   Is Kid Chat Safe? 171
   How to Make Your Kids Safe Online 171

15 Chatting for Fun or Profit — 175

Business on the Net and Beyond 176
   Newsgroups and Boards 176
   FAQs 179
   Advertising on the Net 179
   Can I E-Mail Everyone Instead? 181
Networking Among Newsgroups and Boards 181
   Survey Says 181
   Job-Seeking Tips 182
Finding Business Chat on the Chat Lines 182
   Enroll in Online School 183

16 Online Dangers — 185

It's a Jungle Out There 186
   Guard Personal Information 186
   Keep Your Passwords Safe 186
   Watch Out for Free Offers 187

The Complete Idiot's Guide to Sex, Lies, and Online Chat

      Don't Get Involved with Illegal
         Software Distribution 187
      Get Virus Protection 188
   More Heinous Dangers 188
   Handling Online Harassment 189

17 Online Troubleshooting — 191

   Hey—Something's Wrong! 192
      My Screen's Stuck 192
      I Just Got Thrown Off! 193
      Speed Needs 194
      Something's Wrong with My Phone Line 195
      Other Problems 195
         My modem's lights don't come on (external). 196
         The screen says "Device not present" or
         "CTS signal not detected." 196
         Nothing happens after my modem dials. 196
         My modem won't call at its fastest speed. 196
         When I connect to a BBS, I get gobbledygook
           on my screen. 196
         I see strange characters instead of the BBS
           menu when I call. 196
         My online text is missing letters. 197
         I'm seeing two of everything I type. 197
         I can't see anything I'm typing. 197
   How to Holler for Help 197

Part 4: Confessions of an Online Junkie — 201

18 How to Become an Online Addict — 203

   Confessions of an Online Addict 204
      I'm Exaggerating... Sort Of 204
      Just How Addictive Is It? 206
      Seek Treatment 206
   What to Do When They Close Your Account 207
      Online Billing Horror Stories 207
      So What if You're Addicted
         and They Close Your Account? 208

19 The Good, the Bad, and the Ugly — 211

- My Best Chatting Advice 212
  - Lurk First 212
  - Try Different Channels 212
  - Try the Less-Populated Channels 213
  - There's More Chat During Peak Times 213
  - Find Things You Have in Common
    with Other Users 214
  - Use Humor 214
  - Keep Up Relationships Through E-Mail 215
  - Take Time to Help Other Newbies 215
- Weeding Out the Bad Stuff 215
  - Learn to Handle Online Rejection 215
  - Online Rudeness Is a Fact of Life 216
  - Learn to Deal with Cyberviolators 216
  - Expect to Encounter Some Private Messages 217

20 Rating Online Chat — 219

- Rank and File 220
  - The Best and Worst of the Commercial Services 220
  - The Up-and-Comers 221
  - The Best Places to Chat 221
  - The Worst Places to Chat 222
- Top-Ten Lists 222
  - Ten Ways to Save Money Online 223
  - The Ten Most Popular Opening Lines 223
    - Top Ten Pickup Lines (Male) 224
    - Top Ten Pickup Lines (Female) 224
  - Ten Ways to End an Online Conversation 225
  - Ten Ways to Start an Online Fight 225
  - Ten Ways to Respond to Instant Messages 226

The Important Extra Stuff — 227

- UNIX Command Summary 227
  - Understanding UNIX Commands 228
  - UNIX Command Table 228
  - Some Useful IRC Commands 229

Phone Numbers to Reach All the Big Online
  Services Fast 229
    CompuServe 230
    America Online 231
    PRODIGY 232
    GEnie 233
A List of Internet Service Providers 234
A List of BBSs 235
Tips and Tricks for Buying a Modem 237
  How to Read a Modem Box 237
  Ye Olde Standards 238
    Bell Standards 238
    The MNP Standards 238
    CCITT Standards 239
    Speed Bumps 240
    Summing Up Standards 240
  Who's Hayes and Why Are All the Other
    Modems Talking to Him? 242
  Does It Fax? 242
  Miscellaneous Modem Features 242
  Where to Shop 243
  Money-Saving Tips 244
    Free Software? 245
    Ya Gotta Have a Manual 245
    Watch Out for Warranties 245
    Does It Include an Online Service Hookup? 245
    Brand Names to Look For 246
  Make a Shopping List 246
Shopping for Software 246
  Software Features You Need to Know About 247
    Terminal Mode 247
    Settings Mode 248
    File Transfer 248
    The Proper Protocols 248
    It's Not in the Script 249
    Miscellaneous Features 250
  What's Hot and What's Not in
    Communications Software 250
    How to Read the Software Box 250
    Your Modem Came with Software? 251

Searching for Software You Didn't
    Know You Had 252
  Where to Shop for Software 253
Feeding and Caring for Your Modem 253
  Spills, Chills, and Dust Pills 253
  The Surge Splurge 254
Going One-on-One, Modem-to-Modem 255
  How Does It Work? 255
    Host or Remote? 255
    Practical Parameters 256
    Making the Call 256
  When Things Go Wrong 257
Quit Reading This Book and Go Online 258

Speak Like a Geek: The Complete Archive   259

Index   263

Preface

Help Me—I Just Want to Communicate!

What's the matter? Heard about the chat phenomenon, but can't figure it out yourself? Can't find your way online? Have you taken a wrong turn on the information highway? Don't dismay; this computer technology can be very confusing—especially such a hot topic as online chat. The technology seems to be changing overnight, and the world of online communications is no exception. Every time you turn around, there's a new service to join or a faster modem to buy. The worst part is that nagging feeling that you're missing out on something. The point is, this stuff can really give you a headache.

Isn't it about time you picked up a book that can really help you sort it all out? Believe it or not, you are holding a book that can soothe your technological troubles away: *The Complete Idiot's Guide to Sex, Lies, and Online Chat* is the cure you've been looking for. In this book, I'll give you the low-down on how online chat really works (including tips for finding chat channels on BBSs, commercial services, and the Internet) and plenty of advice for jumping into it all yourself. You'll also discover the mysterious motivations that bring people online, such as cybersex and secret online personas, plus tips for dealing with the people you meet (like sending private messages and flaming). You'll get a thorough grounding in netiquette and learn how to cultivate your own online relationships. If you ever wanted to find out what was going on online, this is the book to tell you all about it.

So don't waste another minute being tormented by technology and wondering about the online chat phenomenon—read this book for instant relief. (Plop, plop, fizz, fizz.) Aren't you starting to feel better already?

Sherry Kinkoph

Introduction

I take it you're curious about online chat? That's why you picked up this book, right? (Or was it the catchy title that caught your eye?) Maybe you've been hearing about the online world and the Internet, or reading about how you can meet people electronically. Or maybe you're looking for an online romance, or just to meet up with other online users who share the same interests. Perhaps you want to connect to friends and relatives using your modem and an online service. In any case, trying to make heads or tails out of online communications can be a little overwhelming. Don't worry, this book can help. Welcome to *The Complete Idiot's Guide to Sex, Lies, and Online Chat*. Quite a title, eh? I knew it would grab your attention.

Let's get one thing perfectly clear, up front and center—I know you're not an idiot. Sure, this ever-changing computer technology can make you *feel* like an idiot at times, but get used to it. This computer stuff is changing constantly—*constantly*, I tell you. There's no way anyone can keep up with it—and who would want to anyway? It's evolving faster than a Steven Spielberg plot. So just relax, you don't need the stress of trying to become a modem guru or a communications expert overnight. Sit back and learn what you need, when you need it—without all the mind-numbing technical ying-yang.

The topic at hand is online chat. This book will explain all about communicating in cyberspace—including how to hook up with an online service, where to look for a good BBS, and tips for finding an on-ramp to the information superhighway. This book covers everything from what you need to get online to what you should do when you get there. You'll discover how to find all the hip chat areas, and get a first-hand account of what actually goes on out there (you're dying to know, right?). But that's not all—for a limited time only, we'll also tell you how to avoid online dangers, troubleshoot when your lines get crossed, and traipse through the intricacies of online etiquette.

As with anything centered around computers, online communications can be a little intimidating. There's a lot to know about the subject. Things like what to do when someone flames you, how to pick a good handle, and how to send an instant message. Yes, it's a whole new lingo to deal with. But that's why this book will come in handy. You'll learn this lingo and master online chat all at the same time. Plus, you'll have fun doing it. That's right—I said *fun*. Learning about the various paths to online communications doesn't have to be so technical and boring, you know. Lighten up and laugh a little!

How Is This Book Going to Help?

Basically, this book will help you in the following ways:

- ➤ It will explain all the basics you need to know about going online. (Don't for a minute think you have to know *everything* about this stuff anyway.)
- ➤ It will clarify costs and expenditures for the various services, examine the different GUIs available, and even give you some important information about modems and modem software.
- ➤ It will take you through the necessary steps for logging onto BBSs, commercial services, and the Internet.
- ➤ It will give you the lowdown on who's online and what they're doing.
- ➤ It will open up a world of possibilities as you learn how to use online chat to meet people from around the globe.

How Do You Use This Book?

Well, I suggest you read the parts that interest you, or that you want to know more about. There's no need to read this from cover to cover, unless you've got some major free time on your hands, or can't find anything else to entertain you (like when your cable TV goes out). The book is divided into four sections.

Part 1 is all about where to find online chat. It covers the nitty-gritty, what-are-all-these-places-anyway stuff. It explains the differences between commercial services (like CompuServe and America Online), BBSs (bulletin board systems), and the infamous Internet, as well as how to sign up for an account with each.

Part 2 will help you with the rules and regulations that govern online life. You'll find chapters detailing the ins and outs of online behavior, how to convey emotions in your text-based conversations, and how to work bizarre acronyms into your live discussions to make yourself sound like a seasoned pro.

Introduction

Part 3 takes you through the various scenarios you'll encounter online, including details about what it's like to log on as a female, a male, and a genderless person. This section explores what's really happening online, and what kinds of things you'll encounter in your own online adventures. Yes, this is also where I tell you about cybersex (I could tell you were wondering about that).

Part 4 gives you tips for saving money online, suggestions for other methods of online communication, and advice for avoiding online addiction (it can happen to you!).

In explaining all of this information, there are times you'll need to type something in. When this happens, you'll see a change in book conventions. Anything you need to type in will appear like this:

Type this in

If there's any variable information to be typed in, such as your own names or figures, it will appear in italics like this:

Type this *number* in

In addition, you'll find extra boxed information scattered throughout the book to help you with terminology, boring technical background, shortcuts, and other tips. You certainly don't have to read these little boxes, although I did work awfully hard putting them together for you (and will be *crushed* if you don't read them...). But if you want to understand more about a topic, you'll find them very handy.

> **Look! A Shaded Box with a Geek in It!**
>
> These boxes will contain technical twaddle that may make you drowsy. Read them only if you're planning to appear on *Jeopardy!* (the game show for people who wish they'd been born computers) or just want some geeky background information about the topic.

> **Another Shaded Box!** You'll find easy-to-understand definitions of computer terms, tips for shortcuts, and warnings and cautions in these boxes to help keep you "online" and out of trouble!

Okay. That's everything about this book. If you bought it already, you're all set to get going. If you haven't bought the book, but are one of those people who reads the introduction before making a purchase, then stop wasting time and go pay for it before the store clerk starts giving you the evil eye.

Acknowledgements

Yes, yes, yes... here's the part where I thank all the members of the Academy for awarding me. Special thanks to Barry Pruett for believing that this idea could actually make a good book and for recognizing a hip thing when he sees it. Thanks to Marie Butler-Knight for daring to publish it. Thanks to Melanie Palaisia for making sure it was interesting to read, and to Barry Childs-Helton for making sure it was grammatically acceptable. Also, thanks to Kelly Oliver for her enthusiasm about the subject matter and her efforts to get it into production. And... (good grief, when will she stop?) to all the wonderful production people who slave away at these computer books day and night to get them to the printer. And... (someone please shut her up!) to Scott Parker, the technical editor, for slogging through it all and making sure it was correct. Let's see, I think that's everybody. No, wait, I forgot Joe Kraynak for adding to my silly top ten list of pickup lines... okay, that's all. (She walks off stage, clutching her newly won Oscar and weeping uncontrollably.)

Trademarks

All terms mentioned in this book that are known to be or are suspected of being trademarks or service marks have been appropriately capitalized. Que Corporation cannot attest to the accuracy of this information. Use of a term in this book should not be regarded as affecting the validity of any trademark or service mark.

Part 1
Straight Talk About Chatting

Pssst… over here. You have a real serious look on your face, like you're trying to figure something out. Oh, I get it… you're looking for information about online chat! Maybe I can help—tell me what you want to know. What is online chatting? Where did it come from? Why is it here? How do you start doing it? Good grief, you're full of questions, aren't you? Well, you've come to the right place. In this first Part of the book, you'll find answers to many of these questions. You'll learn all the nitty-gritty details about going online to chat—including costs, tips about billing and sign-on procedures, how to find an online service, and how to drive down the information superhighway without getting a speeding ticket. Sound like fun? There's only one way to find out: turn the page. And quit looking so serious!

JERRY REALLY GETS INTO THE ONLINE CHAT ROOMS.

Chapter 1

The Least You Need to Know About Online Chat

Welcome to the first chapter. I'm sure you're really curious about this concept called *online chatting* and what it's all about. It's about talking to other computer users with your own computer through a modem or network connection. Sounds intriguing, doesn't it? Let's stop right here and run through a list of the top ten things you need to know about our subject matter before you dive into the rest of the book. Mind you, as you read through this list, you'll come across terms that don't mean diddly to you. Don't despair, I'll explain everything in the chapters to come.

Ladies and gentlemen... (could we have a drum roll here, please?)... the top ten things to know about online chatting:

10. You can chat on BBSs, commercial online services, or on the Internet.

In case you were wondering *where* all this chatting takes place, it's found on bulletin board systems (called BBSs), commercial online services (such as PRODIGY, CompuServe, or America Online), and on the Internet (a giant network of networks). Once you establish accounts or connections to these resources, you can go online and chat with fellow users anytime. You can also chat (so to speak) via message-posting and e-mail. I'll tell you all about finding these cyberspace locations in Chapters 5, 6, and 7.

9. You have to have some sort of connection to chat.

Obviously, you and your computer must be hooked up to the chatting source in order to chat (what astounding logic, eh?). You can make such connections with a modem, or through a network. For example, to talk in the Chat areas on the PRODIGY service, you have to call them up (assuming you have an account) with your computer's modem and establish a link in order to engage in online conversations. Sound complicated? It's not. I'll tell you more about connecting in Chapters 3 and 4.

8. When you first start out, it's best to watch what's going on before joining in.

Being the wise consumer that you are, you should first scope out the chatting area you connect to. Lurk around and read what everyone else is saying. Find out what they're talking about—if it's a subject you're interested in, or if it's appropriate for you. Once you feel comfortable, then dive in and start adding your own input. As usual, there are exceptions to this tip, but you'll know 'em when you run across 'em. Read all of Part 3 for more details about jumping into online conversations—and what to expect.

7. You'll find a wide variety of subjects discussed online.

Just what do people chat about online? Everything under the sun... you'll find conversations going on about all manner of topics and ideas, as well as lots of people just shootin' the breeze. It's not uncommon to go online at any given moment and find flirtatious chatting, serious political debates, simple let's-gather-by-the-water-cooler discussions, technical information exchanges, or all-out weird stuff for the professionally deviant—oh yeah, and there's also cybersex, although that sometimes falls into the previously mentioned category. It's a free-for-all in cyberspace when it comes to topics to talk about. Because it's so open, you really need some groundwork before venturing out. Chapters 11 and 12 of this book give you a first-hand account of what goes on out there. Chapter 16 even discusses the dangers you'll find online.

6. Mind your cyber Ps and Qs.

Just because you can talk about anything under the sun doesn't mean there aren't *some* rules to follow. There is a certain etiquette online, and depending on the online service or area you're using, different proprietary standards apply. It's not exactly all-out anarchy, you know. The people you communicate with can't see you or hear your voice, but that doesn't mean you lose all sense of diplomacy or common courtesy. For a rundown of online manners, take a look at Chapter 8.

5. If you're going to talk the talk, you've gotta learn the lingo.

As with any subculture that rises from new technology, there's a lingo to learn. If you're going to be hip online (and who wouldn't want to be?) and with computers in general, you need to know how to talk the talk. In the case of online chatting, the lingo involves emoticons and acronyms. *Emoticons* are used to express emotion (like humor) online. Since cyber-chatting is expressed through typed words, it's often necessary to add symbols suggesting facial expressions. You'll learn about these in Chapter 9. There's also a set of acronyms that you'll see frequently sprinkled in online conversations. Chapter 10 explains what each of these mean—and how to use them in your own conversations.

4. Not everything is as it seems.

Now, get this straight—*nobody* can see you or hear your voice online. You don't always know who you're really talking to. Part of the appeal of online conversations is that you can be whoever you want to be; you don't always have to be *you*—you can be anybody. Although a lot of cyberspace inhabitants don't like this aspect of online chatting (and would prefer that you be who you say you are), it's still an appealing part of online communications. The downside of this, however, is that the nice guy (or gal) you struck up a conversation with might not really be a guy (or gal) at all—I think you get the picture. On the other hand, that guy (or gal) you're chatting with may, in real life, be a big celebrity or something. You never know in cyberspace! Chapter 11 tells you how to handle these situations when they arise.

3. Get a handle on your handle.

An important part of going online with many services (including BBSs, commercial services, or the Internet) is choosing a handle. Remember the CB craze back in the '70s? You installed a CB (Citizen's Band radio) in your car or truck and used it to talk to complete strangers while driving down the open road—remember all that? That's what online chatting is like today. It can be just like the CB craze—you can make up a nickname to identify yourself when you go online. They call these nicknames "handles." Handles play a crucial role in your online experience, as you'll see in Chapters 4 and 12.

2. Talk is not always cheap.

When it comes to online communications, your connections can cost money. When you sign up with a commercial online service, there are fees to be paid. Some services designate the chatting feature as an extra service and make you pay more to use it. Others charge by the amount of time you spend connected to their service. You really need to be aware of the costs involved, and you need to know what to expect in your own bill-paying. Chapters 2, 4, and 5–7 go over costs involved with online chatting. Chapter 20 even offers some tips for saving money.

1. Online chatting is as simple as talking... almost.

Finally, the most important thing you need to know about online chatting is this: it's as easy as talking... that's what makes it so much fun! Everybody likes to talk, or *would* like to when they can get a word in edgewise. Online chatting is talking... using your computer instead of your mouth. Rather than vocalizing your thoughts and ideas, you type them instead. Best of all, you don't even have to be a speed typist. You can talk to people all over the globe with your online connections. So what are you waiting for? The whole world is at your keyboarding fingertips—get going!

Chapter 2

What's All the Fuss About?

In This Chapter

- ➤ Online chatting defined and explained
- ➤ Find out where you can chat
- ➤ Learn how much chatting costs
- ➤ Some compelling arguments about our sociological need to communicate with each other

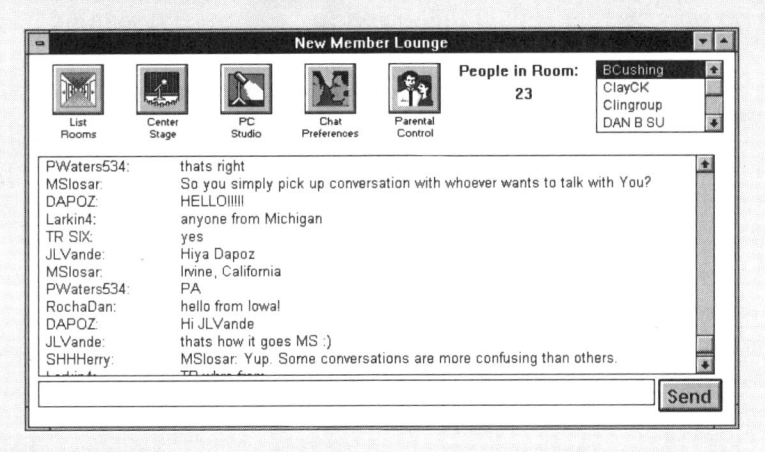

Part 1 ➤ *Straight Talk About Chatting*

Online chatting is hip. In fact, it's probably the hippest thing you can do with your computer since they invented the printer (or screen savers—whichever *you* think is more hip). Everyone's talking about going online, surfing the Net, and meeting people. You'll find magazine and newspaper articles from around the globe covering this new phenomenon. Thousands upon thousands of people log on to BBSs, commercial services, and the infamous Internet every day to find out what's going on and to strike up conversations with fellow cyberspace travelers. Even celebrities, ranging from Rush Limbaugh to Howard Stern, are cruising this electronic highway and hailing its merits to anyone who'll listen.

Why is it so hip? That's what I'm about to tell you in this chapter.

> **What's This "Cyberspace" Thing?**
>
> You'd better get used to seeing this word a lot, both now and in the future. *Cyberspace* is one of those trendy little catch-words for describing the vast electronic domain that includes the Internet and all the various network connections and services. Any time you see the word "cyber" in front of something, it's usually describing a computer-related thing or activity. It's also a snappy way to describe the various online areas, so by all means, use the word as much as possible to impress people who aren't as computer-literate as you are.

What Is Online Chatting?

How can I possibly describe something so exciting, so vast, and so mind-boggling? Online chatting is a whole new way of communicating. It's radical, educational, and inspirational. It's action-packed, weird, fascinating, and exhilarating. It's also very addictive. How do I know all this? My name is Sherry, and I'm an online junkie.

I was online for about month before I discovered chatting. The very first commercial online service (more about these later) I tried was CompuServe. I started using the service like everybody else—checking out features like forums, looking at news reports, downloading files, and so on. One day, I stumbled onto CompuServe's chatting feature, called *CB Simulator* (a reference to the '70s Citizen's Band radio craze). As I wandered around the feature, I found all kinds of conversations going on, right before my very eyes. It was absolutely mesmerizing. The conversations were from actual people logged on at the same time I was. People from New Zealand to Alaska were talking up a storm, as if they were in the same room together. It didn't take long for me to jump into the conversations as well, and from then on... I was hooked.

So what *exactly* is online chatting? Good question. Basically, online chatting is talking with other computer users through your own computer. Using your modem or a network hook-up, you can contact other computers that can access BBSs, commercial online services, and networked Internet computers, and "chat" with other people who are using them too. But it's not your normal method of conversing—it's communicating via your keyboard. *What?* Instead of opening your mouth and uttering words, you use the computer keyboard to type your thoughts on the computer screen for anyone else to read and respond to. Pretty cool, eh?

There are several ways you can chat with everybody out there in cyberspace. One way to chat is by posting messages on electronic *message boards* and *forums*. These are areas on an online service, such as CompuServe, where people who have similar interests gather to leave notes for each other to read. You can also chat by sending *electronic mail* (called *e-mail* for short) messages back and forth to other users. This is a more traditional form of correspondence, like letter-writing.

Both message posting and e-mail are great ways to talk to others online, but they take a lot of time and energy to do; you have to log on, compose a message, then *post* it or send it. You won't get an immediate response, either. You may have to log back on in a day or so and see if there's a response to your posted note or e-mail message. But hey, it's still communication, right?

What's a Message Board?

It's an area online where you can post messages or notes for others to read. I suppose you could think of it as a piece of electronic corkboard with lots of push pins and thumb tacks. Most message boards are set up for specific topics and interests; for example, you might find such topics as photography or computer games. Message boards have different names on different online systems. BBSs and commercial services may call these areas *clubs*, *forums*, or just plain *message boards*. Internet users call these areas *newsgroups*. Regardless of the name, the purpose is still the same—to leave messages for others to read and respond to. You'll find more details about using message boards as you keep reading.

By far, the hippest, hottest, most exciting method of online communication is *real-time chatting*. Real-time chatting means that your conversations happen now, in real time—no waiting. When you log onto a BBS, a commercial online service, or the Internet and find your way to the real-time chatting area, you can immediately start talking to

Part 1 ➤ *Straight Talk About Chatting*

> **E-mail (electronic mail):** Used to send personal correspondence to others who are online or who are using the same network system. It's similar to regular mail; you can use e-mail to send and receive messages. And guess what—there are no stamps involved.
>
> **Real time:** The actual time that is taking place now, even as you read this.

other people who are using that feature at the same time. Everything you type and send is immediately read by everyone else logged onto the chatting area. It's spontaneous, sometimes chaotic, and always tons of fun.

By now, some of you may be wondering, "What's the difference between online chatting and making a simple phone call?" There are several differences. For one thing, you usually know who you're talking to with a telephone call (except when it's a wrong number or those anonymous salespeople who call you while you're trying to eat dinner). With online chatting, you don't really know *who* you're talking to, at least at first. Initially, all you know about your online conversant is a name or handle (more on this in Chapter 4).

Another difference between phone calls and online chatting is that with a regular phone call, the person's voice on the other end of the line generally tells you whether it's a male or female you're conversing with. Not so with online chatting. There is no audible "voice" to give you a hint as to the gender of the person you're talking with. Often, online names or handles are misleading too. Just because the name on the screen says "Bob" doesn't necessarily mean it's a guy you're talking to. It could be woman, child, or an extra-terrestrial. You may never know!

Yet another difference is cost. A lot of people find it cheaper to talk to faraway friends and relatives online, rather than with a long-distance phone call. You can also chat online with lots of people at once, though I guess that's not very different from a conference telephone call (not that I can perform a conference call with my home phone anyway). However, the biggest difference between online chatting and phone chatting can be summed up in one three-letter word: F-U-N. I'm telling you, this online stuff is *major* fun. Oh sure, I know you can't understand it now, but just wait. Keep reading this book and you'll find out how fun online chatting really is.

Where Do You Find Online Chatting?

Another excellent question. Online chat can be found in a variety of places. Want to know where? Okay, I'll tell you. For starters, you can find chatting features among all the major commercial online services. A commercial online service is an electronic service that lets you to access data and share information. CompuServe, America Online, and PRODIGY are all examples of commercial online services. They offer such things as the

Chapter 2 ➤ *What's All the Fuss About?*

latest news, sports, and weather reports; clubs and forums for exchanging ideas; electronic shopping; and of course, real-time chatting. Commercial online services are available to anyone with a computer and a modem. The catch to commercial services, however, is that you have to pay the fee and set up an account in order to use the service. (You'll learn more about fees and accounts in Chapter 4.)

> **Commercial online service:** A service that offers you a variety of commercial features for your computer (such as news, sports information, electronic shopping, stock reports, and travel information) and access to databases of information and files—all for a fee, of course. You can connect to an online service using your modem.

Things work a little differently with BBSs. What the heck is a BBS? It's short for bulletin board system, and its name really says it all. A BBS is rather like an electronic bulletin board. BBSs are smaller in scale than the commercial services, and they cost less (many of them are free). You'll find a wide range of BBSs out there in cyberspace, ranging from technical support BBSs set up by hardware and software companies, to fun BBSs set up just for playing computer games. Others are simply run by one person out of a garage or basement for anyone to call up and access. All it takes is a modem to connect you to a BBS. What they offer varies greatly, too. Some BBSs are focused on specific hobbies, others are more general. But the most popular BBSs are those offering real-time chat. (I'll tell you more about these BBSs in Chapter 7.)

Another place to find chatting is the Internet. There's quite a buzz about the Internet (or *Net* for short) these days. It seems like everyone and his or her brother wants to get on the Net and check things out. Why? Because it's simply awesome. The Internet is thousands and thousands of inter-networked computers all around the globe. It's a network of many networks that are all connected so they can communicate with each other.

> **BBS:** Stands for *bulletin board system*, a smaller-scale online service that lets you call up with your modem and access files, games, technical information, and other features.
>
> **Internet:** A giant network of many interconnected computers. It's used to connect to computers all around the world and access information.

The individual networks that make up the Internet range from government departments to universities, businesses to libraries, and much more. If you are connected to the Internet, you can access archives, educational databases, medical resources, photographs, videos, and so on. You are also connected to other users, which means you can chat with them. Unlike commercial online services or BBSs, the Internet isn't owned by anyone. (So how do you hook up to it? I'll tell you in Chapter 6.)

11

Part 1 ➤ *Straight Talk About Chatting*

How Does Chatting Work?

I told you where to find online chatting, now let me tell you how it works. Once you've located the chatting feature of the particular service you want to use, you can immediately start talking. Most chatting features work similarly. You're presented with a blank screen or window that fills up with conversational lines. As it fills, the conversation scrolls along so you can keep reading it. Let me show you an example. Here's what the chatting feature looks like on America Online.

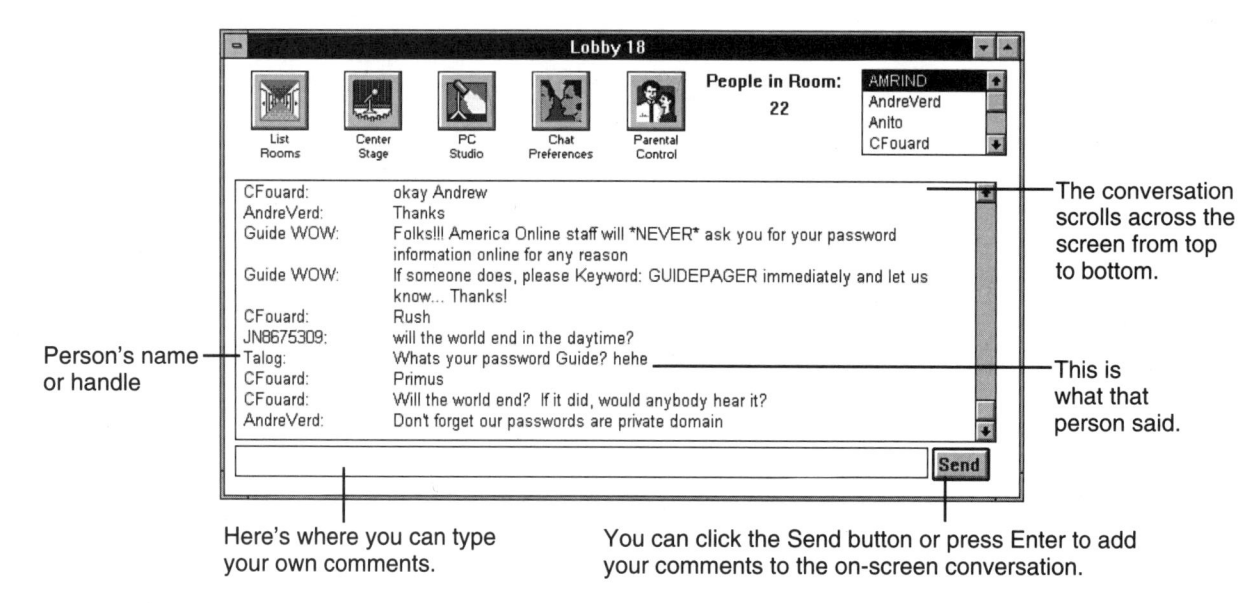

Here's an example of real-time chatting from America Online. It's pretty to look at, isn't it?

What do you think of that? Now take a look on the next page at how chatting appears on the Internet's IRC (Internet Relay Chat).

Chapter 2 ➤ *What's All the Fuss About?*

```
<Kimba> y=e**ipi
<poem> Peppr wwould never ignore You
<zooey> *sigh*
<sierra> imm: just finished dinner.. chilling our for 0.5 hours
<Bob34> howya doin Sarge?
<Peppr> Right Herb...I wouldnt'
<zooey> *sigh*
* Albundy proposes to ZOOEY. Hehehhe
<immigrant> zooey- im in the middle of franney and zooey  right now :)
*** Sulu (~C617331@128.206.2.2) has joined channel #30plus
<Kimba> Peppr's ignoring folk
<Kimba> Peppr's ignofing flok
<mfp> Kimba is back.....yahoo
<mfp> Sulululululululululul
<Albundy> Sulu!!!!!!!!!! my love.
<Prism> bye, all.
*** me3 (dagec@abc.abcde.wfull.edu) has joined channel #30plus
<zooey> immigrant  aren't you that yallie i was talking to
<me3> hi all
<poem> zooey is 29
<Kimba> SULU!!!!
<Peppr> ARGH!!!!
*** mickk has left channel #30plus
<Kimba> mfp!!!!!!!!!!!!!!!!!!
<Salgak> hmm.... zooey is definitiely 29 and sighs a lot
<Sulu> Albundy!!
<Sarge> Bob: Still having terminal probs... Sent a msg to help!
```

Person's name or handle — *Peppr*

This is what the person said.

*Depending on where you're chatting, the interface may look different.
This is what the Internet IRC may look like in a UNIX format.
Can you follow the conversation?*

Here's what's going on: as the conversation scrolls along on your screen, assuming there's some chatting taking place, the name of each person who speaks appears to the left of the text he or she typed. It sort of looks like a script for a play or a movie. The number of people talking also affects what happens on your screen. If everyone is talking about the same thing, then the text will probably appear in a logical order. Everyone takes turns and you can easily follow the conversation.

13

But, if some chatterers are carrying on separate conversations, the lines of text can appear very mixed up and without any logical flow. You have to learn to read the dialog and associate it with each person who "spoke" it. It's a little tricky sometimes, especially if there are lots of people chatting. This scenario is comparable to being in a crowded room with everyone talking at once.

Remember, the chatting that goes on is real-time, there's no delay. When you stumble into a chatting area where lots of people are talking, speed can sometimes play an important part of your conversation. The fastest typists can convey their responses faster than others. Spelling errors, however, are a common sight among the scrolling text you'll see (they've been left as-is in the IRC example to give you an idea). If you type too fast, you may goof up and send a misspelled word for everyone to see. Thankfully, most of your fellow online conversants are sympathetic to this problem, and will readily forgive you when you misspell something in your rush to communicate.

How Much Does It Cost?

Aha, now we shall see the real story about this new phenomenon—how much it costs. The cost of chatting away your time online varies, depending on the service. BBSs are probably the most affordable ways to chat. They usually let you join for a small fee, or sometimes free of charge. Because there are so many different kinds of BBSs, there are many different kinds of costs. You'll find basic subscriptions that may cost $35 a year, or rates like $1 a minute. It will really vary. Fortunately, you can easily find out the cost of a BBS the first time you call it up with your modem.

The commercial online services are a bit pricier, but they're often easier to use. You'll find that monthly rates start at about $8.95. Be careful, however; with some of the services, the chatting feature costs extra to use. (You'll find more about online services costs in Chapters 4 and 5.)

If you're chatting on the Internet, your cost varies a *lot*. If you're at a university, for example, your Internet connection might be free. If you're really lucky, your company has bought a connection, and you can use it to go online. (Keep in mind that not all business connections will let you access the chatting option on the Internet.) But if you're not so lucky, then you have to hook up to the Internet via an Internet provider. Providers offer you a gateway to the Internet, often with a friendly-looking interface. The price of accessing the Internet through a provider will vary vastly (more on this in Chapter 6).

If you're using your modem or an Internet service provider to get online, remember this: you're tying up phone lines, and that's going to cost you one way or another.

Because there are so many different price scenarios, there's no way I can tell you how much you're going to spend. I can tell you, however, that when it comes to online chatting, people do tend to get carried away; it can be amazing how much time and money they spend online. There are plenty of billing horror stories out there, so consider yourself warned.

Who Exactly Participates in This Online Chatting?

Anybody… anybody with a modem or an Internet connection, that is. You'll find a variety of people online chatting, including scientists, educators, business people, geeks, cheerleaders, kids, hermits, celebrities, criminals, clergy members, deviants, mothers, and people just like me or you; there really is a broad spectrum. There's also a broad spectrum of locations that people are connecting from. You'll find yourself online with computer users from every country in the world, and even those claiming to be visitors from another solar system.

Not only will you find people from all walks of life, you'll also find lots of different personality types. For those of you researching the online chatting craze, you might think that only the social butterflies among us are drawn to this online activity. Not so. There are plenty of shy people, intelligent people, wackos, and loudmouths online. Again, you'll find a full gamut of personality types chatting at any given moment.

You might be interested to know that the majority of people online are male. Why? Without getting into a drawn-out discussion on gender and roles, males in our population have typically jumped into this computer technology first, and are therefore more prolific than females online. This little fact can have its advantages and its disadvantages. I'll show you this side of the world of online chatting in Chapter 12.

It's not just adults that get online and chat; kids and teens do it too. I can't even count how many 9- to 13-year-olds I've met and had wonderful conversations with. These little people are tons of fun online (except for the bratty ones), and they're pretty good typists to boot. But there's nothing worse than being in the middle of a conversation with a 9-year-old who suddenly has to log off because his mom told him to go clean his room.

Teens are into chatting big time, not that this should surprise you. Some of the most popular chatting rooms you'll come across are teen-oriented. Yes, the conversations in these areas are a little strange, but hey—they're teenagers, what more do we need to say?

Who else goes online to chat? People who are looking for people. This ranges from computer users looking for technical help from their peers to love-starved people looking for romance. The chatting areas are hopping with users sharing like interests, whether it's a hobby, game, or computer dating. There's also a lot of strange, perverted stuff going on in the chatting areas too, and plenty of strange, perverted computer users doing it. Of course, that category doesn't include me or you, right?

So What's the Big Attraction About Online Chatting?

By now, you skeptical readers out there are probably scratching your collective heads, wondering and muttering something like, "Talking by using your computer—what's so hip about that?" Well, there's nothing worse than an un-hip skeptic. Online chatting is just plain fun. With it, you can meet new friends, get help with problems (computer and otherwise), compare hobbies, or fall in love (it worked for Rush Limbaugh).

Communicating with the written word, even if it is typed in quickly onto a computer screen, is an amazing thing. It doesn't matter if you're a terrible writer or a brilliant conversationalist—the ability to reach out using your own computer is truly a mind-boggling concept. Never before has the global community been so connected. Not only are we connected, but our communication is instantaneous. Think back on the many ways we've communicated in the past—through messengers, carrier pigeons, the Pony Express, mail carriers, the telephone system, radio, walkie-talkies, UPS drivers, television, and now computers. Isn't that astounding? And it's not stopping here—the future of this technology knows no bounds.

You skeptics are shaking your heads again, saying, "Why whittle away your time with all this chatting nonsense?" Darn it, we're reaching outside of our own little worlds and touching other lives, that's why. So what if it's not always productive? So what if it's not always educational? So what if it can really run up your credit card bill? We chat because we can, we chat because we are compelled to, we are driven to exchange thoughts and ideas with others… and because we're hip to the latest technology craze.

The Least You Need to Know

In this chapter, you learned what online chatting is all about. To be more specific, you learned:

- ➤ Online chatting is talking with other computer users using a modem or network connection.
- ➤ You can chat with others by posting messages on message boards or by sending electronic mail, but the most spontaneous method is real-time chatting.
- ➤ Chatting features are commonly found among BBSs, commercial online services, or the Internet.

Chapter 2 ➤ What's All the Fuss About?

- ➤ Online conversations scroll across your screen from top to bottom, with each person's text identified next to that person's name or handle.
- ➤ Online chatting costs vary greatly, depending on which service you're using.
- ➤ As for why everyone's chatting, it's because it's the hippest thing to do online—and you do want to be hip, don't you?

Chapter 3

Online Options: What's the Difference?

In This Chapter

- ➤ Discover what nifty things an online service can offer
- ➤ Find out how BBSs work
- ➤ Learn what it takes to hook up to the Internet
- ➤ Get the scoop on online GUIs

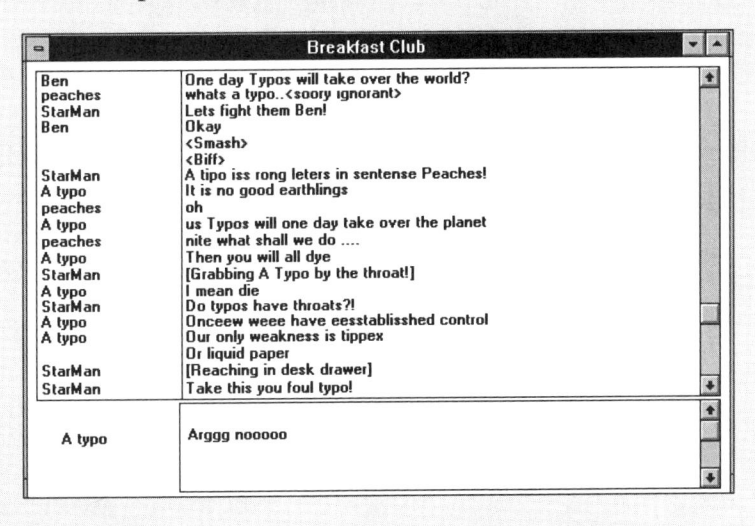

	Breakfast Club
Ben	One day Typos will take over the world?
peaches	whats a typo..<soory ignorant>
StarMan	Lets fight them Ben!
Ben	Okay
	<Smash>
	<Biff>
StarMan	A tipo iss rong letters in sentense Peaches!
A typo	It is no good earthlings
peaches	oh
A typo	us Typos will one day take over the planet
peaches	nite what shall we do ....
A typo	Then you will all dye
StarMan	[Grabbing A Typo by the throat!]
A typo	I mean die
StarMan	Do typos have throats?!
A typo	Onceew weee have eesstablisshed control
A typo	Our only weakness is tippex
	Or liquid paper
StarMan	[Reaching in desk drawer]
StarMan	Take this you foul typo!
A typo	Arggg nooooo

Even as you're reading this, there are thousands of people out there in cyberspace chatting away... without you. If you want to join them, then you'd better figure out how you're going to get online and what option you're going to use. I briefly told you about three online options in the last chapter, but you should become better acquainted with them in order to determine which chatting avenue to pursue. Now it's time to find out the subtle differences between each one, and what makes them tick. In this chapter, I'll explain those differences, and even include a list of pros and cons for using each one.

Online Services: The Big Players

Commercial online services can be compared to television. With television, you can tune into the major networks, like CBS, ABC, and NBC (possibly Fox, depending on your viewpoint), or choose from a wide range of smaller local or cable channels. The vast majority of the viewing audience is tuned into the major networks. Why? Because they offer something for everyone; news, weather, comedy, drama, and sports are available for anyone to watch (besides, not everyone has cable). The commercial online services are a lot like the major network channels. They appeal to a wider audience, and try to offer something for everyone.

What Do They Offer?

A typical online service lets you dial up and read the latest news, weather, and sports reports. Other features include stock market reports, online banking, art galleries, and even magazine racks. Commercial services let you access databases of information, such as encyclopedias and libraries. You can even make travel arrangements, which is pretty cool when you're fed up with your computer and feel an urge to fly off to the Bahamas. A real perk, though, is the ability to download all kinds of files, ranging from games and shareware programs to articles and text files (but not copyrighted computer programs—that's illegal).

Download To copy a file from another computer onto your computer

Upload To copy a file from your computer onto another computer.

You can also find special interest areas for exchanging notes with other users with similar interests (these areas go by many names, such as message boards or forums). You can even shop for stuff online, and there's no cart to push. Online services are improving their features all the time and adding new ones as they develop, such as gateways to the infamous Internet. Good old e-mail, however, is a staple of any service, and most commercial services let you connect not only with others using the service, but with people on other online services or the Internet as well. Then, of course, there's real-time chatting, which you'll see more of later in this book.

Chapter 3 ➤ *Online Options: What's the Difference?*

Online services charge a monthly rate for usage. They're more expensive than BBSs, but they offer a whole lot more. With most online services, a typical monthly fee ranges from $10-$15. You can incur additional costs when you dial in at different modem speeds or when you use any of the service's "extra features"—which, sadly enough, includes chatting. If you shop around for a deal, you may find that some online services offer you the first month at no cost, or they set you up with free hours as a new user. Be a good consumer and do your homework in terms of checking out prices for the different services, and then weigh those prices against what you expect to use the service for. (You'll find exact costs for each of the big services mentioned in Chapter 5.)

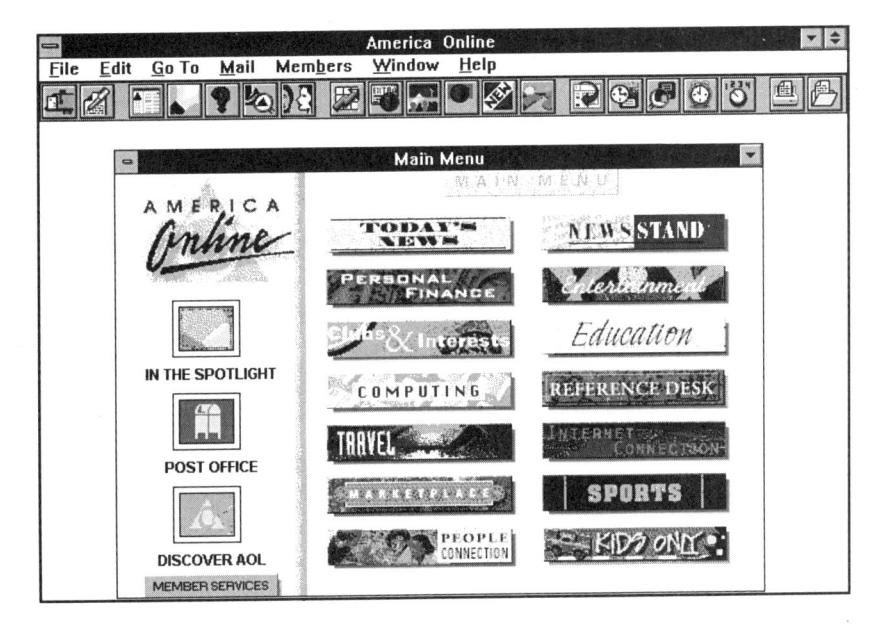

Here's what America Online looks like.

Who Runs These Services?

And who are the big commercial online services? CompuServe, PRODIGY, America Online, and GEnie are some major players. Others have started up recently, like Apple's eWorld, but they're still in the beginning stages. You'll find all these services heavily advertised in computer magazines and computer books. The commercial online services are typically run by big companies. For example, PRODIGY was started by a joint effort between IBM and Sears Roebuck Company; GEnie is run by General Electric.

In terms of how they work, there's usually a central computer, or computers, that you can connect to. Online services have "branch" offices you can call up and get direct access without the price of a long distance phone call. These branch offices are typically known as *local access numbers*. A local access number is simply a local phone number your modem can dial that will hook you up with the big computer running the service.

So, How Would I Use a Service?

The key to using an online service is to set up an account. You can do this by contacting the service by modem or voice phone (look for phone numbers for specific services in Chapter 5). Just give them your credit card number (preferably one that's not run up to its limit); they'll give you a password and a local access number to use, and you're ready to go—just about. Some of these online services have startup kits you can purchase in computer stores. Many of them, like PRODIGY or America Online, require *service-specific software* in order to use the service. You can download the software using your modem, or you can have the service send the software to you on disk. Then, you just install it onto your own computer.

> **Local access number** A local phone number your modem can dial to hook up with an online service, without incurring long distance charges.

What does the software do? Usually, it gives you a nice-looking computer screen. This is called a *graphical user interface*, or *GUI* for short. A GUI gives your computer screen a friendlier face (more on this concept coming up), and makes the service easier to handle. Not all the commercial services require software. For example, you can log onto CompuServe using your own modem's communication software... it just won't be very pretty to look at, that's all.

> **Service-specific software** A program created just for use with a particular online service.

That's what online services are all about. Any questions? Good. You'll find specific steps for contacting the commercial services in Chapter 5, including figures of what each service looks like.

To Be or Not to BBS?

BBSs, or *bulletin board systems*, are like small-scale online services. They don't offer nearly as much stuff as the big online guys, but they're just as much fun. If commercial online services are like major network television companies, then BBSs are like local channels. They're usually more focused in what they offer, and sometimes they don't operate 24 hours a day.

The beauty of BBSs is that you don't need special software to use them. They use text-based menus and commands to access the various features. Features range from archives (online libraries) of files to download, to message posting areas, to e-mail... and of course, real-time chat. BBSs aren't for everyone, however. They're not as slick-looking and easy to handle as the big online services. Yet they do have a lot to offer in their own unique way, and many of them are free of charge. You can't say that about the commercial online services!

```
[S1]D-Menu>
   || CONference....Conference Channels    EMAil......Electronic Mail System ||
   || MESsages.....Public Message Bases    ADS................Classified Ads ||
   || DATabase.....Information Database    MAGazines.......Magazines Online  ||
   || BBS..................BBS Lister      DIRectory..........User Directory ||
   || PROfile..........Account Profile     CREdit..........MGS Credit Center ||
   ||                                                                        ||
   ||       /CHAt    /LASt   /LOGoff   /MENu   /SYStem   /TIMe   /USErs   /XMIt ||
   ||  Type /GLObal for a complete listing of all global commands available  ||


[S1]D-Menu>
```

Here's an example of what a BBS looks like. To choose a menu item from this BBS, at a prompt, you have to type the first three letters of the selection you want to make.

Who Runs These BBSs?

There are zillions of BBSs out there, and I'll bet you'll find a few local ones in your own area to try. BBSs are run by a variety of people. Some are run by individuals just for the sheer fun of it; others may be run by large companies with giant computer systems. Anyone can run a BBS. You can even start your own BBS if you have a computer, a modem, and a version of BBS software that turns the computer into a host for other modem callers.

The larger companies tend to use several computers or a really big minicomputer or mainframe to run a BBS. They also have numerous phone lines and many modems. That equals lots of money. Smaller BBSs rely on personal computers—and lots of the owner's free time—to manage everything that goes on with a BBS. Some of these smaller BBSs are very hard to connect to. That's because they don't have a lot of modems and phone lines to use. Regardless of the size of the BBS or who runs it, you'll find many different kinds of BBSs to choose from.

The Many Faces of BBSs

If you're a new computer user, you may already be acquainted with *technical support* BBSs (I had to call one up several times when I installed my first modem). These are staffed by technical experts who are ready and waiting to answer questions about your hardware or software problems. Most hardware and software manufacturers run small technical support BBSs. When you call up these folks (via your modem), you can access software files and support files for making your computer easier to work with or to fix a problem. You can type in messages detailing your computer problem, and they'll answer your message with a solution to your problem. They'll sometimes do a sales pitch on you, though, by recommending files that are included in upcoming releases or products.

> **Operating system** The software that tells your computer to behave like a computer. An operating system provides the most basic instructions for making the computer work with data and devices (like the mouse, or keyboard). For example, DOS is a famous operating system.
>
> **Service provider** An organization that provides access to the Internet, usually for a fee.

A second kind of BBS is one run for a profit. Of course, this kind of BBS costs you some money to use, but it's not usually as much as the commercial online services. Because money is involved, these types of BBSs work a little harder to make sure you're getting a good value. You'll find the latest features, the best files, and lots of advertising going on. If they didn't offer you the cutting-edge stuff, you wouldn't call them up again, so they do scramble to satisfy the customer.

A third kind of BBS is the "just for the fun of it" kind that individuals or small groups run. Most BBSs fall into this category. You'll find these BBSs run the gamut from community focus to individual interests and hobbies. Some of the more exciting BBSs I've stumbled across are the ones that offer great games to play.

A fourth kind of BBS is the one run on your company's computer network. This kind of internal BBS is used to post messages, send memos, and access files and reports.

How Do I Get Onto a BBS?

The key to using a BBS is to simply call one up. You usually have to go through a sign-on procedure and make a few adjustments to your modem or communications software settings to get in sync with the BBS computer. The sign-on instructions may vary from one service to another, but usually they are simple and self-explanatory. It may take you a while to figure out how to use the BBS, but once you do, you'll find it's a lot of fun.

So, where do you find all these great BBSs? Look in the back of computer magazines, check out area computer clubs, or—best of all—pick up the latest copy of *Boardwatch Magazine* or *Computer Shopper* magazine. Both of these publications list BBSs from all around the globe. (Chapter 7 mentions some specific BBSs to try.)

Internet: The Open Road on the Information Highway

You can't go anywhere today without hearing about the Internet—the so-called information superhighway. Everybody's talking about it (or at least all the hip people are), and everybody wants to take a drive on it. The trouble is, this is one treacherous highway to traverse. Why? Because it's just so darned confusing.

What's So Confusing About It?

You see, the Internet *isn't* an online service or a BBS, and nobody owns or administers it. It's a network of many networks, and it can connect you to thousands of computers. The confusing part is finding your way along this network to get where you want to go. Much of the Internet is based on UNIX, a *command-line operating system* that's not always easy to use. (With command-line systems, you have to enter commands at a prompt to tell the computer what to do.) Thankfully, if you're connecting to the Net through a service provider, they'll make it a little easier to use the Net by giving you a menu system or a graphical user interface.

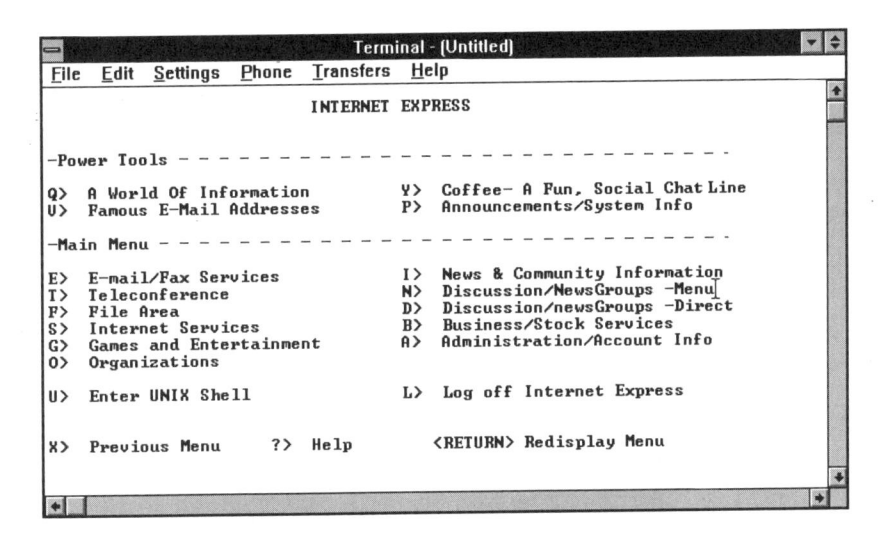

```
┌─ Terminal - (Untitled) ─────────────────────────────────┐
│ File  Edit  Settings  Phone  Transfers  Help            │
│                    INTERNET EXPRESS                     │
│                                                         │
│ -Power Tools - - - - - - - - - - - - - - - - - - - - -  │
│                                                         │
│ Q> A World Of Information      Y> Coffee- A Fun, Social Chat Line
│ U> Famous E-Mail Addresses     P> Announcements/System Info
│                                                         │
│ -Main Menu - - - - - - - - - - - - - - - - - - - - - -  │
│                                                         │
│ E> E-mail/Fax Services         I> News & Community Information
│ T> Teleconference              N> Discussion/NewsGroups -Menu
│ F> File Area                   D> Discussion/newsGroups -Direct
│ S> Internet Services           B> Business/Stock Services
│ G> Games and Entertainment     A> Administration/Account Info
│ O> Organizations                                        │
│                                                         │
│ U> Enter UNIX Shell            L> Log off Internet Express
│                                                         │
│ X> Previous Menu    ?> Help    <RETURN> Redisplay Menu  │
└─────────────────────────────────────────────────────────┘
```

Here's an example of what the Internet can look like.

Part 1 ➤ *Straight Talk About Chatting*

How do you connect to the Internet? If you're really fortunate, you may already have a free connection. These are usually found on university and government computers. There are also corporate-sponsored connections that some employees can use for free. Some BBSs and online services offer limited usage of the Internet, too. If you can't find a free on-ramp to this information highway, however, you may have to look for a service provider.

> **What's an On-Ramp?** When I say on-ramp, I'm referring to your access or connection to the Internet. So, when you see the word on-ramp, just think "connection."

An Internet *service provider* is the owner (whether a person or company) of a computer that's hooked up the vast network we call the Internet. That person or company lets you dial into this computer and use it to connect to the Net. There are two kinds of service providers, Free-Nets (exceedingly rare) and commercial service providers (the norm). In some places, usually big cities, you can find civic organizations or generous benefactors who will let you use their Internet connection for no cost. But chances are you won't find one of these. Instead, you'll have to shop around and sign up with a commercial provider who, for a fee, can give you an account and a password and let you onto the highway. Consider this a tollbooth approach. Where do you find these providers? Check with your local computer clubs, computer magazines, and books. (I'll give you some specific ones to try in Chapter 6.)

Once you've found an on-ramp, you're ready to cruise. You'll find a variety of places to go and things to see on this superhighway; just make sure you bring along a map. You can dig up message boards, called *newsgroups*, and post messages on specific topics. You can download files with FTP (File Transfer Protocol). You can look up stuff with Gopher, Mosaic, Archie, and other such programs. You can travel through linked hypertext documents with World Wide Web. (Hypertext is a system in which documents are linked by subjects.) You can telnet into someone else's computer and use their system. You can also e-mail people and chat using IRC (Internet Relay Chat).

> **Need More Internet Info?** If you're looking for in-depth information about the Internet and how to use it, try these other titles: *The Complete Idiot's Guide to the Internet* and *The Complete Idiot's Guide to USENET Newsgroups*.

Despite how baffling the Internet can be, especially to new users, it's still the best way to find files and information, and it's a great way of connecting you to computer users across this cybergalaxy.

Chapter 3 ➤ *Online Options: What's the Difference?*

Online Options: Pros and Cons

In the previous paragraphs, I gave you the lowdown on the various ways you can transport yourself into cyberspace: commercial online services, BBSs, and the Internet. Which route is for you? I recommend starting off your chatting adventure with a commercial online service. They're usually the easiest to use, even if they do cost more.

Chatting on a commercial service is relatively painless, even for newbies. With many services, like America Online, the chatting areas have specially designated guides to help new people figure things out. These guides are experienced online users who can answer your questions and give you directions and tips. Besides asking online officials, you'll find that just about everyone else on the commercial services is willing to help you out too. In fact, that's another "pro" about commercial services: their users are very friendly, sometimes friendlier than users of BBSs or the Internet.

> **Newbie** A person who's a beginner online or who's new to the online world. In some areas, like the Internet, the word newbie can be a little derogatory. But so what if you're a newbie? Everyone's a newbie at first.

The downside of using a commercial online service, however, is the cost. They're more expensive than BBSs. But, back on the upside, they have more members than BBSs, so you can potentially meet more people.

You know what? Now would be a good time to look at a table of pros and cons regarding the three online options. That might help you pick out the route you want to go to online chat.

Online Option	Pros	Cons
Commercial services	Easy to use (simple to navigate, lots of visual elements)	Somewhat expensive (monthly cost plus charges for connect-time and use of extra features)
	Great GUIs available	You may have to install software.
	Lots of online help (both in technical help and text files)	Limited Internet access, in most cases (newsgroups and e-mail)

continues

Continued

Online Option	Pros	Cons
BBSs	Tons of chat areas for all kinds of topics	
	Cheaper, sometimes free	Menu-based interface (not very visual or intuitive)
	Lots of variety (local to national, ranging in focus)	Some text commands needed
	Homier feeling	Sometimes too exclusive
	Internet access	Sometimes Internet access is limited (newsgroups and e-mail)
	Chat channels are some of the most popular features of any BBS	
Internet	Potential to talk to millions of people (IRC offers hundreds of chat channels)	It's the hardest to use (navigation is tough, and some UNIX commands are required)
	Lots of diversity (connect to people from all over the world)	Sometimes difficult to find an on-ramp (lots of service providers to choose from)
	It's got everything! (access to databases, files, e-mail, and more)	Not exactly a friendly atmosphere (tough on newbies)

Gee, You've Got a Nice-Looking GUI

I brought up the term GUI a lot in this chapter, so I'd better explain what it's all about. The vast majority of us are visual by nature; that is, we prefer to operate in a visual world rather than an abstract one. Thankfully, today's computers employ a lot of visual elements in their operation, but it wasn't always so. For a long time, computers and programs were command-driven. Ever work with DOS or UNIX? Then you know what I mean. *Command-driven* (or *command-line*) interfaces require you to type in commands at a prompt in order to get your computer to do anything. The only way you could communicate with your computer was through this prompt. The prompt usually appeared on an all-black screen, and it glared at you, daring you to type something in so it could refuse you by not understanding what you typed. A lot of people found this very frustrating—and still do.

Command-driven interfaces are well and good, but in order to use them efficiently, you have to memorize all the various commands and remember how to type them properly. Most of us don't like doing this. Thankfully, programmers came up with the graphical user interface, commonly known as a *GUI*. Rather than interact by typing commands, a GUI lets you select commands from menus, icons, dialog boxes, windows, and other elements. The neat part about working with GUIs is that you can use your computer's mouse. To select on-screen items, you point-and-click with the mouse. This method of getting around is more intuitive than entering commands at a prompt—and with just a little practice, it'll become second nature to you.

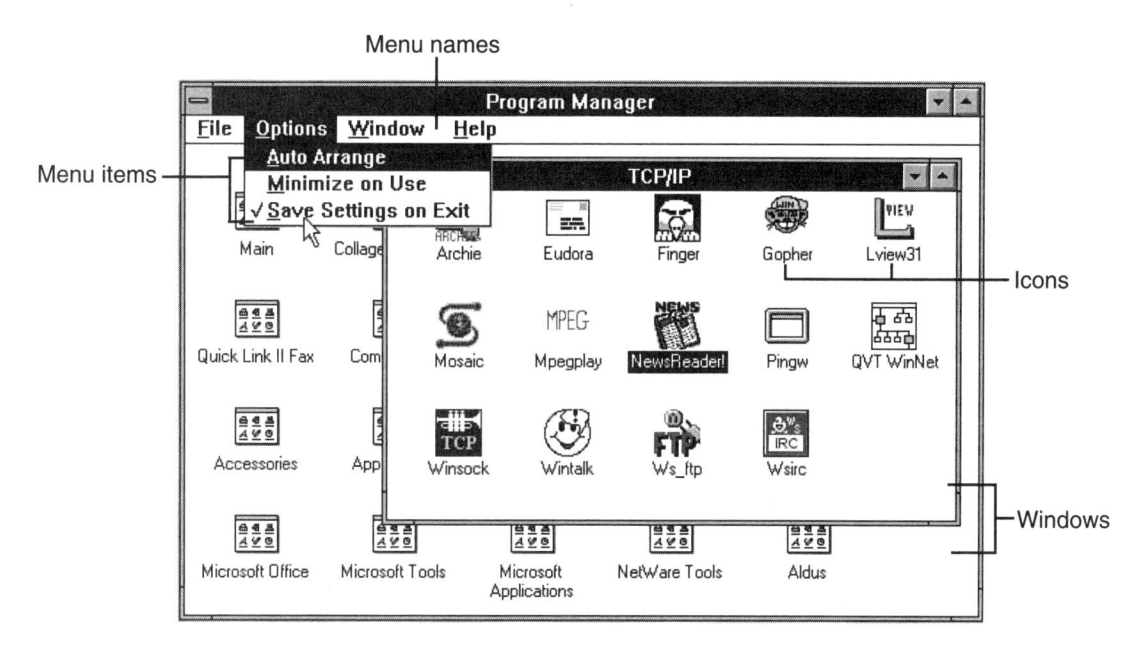

The Microsoft Windows GUI.

Care for Some GUI History?

One of the first GUI interfaces people got excited about was developed by Apple Computers for the line of computers they called Macintosh. The Macintosh computer was very successful, and lots of people found the innovative interface to be the answer to their computing problems. It wasn't long before everyone else jumped on this GUI bandwagon. The IBM computers and IBM-compatibles soon had several GUIs available, such as GeoWorks and Windows. In case you haven't been paying attention in the last couple of years, Windows won over this GUI market; just about every IBM-compatible computer sold today has Windows installed on it.

GUIs really make it easier for you to use your computer. The same theory goes into making it easier for you to use online services and the Internet. You'll encounter all kinds of GUIs with nifty icon buttons, windows, and other elements for navigating the service.

Icon A tiny graphical picture that represents a program, a command, or a feature. To select an icon, you just click on it or double-click on it, depending on what type of software or system you're using.

In fact, you can't even get online with some services (like PRODIGY and America Online) without installing their special GUI software on your computer.

When it comes to the Internet, most service providers you subscribe to use GUIs to make the Internet easier to navigate... and it's a good thing. It's a whole lot harder to navigate by typing in UNIX commands at a glaring prompt. Even the special software used to run a BBS makes it easier for users to get around and select the various features. I'm telling you, without GUIs, we'd be lost, or at least very frustrated.

The Least You Need to Know

You've armed yourself with a great deal of knowledge by reading this chapter. You can now explain the subtle differences between commercial online services and BBSs to all your friends and relatives, who will, in turn, stand amazed at your expertise (trust me, that glassy stare *is* amazement...).

- ➤ Online services offer something for everyone, and therefore have a very large subscriber base.
- ➤ BBSs are like small-scale online services, without as many broad features, but more focused on specific hobbies or interests.
- ➤ There are all kinds of BBSs, ranging in size and scope. There are thousands upon thousands of BBSs around the world.

- The Internet is not like a commercial service or a BBS; rather, it's a giant network of networks, connecting individual computers all over the world.
- If you can't get on the Internet for free, find a service provider to use instead.
- The fastest way for a novice to start chatting fast is with a commercial online service. They're easier to navigate and use.
- GUIs play a big role in the online world. A good GUI can really enhance your online experience. Most commercial online services utilize GUI software to make their systems easier to use.

Chapter 4

Getting Plugged In

In This Chapter

➤ Learn what you need in order to go online

➤ Find out what kind of sign-up procedures you'll encounter

➤ Ideas for creating the perfect handle

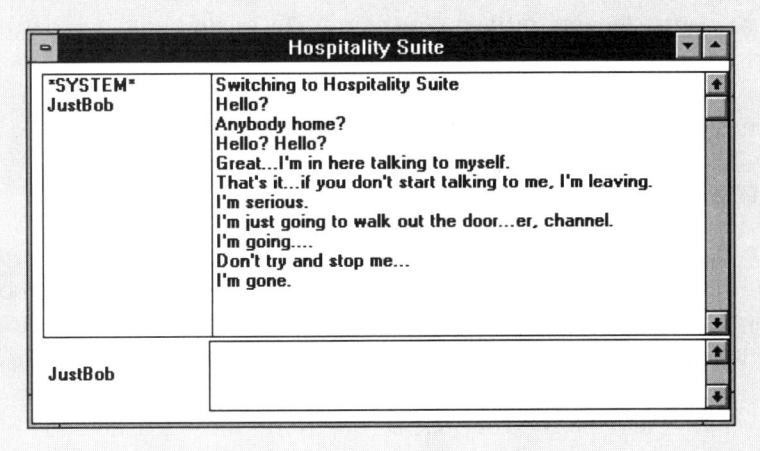

```
┌─────────────────────────────────────────────────┐
│                Hospitality Suite                │
├─────────────────────────────────────────────────┤
│ *SYSTEM*   Switching to Hospitality Suite       │
│ JustBob    Hello?                               │
│            Anybody home?                        │
│            Hello? Hello?                        │
│            Great...I'm in here talking to myself.│
│            That's it...if you don't start talking to me, I'm leaving.│
│            I'm serious.                         │
│            I'm just going to walk out the door...er, channel.│
│            I'm going....                        │
│            Don't try and stop me...             │
│            I'm gone.                            │
│                                                 │
├─────────────────────────────────────────────────┤
│ JustBob                                         │
│                                                 │
└─────────────────────────────────────────────────┘
```

Now that you know what online chatting is all about—and the various online options to pursue (assuming you read the previous chapters)—it's time to give you the details for getting started online yourself. What kinds of details? Oh, stuff like how to sign up for an online account, how to create a handle, what to expect on your online bills... we'll go over details like these, and more, in this chapter.

How Do I Start Talking—Fast?

Okay... the first thing you need to do is to determine which online option to use as your avenue to chat. Are you going to go online with a commercial online service, a BBS, or the Internet? How do you determine this? Well, what's your situation?

- What is your monthly budget?
- Are you going to chat using your modem or are you connected somehow through a network?
- Are you planning on using the Internet a lot, or will an online service or BBS suffice?
- What other features besides chatting will you use? Do you plan on doing some online shopping, investing money, doing research for school or business?

Probably the most common route to chatting is with a modem. A modem can connect you to any element in the online world. The second route to chatting is with a network connection. If, for example, your company computers are networked and have an Internet hookup, you can chat on the Internet (if it's allowed, that is). Let's stick with the first scenario for now, since it's most common.

Modem Mayhem

In this section, I'll share some tips with you about modems, but helping you choose and set up your modem is really a huge topic in itself, enough to fill an entire book. In fact, it does! If you're fairly new to the world of modems and computer communications, you might want to pick up that book to help you set up your modem and make it work. Try to get your hands on a copy of *The Complete Idiot's Guide to Modems and Online Services*. It will help you solve all your modem start-up questions, including how to find the perfect modem and what to do with it once you've brought it home.

What Exactly Is a Modem, Anyway?

Modem stands for *modulator/demodulator*. It's a device that allows you to communicate with other computers by way of ordinary telephone lines. A modem can turn computer data into a format that can be sent through a phone line; the receiving modem takes that signal and changes it back into computer data. There are two kinds of modems: internal and external. Internal modems plug into your computer's motherboard, inside your computer. An external modem sits outside your computer and is connected with cables.

An essential element of a modem is its speed, or ability to send data quickly. Speed is measured in *bps* (*bits per secoMnd*), which is the number of bits that can be transferred through the telephone line each second. A modem's speed is often incorporated into its name. Today's modems transmit at rates anywhere from 9600 to 28,000 to 33,600 bps, and are getting faster all the time. They're evolving so fast, it's exceedingly difficult to keep up with them!

If you just bought a new computer, it might already come with a modem installed internally. If not, you'll need to go out and buy one (external or internal). You'll find modems galore at your local computer store, electronics store, or office superstore. You can also order a modem through computer catalogs (look for bargains among the various advertisements in the back of computer magazines).

What Kind of Modem Should I Use?

Well, that depends. Do you want a modem that sits alongside your computer with pretty lights that flash? Or, would you rather have your modem tucked away inside the deep recesses of your system unit? If you purchase an external modem, it's easier to install and easier get to if something goes wrong with it. Plus, it's completely mobile—you can take it with you and plug it into other computers. On the other hand, it's more easily damaged, along with anything else sitting among the stacks of stuff on your desk or table, and it can easily be stolen.

An internal modem is a little trickier to install—you have to open up your computer's guts to plug it in. But once installed, it's not as prone to spilled beverages or dust as an external modem is. The downside it that you can't easily get to it if something's wrong, and there aren't any lights that flash to tell you it's working.

Part 1 ➤ *Straight Talk About Chatting*

What kind should you buy? Well, how much do you want to spend and how fast do you want to go? You ought to know that modem speed can make a big difference in your connection to cyberspace. It's best to use a higher-speed modem, such as 14,400 bps. If you haven't rushed out in the past year or so to purchase a higher speed modem, you might want to consider it before jumping online. The prices of higher-speed modems have really come down in recent years. In fact, you won't even find modems like 2400 bps or slower, unless you're in a pawn shop or something.

Higher-speed modems are most useful when you plan on downloading files from various cyberspace locations. The faster your modem speed, the less time it takes to download data. This is something to consider when purchasing a modem. If you're going to use a modem strictly for connecting with others through chat and e-mail, then speed isn't a priority for you. However, if you change your mind later and want to get more use out of your modem, a slower-speed modem will not be able to meet the challenge.

The Mind-Boggling World of Communications Software

A modem isn't much good without communications software to make it work with your computer. Most modems today come with free software, or you can buy a better program at your local computer store.

The communications software lets your hardware (in this case, your modem and your computer) talk to each other. The software is used to store modem numbers to dial, issue modem commands, and instruct your computer how to communicate with the modem itself as well as any other modems you dial up. So, basically, software instructs your modem on what to do and when.

> **Look for Service-Specific Software**
> If you've decided to get online with a commercial service or an Internet provider, you may luck out and get some service-specific software (see Chapter 2) to get you going. This service-specific software controls a lot of the settings for you, so you won't have to worry about it, lucky dog!

When you work with communications software, you have to learn about settings. Settings control how two modems exchange information. Settings can determine how a file is uploaded or downloaded, how your terminal behaves, or even how loud your modem speaker is set (if you happen to have a modem speaker). Settings can be a little tricky, especially for a novice, so be sure to consult your communications software manual for help. (And be sure to pick up a copy of *The Complete Idiot's Guide to Modems and Online Services*. It will help you with your software settings too. Good grief, it's another shameless plug!)

Chapter 4 ➤ *Getting Plugged In*

How Do I Sign Up and Sign On?

Well, now... you know about modems and communications software, now what? The next step to take is to get yourself online. Depending on which online option you've decided to pursue, there are several different sign-on procedures you'll run into. How you sign up with a commercial service will differ from how you sign up with a BBS. And the various routes to getting on the Internet differ even further. In the next few paragraphs, I'll give you a brief look at what it takes to go online with the various online options. Knowing what you're going to be expected to do in the sign-up process can help you determine which online option to use yourself. Be sure to read Chapters 5, 6, and 7 for exact details and procedures for logging onto commercial services, the Internet, and BBSs.

Commercial Services: All It Takes Is a Credit Card

If you're going online with a commercial service like CompuServe, you have to set up an *account* first. This means you have to contact the service, by a regular phone call or by using your modem, and then give them your credit card number (in Chapter 5, I'll give you some specific phone numbers to try). In return, the service will set you up with a password and a local access number (phone number) to connect you with the service. With some services, you also have to pick a *package*—in other words, figure out how you want to be billed and for how much.

Here's something else you ought to know when signing on with a commercial online service: many of these services entice new users with special offers. For example, for quite some time now, America Online has been offering 10 free hours (online) to new users. PRODIGY sometimes offers free hours if you can convince a friend to sign on too. If you just bought a brand-new modem or computer, there may have been some special offer coupons included in the packaging. Also look for special offers in magazines and the backs of computer books.

> **Do I Have to Use My Credit Card?** What's the matter, are you maxxed out already? You can work out other kinds of billing arrangements, but you'll have to personally contact the service to find out what options are available. Using a credit card is by far the quickest method to getting online, but that doesn't mean it's your only option.

Be sure to find out what kind of fees and prices are involved before committing to the service. You'll run into monthly membership fees, hourly connect fees, and even special services fees. Why so many fees? Wake up, pal, this technology stuff is never free, especially when there are big bucks to be made. Did you think you could just have your computer call all over the universe for no cost at all? These commercial online services are definitely in it for the money. Oh sure, they give you lots of nifty things to do while you're online with them, but they put all the fun stuff in the extended services part and charge you more to use 'em. And of course, the chatting feature is usually among the fun stuff, so you'll pay extra to use it. Was this a shrewd business move, or just plain orneriness? You decide.

Anyway, once you've taken all these steps and you have an account, you're ready to dive into cyberspace. You just call up the service, use your password, and bingo—you're in like Flint. (Who is Flint, anyway?) Read Chapter 5 for information about each of the big commercial services and what they look like.

The BBS Way: Fiddle with Your Software Settings

Signing up with a BBS is a little different from picking a commercial service. You have to decide which one to call and then, once you've got a hot little number in your hands, you instruct your modem to dial it up. You'll probably have to make a few adjustments on your modem settings the first time you try. Not all BBSs use the same communications settings. You may have to indulge in a little trial-and-error juggling to get your connection just right. And, unlike some of the commercial services with their fancy service-specific software, you'll be the one responsible for fiddling with the settings—your software won't figure it out for you. (I'll give you tips for dealing with the various settings in Chapter 7.)

When you connect with a BBS for the first time, you'll be asked to answer a bunch of questions. Sometimes the questions are rather technical in nature. This is part of the sign-up routine. For example, you'll encounter your basic questions—name, address, and phone number—as well as questions about which kind of modem you're using and how you're going to pay for membership (unless it's a free BBS). If it's a fee-based BBS, you'll need to have your credit card handy. Most BBSs I know offer you a chance to visit the service to see what it's like before making a commitment to pay for it. Of course, as a visitor, you won't be able to do much more than look around. Once you've been through the sign-up procedure, you can then wander around and discover what features the BBS has, or make a beeline to the chatting area.

Internet Sign-Up: Every Which Way But Loose

This one's a doozy, whatever a doozy is. Since the Internet doesn't work like a BBS or an online service, it's a little harder to sign up and sign on. As I've told you previously, there are many different ways you can get onto the Internet. If you're networked into the Internet with a permanent connection, you won't have to worry about modem speed, long distance charges, and tied-up telephone lines. But if you don't have a free or permanent connection, you'll need to sign up for an account through a service provider.

Remember, a service provider is a company or individual who lets you use their computer to get onto the Net—for a fee, of course. There are two specific ways you can connect to the Internet using your modem. One way is with a *dial-in terminal* connection. This lets you use your modem to call up another computer (the service provider) that's actually connected to the Internet. The service provider's computer is known as the *host* computer in such a scenario, and your computer acts like a *dumb terminal*. No, I'm not name-calling; this simply means your computer doesn't do any thinking on its own when connected to the host—the host computer does all the work.

Sound good? If you sign up with a service provider for a dial-in terminal connection, it's fairly cheap, usually less than $20 a month. However, you're never really connected to the Internet with your own computer. Bummer, huh? And you're stuck with whatever Internet-based software programs your host computer has.

> **Use Your BBS Internet Connection!**
> A lot of BBSs let you access the Internet too. Sometimes the access is limited—like only allowing e-mail activity or newsgroups—but it's still access. Many of the commercial online services let you do this, too. Be sure to check out these resources; they may offer you all the Internet access you want.

If you'd rather have full-fledged (no restrictions) Internet access with your own computer, then you need to sign up for a *dial-in direct* connection. It lets you and your modem dial up the service provider's computer but still use your computer's power. In other words, your computer remains active and doesn't act like a dumb terminal. When you have a dial-in direct connection, your computer, through the host, actually connects to the Internet. You may see this type of connection referred to as a SLIP, CSLIP, or PPP. (More on these in Chapter 6.)

While a dial-in direct connection is good, it does come with a higher price tag. You can probably find such a provider for less than a $50 startup fee and $20 monthly fee—just shop around. I'll list some specific service providers for you in Chapter 6.

When Do They Send a Bill?

If you've signed up with a commercial online service, you'll receive a monthly bill as part of your credit card bill (depending on which credit card you used to pay for this little computer hobby of yours). If you'd like to see a detailed breakdown of your online expenses for that service, you can usually log on and look up your account information. There are other ways you can set up billing, but you'll have to check with the individual service you're using for billing policies and procedures.

Part 1 ➤ *Straight Talk About Chatting*

> **Give Me an Example!**
> Okay. With CompuServe, for example, you can type in the Go-word **BILLING** to review your monthly bills. This command will bring up CompuServe's customer service area and let you examine your monthly charges.

Fee-based BBSs may have yearly membership fees or monthly fees, depending on what you signed up for. There's a wide range of billing procedures among the thousands of BBSs out there. Always make sure you understand how the billing works before committing to the service, to avoid later confusion (and expenses you weren't expecting to pay).

Internet service providers may vary in billing procedures, too, but most are monthly. Since you typically use a credit card to sign up for these, the cost will be reflected in your monthly credit card bill.

Get a Handle on Your Handle

Once you've figured out how to get online, you might want to take a second and come up with a handle for yourself. A *handle* is an online nickname. Why would you want one? Because you're online with thousands and thousands of other users, and you want to be identified, right? Or maybe you'd rather not let everyone know who you really are... whatever the case, it's time to get a handle on handles.

Handle History

For those of you who aren't too hip with cultural trends, I'm going to stop and explain this handle stuff for you. Remember that big CB (Citizen's Band radio) craze I told you about from the '70s? (Yeah, I know I already mentioned this, but I'm telling you again, darn it. I'm doing you a favor in case you fell down and hit your head between Chapter 1 and this chapter and have been suddenly afflicted with amnesia.) Everybody ran out and bought a CB to put in the car or truck. Then, whenever you traveled anywhere in your vehicle, you could listen to people chatting on their CBs, as well as chat with everyone yourself.

What was the big deal about that? Well, for one thing, it was before cellular phones hit the scene; using your CB was a lot like making a phone call. If you ever got into any road trouble, you could contact other CB users for help. CBs were great for whiling away the hours on the open road. CB users gave themselves nicknames, called *handles*, to identify themselves while on the air. These handles ranged from vehicle descriptions, point-of-origin nicknames, and more. It wasn't uncommon to drive down the road and

40

talk to people named "Big Mama" and "Lone Wolf." There was a certain feeling of camaraderie in being able to communicate with your fellow travelers.

The CB craze died off quite a bit, though it's still alive among truckers. But perhaps you'll be happy to know it's been reborn in cyberspace. Like the CB days of yesteryear, there's a feeling of camaraderie in being able to talk to other computer users, hollering for help when you have hardware or software trouble, or just shootin' the cyberbreeze. And the use of handles is still a strong tradition.

Where Do You Use Handles Online?

Handles are fairly common among all online areas. They're primarily used in the chatting areas. Why is that? Because it's fun, darn it. (Do you really need a better reason than that?) Actually, it's rather nice to let your creative juices flow and give yourself a nickname instead of using your real name. Anonymity can really empower you sometimes, too. Here's your chance to be anybody you want; male, female, or gender-unknown. You really ought to think about using a handle when the opportunity arises.

In most cases, you choose a handle when you enter a chatting area. This is common among BBSs and online services. Depending on the service you're using, some may even ask you to type in a handle before you can even get started chatting. In other cases, you can choose a handle before you even log on.

What Handle Should I Use?

Be creative. Be whoever you want to be, but keep in mind that your handle should be appropriate for the chatting area you're going to use. For example, if you're about to enter a BBS discussion group that's talking about nuclear physics, it's probably not a good idea to call yourself "StudMuffins." You probably won't be taken very seriously if you do.

When it comes to handles, the sky's the limit.

> **Wait, I'm Confused!**
> Using a handle is different than signing up, just in case you're getting confused. When you first set up an online account, you need to use your real name. Handles come later, like when you're using the chat feature.
>
> And another thing, the terms *log on* and *log off* are just ways of describing the action of turning your computer on or off, or connecting to a service. When you log onto a service, you go through the signing on procedures (like entering your password or ID number). When you log off a service, you go through the signing off procedures (like selecting the exit command or button).

It's your chance to be clever, simple, or insane. And depending on what you plan on doing online, your handle can also be very suggestive... if you know what I mean. I've seen a lot of good handles out there. People really do get creative with this stuff. Some are downright funny, too. I saw one the other day on the ImagiNation Network for *INeedAName*. I wish I had thought of that.

> **Choosing a Name** With some services, you may be asked to create an on-screen name as soon as you sign up. Be a little cautious with this. Don't just type anything; give it some consideration. You may get stuck with your first on-screen name forever, which is the case with America Online. Sure, they let you choose some other names to use as well, but your first one is permanently part of your account. I thought you might want to know this before typing in something like *SWEETUMS* or *MR. LOVE*.

Now that the online world is getting so popular, it's getting harder to come up with a really clever handle because all the good ones are taken (this depends on how populated the online service or BBS is). I was on America Online one day and accidentally deleted my favorite handle (it was entirely my fault, I didn't read the directions), then I spent 15 minutes trying to add a new one. It seemed that every clever one I could think of was already taken. I was very frustrated. The best I could come up with that day was *KnotKiddin*. If you have the same trouble, I suggest you sit down with a big, fat dictionary or a thesaurus and see what you can do.

If you'd rather not think of a real creative one, you can always use your own name or a variation of it. For example, if your name is already in use by someone else, add a number to it, like *Bob2001*. Or if you don't like that, try fiddling with adding additional letters. For example, I used *SHHerry*, instead of regular old *Sherry*. Others I've seen include TheBobMan, MrBob, MisterBob, Bobbaran, DrBob, VIPBob, BobOrRob, CallMeBob, BobTheBlob, BobMeister, and the ever-popular JustBob. Try any of these out on your own name.

Things can get really interesting if you start using different kinds of names, assuming different identities, and such. You'll find out more about this in Chapters 11 and 12. However, I'd try to stay away from anything too vulgar or obscene when it comes to a handle. It's not always acceptable, regardless of how many fellow deviants you think are online with you, and it may encourage some unpleasant responses from other chatters you encounter. Of course, if that's what you're looking for, then hey—lottsa luck. (Just remember, there are people in charge of the various systems, and they might just kick you off for using too vulgar of a name.)

There are a lot of great handles that consist of a play on words, or that use numbers and words together, like *Deton8* (get it?). One of my all-time favorites I ran across on America Online was *DonPerryOn*. Now that's what I call clever. (I'm a sucker for a good handle, even though I don't always use a clever one myself.) The point of a handle is to create interest or express something about yourself. That's what the early CB users of yesteryear did with their handles, and that's what online users do today.

The Least You Need to Know

For all practical purposes, you're ready to go online. Here's a recap of what you need:

- ➤ If you're not directly wired into an Internet connection, you'll have to find an alternative way of getting online. The most common route is with your modem.
- ➤ With some minor tweaks to your modem settings and your communications software, you can go online with a BBS with a simple phone call.
- ➤ To go online with a commercial online service, you'll need to set up an account first.
- ➤ To access the Internet, you'll need to sign up with an Internet service provider for a dial-in terminal connection or a dial-in direct connection.
- ➤ When the occasion arrives, choose a good handle for your online self.

Chapter 5

Exploring Online Services

In This Chapter

- Find your way to CompuServe's CB Simulator
- Find out what America Online's chat rooms look like
- See what PRODIGY has done with their chatting feature
- Learn what other online services are available

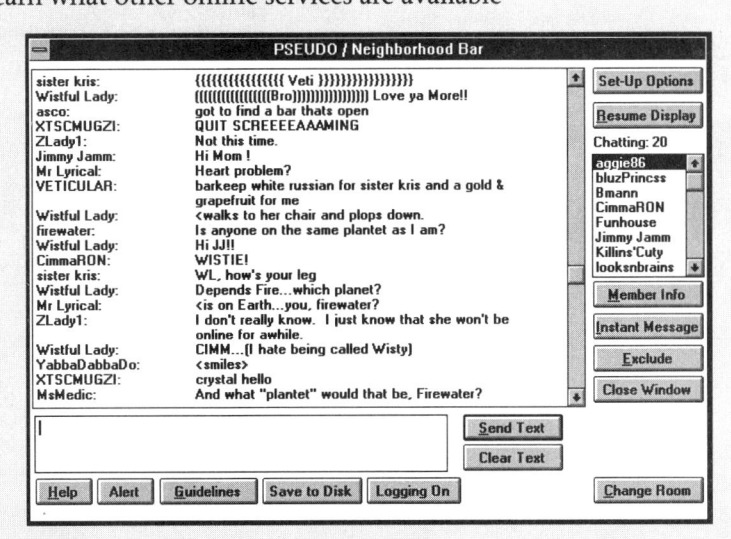

Part 1 ➤ *Straight Talk About Chatting*

Let's see how these commercial online services compare, shall we? In this chapter, you'll see how each of the major services look and work, including all the chatting features. Hopefully, this information will come in handy when you choose a particular online service. Who knows, you may like them all so much you'll want an account on each one. (Only a true online junkie has accounts with every one of them. I should know; my modem never rests!)

CompuServe

Compared to the other available services, CompuServe is an old, established giant. It started up back in 1977 in Columbus, Ohio. In its humble origins, CompuServe was meant to be an information service for a local newspaper. Now, it's grown into one of the most popular online services operating today. What a Cinderella story, eh? Out of all the online services today, CompuServe has a reputation for being the most business-oriented of the bunch.

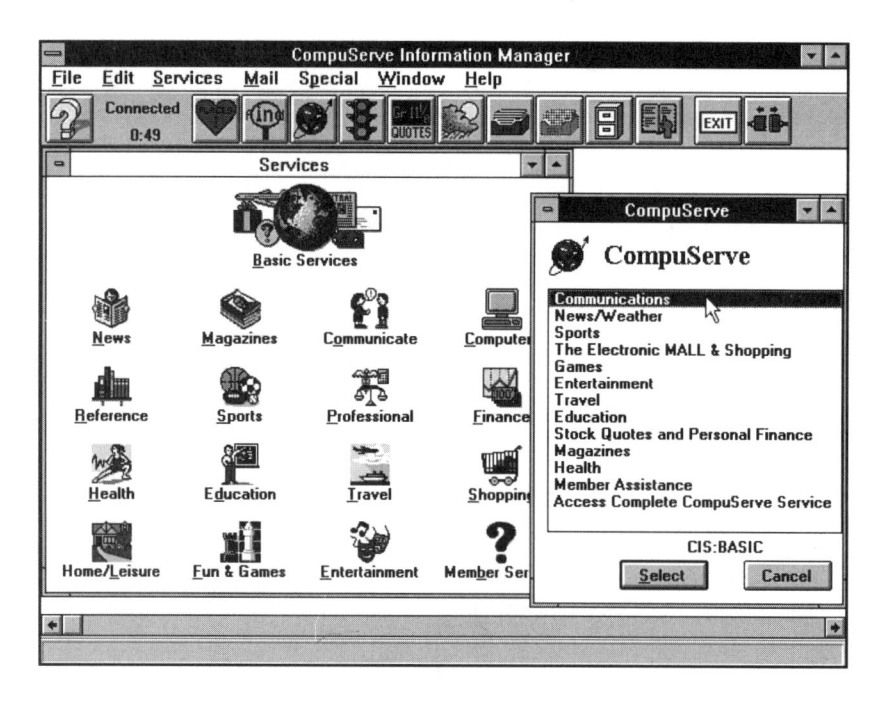

Here's what CompuServe looks like with CIM software. This particular figure shows WinCIM (CIM for Windows).

46

How Do I Get Online with CompuServe?

If you just bought a new computer or modem, there's probably a CompuServe coupon or flier somewhere in the box to help you sign up right away. CompuServe has done a very good job of infiltrating product boxes with advertising propaganda. You'll also find CompuServe advertised in every computer magazine. But if you're looking for a more direct approach—and who isn't?—here's CompuServe's toll-free number: 1-800-848-8199 (that's a regular telephone number, by the way). Just call and tell them you want to sign up for a CompuServe account. Have your credit card handy.

> **CIM:** Short for CompuServe Information Manager. CIM is CompuServe's service-specific software for making the service easier to use. CIM gives you a GUI environment to work in.

When you sign up for an account with CompuServe, they'll give you a password and a user ID number to use when you log onto the service. That user ID number will be your account number, as well as your e-mail address. (Don't lose that ID or you'll have to deal with the modem police.) The final thing you need before actually logging on is a local access number.

To find out your local CompuServe access number, have your modem call 1-800-FINDCIS (or 1-800-346-3247). You'll have to adjust a few of your software settings first, but this number hooks you up to a database of access numbers. (If you still can't find a number, call CompuServe Customer Service direct at 1-800-635-6225.)

How Can I Get a CompuServe Local Access Number?

Before you call, you need to adjust your communications software settings. Change your baud rate to the modem speed you want to use to communicate with CompuServe's computers. Change your communications parameters to **7-E-1** (that stands for **7** data bits, parity set to **Even**, and a stop bit of **1**). Change your **Echo** setting to **Off**, and if your software has a **Duplex** setting, set it to **Full Duplex**. If you don't make any of these changes, you'll get nothing but weird characters on your screen; you won't be able to proceed with the logon.

With your modem, call **1-800-FINDCIS**. After you connect, press **Enter** to arrive at the Host Name screen. Type **PHONES** and press **Enter** to reveal a menu you can follow to find an access number. Just follow the prompts. They should lead you to at least two local numbers you can call to access CompuServe. Be sure to write them both down. When you return to the Host Name screen, type **BYE** and press **Enter** to log off. Now, call CompuServe using one of the access numbers you obtained.

You don't need any special software to get online and use CompuServe. Your communications program will work fine after a little tweaking of your parameters. The folks at CompuServe have an excellent GUI program, however—it makes CompuServe much nicer to look at, and much easier to use. It's called *CIM* (short for *CompuServe Information Manager*), and it's available in several versions such as Windows, DOS, or Mac. I highly recommend that you install CIM when you can get your hands on it. It's available for downloading directly from CompuServe; you *can* go out and buy it (they call it a CompuServe startup kit), but why do that when you can download it for free? I'll tell you more about this CIM stuff in an upcoming section, but for now, I'll assume you don't have it installed on your computer.

Logging Onto CompuServe

Are you ready? Have your communications software call up the local access number. When you see **CONNECT** on the screen, press **Enter** to keep progressing to the CompuServe screen. When CompuServe finally answers, it may say **Host Name**. Type **CIS** and press **Enter**. Type your user ID when asked, and press **Enter**. Type your password and press **Enter**.

Now you're in CompuServe and your meter is running. Your screen doesn't look too pretty, does it? The prompt looks like an exclamation point. To make a selection from the menu, type the number of the menu item you want to open after the exclamation-point prompt, then press **Enter**. If you ever need help, type **HELP** and press **Enter**. If you know where you want to go online, you can use a GO command to get you there fast. Just type **GO** and the keyword (also referred to as quick reference words) of the CompuServe feature you want to use. For example, to get to the chatting feature, type **GO CB-1** (CB-1 stands for Citizens Band 1) and press **Enter**.

> **Need to Find Some CompuServe Keywords?**
>
> Keywords, or as CompuServe calls them, *quick reference words*, are used to "beam" you somewhere fast. Type them to quickly get to a feature you want to use. To see an exhaustive list of quick reference words, you can type **GO COMMANDS**, and then select quick reference words from the menu. You can also just type **QUICK REFERENCE WORDS** to go directly to the list.

```
CompuServe    TOP

 1 Access Basic Services
 2 Member Assistance (FREE)
 3 Communications/Bulletin Bds.
 4 News/Weather/Sports
 5 Travel
 6 The Electronic MALL/Shopping
 7 Money Matters/Markets
 8 Entertainment/Games
 9 Hobbies/Lifestyles/Education
10 Reference
11 Computers/Technology
12 Business/Other Interests

Enter choice !
```

This is the plain old CompuServe menu.

To exit the service, type **OFF** or **BYE** at the prompt and press **Enter**. If you're at a : prompt, type **EXIT** or **QUIT** to return to an exclamation-point prompt, then type **OFF** or **BYE** and press **Enter**.

The CompuServe screen isn't much to look at, but I can help you change that. You need CompuServe's GUI interface—you guessed it—that glamorous software called CIM.

Getting CIM

How do you get CIM? Well, as I said earlier, you can purchase CompuServe startup kits in any computer store, and these include the GUI for CIM. You can also call CompuServe and have them send you the program on disk. Or (here's the best way), you can log onto CompuServe and download the CIM files right onto your own computer. At first, it will look like this is going to cost you 10–15 bucks, but CompuServe will credit your account; you end up getting the software for free. Whatever you do, *get CIM*. You won't be sorry.

To get to CIM software online, use a GO command. Type **GO WINCIM** at any prompt to open the instructions for downloading a Windows version of the software. Type **GO MACCIM** for a Mac version, and type **GO DOSCIM** for a DOS version. Follow the on-screen directions for downloading the files. Depending on your computer system, follow the appropriate steps for installing CIM on your computer. Once you have CIM, you can easily navigate CompuServe by clicking on icons and menus and by selecting items from dialog boxes.

Part 1 ➤ *Straight Talk About Chatting*

Chatting with the CB Simulator

It's time to start talking. All of CompuServe's real-time chatting occurs in the *CB Simulator* feature. The name of this feature harkens back to the CB craze I mentioned earlier. They even call the different areas in CB Simulator "channels" and "bands." At any time of day, you can enter this feature and find live conversations going on, and everyone has an interesting handle.

> **CB Simulator:**
> The name of CompuServe's chat feature. CB stands for Citizens Band, referring back to the CB craze of the '70s. You can chat on CB-1 or CB-2.

If you've got CIM software installed, you can find your way to CB Simulator by clicking on the **GO** button (it looks like a stoplight up on your button bar), typing in **CB-1** or **CB-2**, and then pressing **Enter** or clicking on **OK**. If you don't have CIM software, just type **GO CB-1** or **GO CB-2** at the exclamation-point prompt and press **Enter**.

CB-1 is a more general band (people of all ages use it to chat), and CB-2 is the adult band (for chat that's more adult-oriented). In each band you'll find 36 channels to choose from. Some channels have specific topics, others don't.

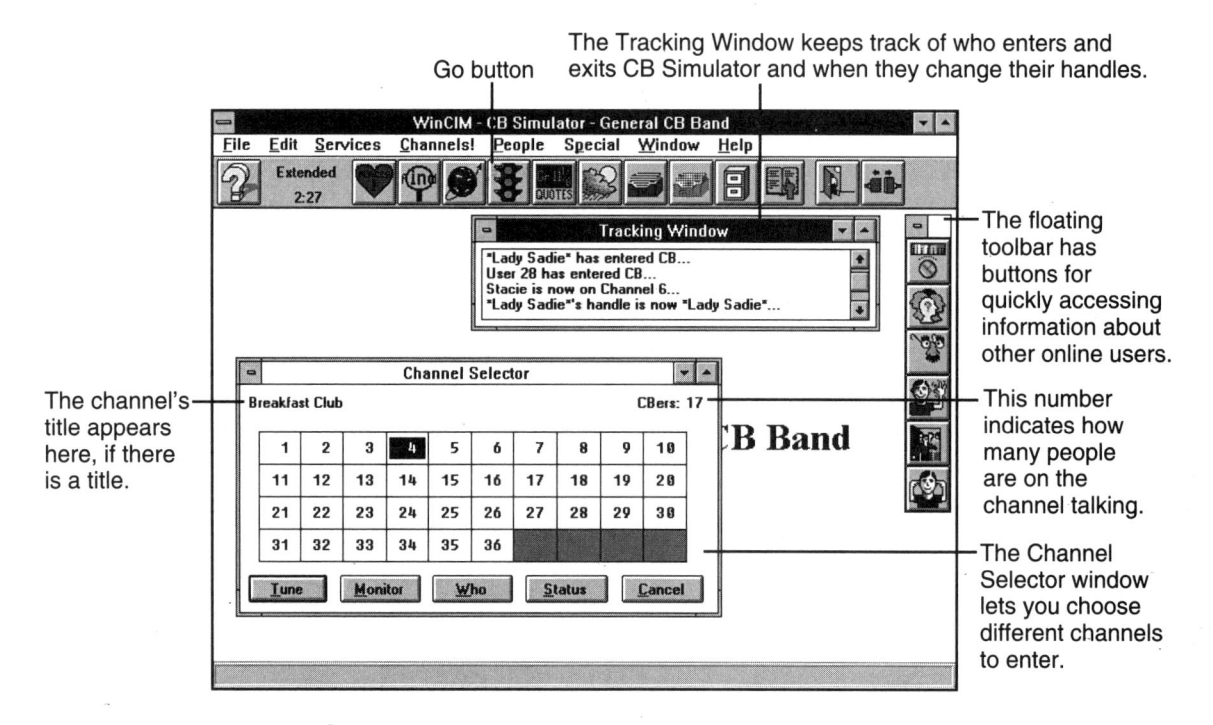

If you're using CIM, you're greeted by this screen upon your arrival in CB Simulator.

- Go button
- The Tracking Window keeps track of who enters and exits CB Simulator and when they change their handles.
- The floating toolbar has buttons for quickly accessing information about other online users.
- This number indicates how many people are on the channel talking.
- The Channel Selector window lets you choose different channels to enter.
- The channel's title appears here, if there is a title.

50

Chapter 5 ➤ *Exploring Online Services*

Pick a channel by double-clicking on it (CIM users) or by entering the channel number at the prompt (non-CIM users).

When you enter a channel, your screen may look like this:

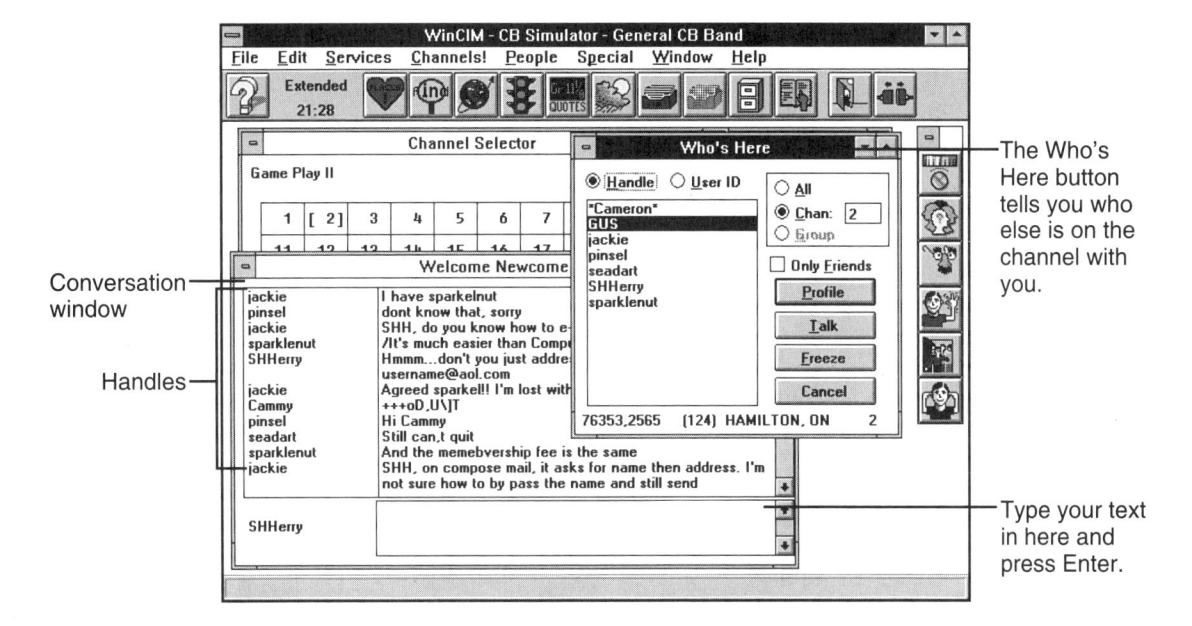

With CIM, the channel you enter looks like this.

You can start talking with others at any time. Just type your text and press **Enter**. You'll probably want to give yourself a handle before you start talking. In fact, if you're a non-CIM user, you'll have to choose a handle as soon as you enter CB Simulator. For CIM users, CompuServe assigns you a handle when you first enter the feature. You're known as *User 00*, with the zeros representing random numbers. Unless you really want to be known as *User 00* online, you need to come up with a name for yourself. To do this, pull down the **Special** menu and select **Change Handle**, or click on the **Change Handle** button on the floating toolbar. In the Change Handle dialog box that appears, type in a name for yourself, and then press **Enter** or click on **OK**.

You can change channels at any time; just click on the **Change Channel** button on the floating toolbar (CIM users) and pick another channel from the window. If you're a non-CIM user, you'll have to use special commands for changing channels. To find out what these commands are, type **/HELP** and press **Enter**. This will list the various commands you can use; each one is preceded by a slash.

To exit the CB Simulator, click on the **Exit** button on the button bar (CIM users), or type **/EXIT** (non-CIM users) and press **Enter**.

Besides chatting with everyone in the various channels, you can also have private conversations and private group conversations. These are separate little windows of dialog (although, not actually windows for non-CIM users) in which one or more people can participate. (If you're not using CIM, private conversations appear in the midst of your scrolling group conversation text, preceded by a special character, like a percent sign.)

> **More CompuServe Communication!**
>
> You can also engage in other manners of communication on CompuServe using e-mail messages and posting notes among the hundreds of special-interest forums. One of the neat features of the forums is that they give you the capability to stop and invite other forum members to chat with you while you're reading notes. Try it yourself sometime!

How Much Is This Costing Me?

You're so practical, always thinking about that bottom line. There are two ways to pay for CompuServe. One is called the Standard pricing plan, and it's $9.95 a month with unlimited connect-time, plus the first month you join is free. If you use any of the extended services, like chatting, it'll cost you $4.80 an hour. The second plan is called the Alternative pricing plan, made especially for people who don't plan to use CompuServe much except for the e-mail service. It costs $2.50 a month, plus hourly connect-time rates ranging anywhere from $6.30 to $22.80 an hour, depending on modem speed.

CompuServe offers four types of services: basic, extended, premium, and executive. The basic services fall under your flat monthly fee and include things like news, sports, and weather. The extended services, which include chatting and forums, rack up an hourly rate in addition to your monthly fee. The premium and executive services, which include a lot of the financial services, rack up an hourly rate plus surcharges when you use them. Now that you know this, be careful about where you venture online with CompuServe—it can really cost you sometimes.

America Online

America Online, or AOL for short, is probably the hippest online service out there. It's also considered the friendliest online service (and they're very patriotic, too). AOL was first created in the mid-'80s for Macintosh users. In 1991, AOL opened its network to other computer systems and has been going great guns ever since.

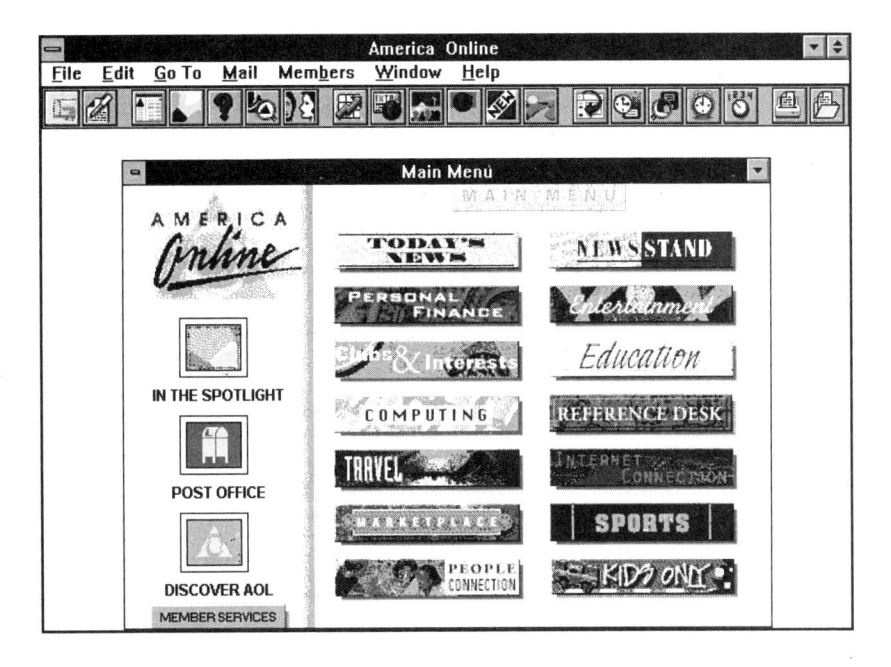

Feast your eyes on the lovely AOL screen.

To use America Online, you have to install its service-specific software and recite the Pledge of Allegiance. (Just kidding, you don't have to recite the pledge unless you really want to.) They have versions for Windows, Mac, and DOS. Each version looks pretty much the same, with menus, icons, and dialog boxes to make selections from. If you just purchased a computer or a modem, you'll probably find an AOL disk somewhere in the box, along with a registration number and a password. AOL gives away its GUI program to lure you into using the service. In fact, they've waged a pretty aggressive campaign to send everyone in America a free startup disk... at least it seems that way. If you can't get a hold of the disk, then call up AOL (1-800-827-6364) and tell them you want an account. They'll send you the software you need or give you a modem number you can call so you can download it yourself.

When you install the software and sign on, you have to type in your registration number, password, and other such account information. You also get an opportunity to choose two local network access numbers to call up AOL with. Once you wade through the sign-on procedure, you're all set to join the rest of us flag-waving, patriotic users on America Online.

Logging Onto AOL

If you're using the Windows version of AOL, just open the America Online program group and double-click the **America Online** icon. If you're using a Mac, open the folder and select the icon. If you're using DOS, switch over to the AOL directory (that's where you installed it, right?) and type **AOL** and press **Enter** to start it up.

As you're logging on, you'll have to select your ID, or handle, from the Screen Name drop-down list, and then type in your password. Hopefully, you wrote these items down and placed them somewhere safe. You're going nowhere fast without them. If you lost them, you'll need to call up AOL and cry about it.

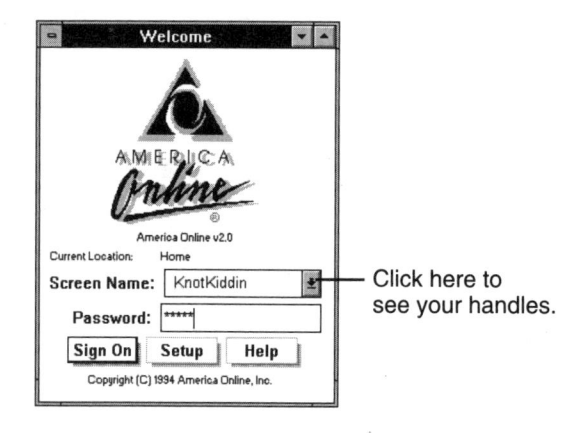

AOL's logon procedure dictates that you select a name and type a password before your modem ever makes the call.

When you log on, you'll be greeted by the opening screens. To exit at any time, choose the **Exit** or **Quit** command. You can pull down the **File** menu from the menu bar and select **Exit** (Windows or DOS) or **Quit** (Mac), or you can pull down the **Go To** menu and choose **Sign Off**. An exiting box will pop up on your monitor; that's where you can confirm whether you really want to exit.

As far as handles go, AOL calls them *screen names*. You can change yours by pulling down the **Members** menu and selecting **Edit Screen Names**. In the dialog box that appears, double-click on **Create a Screen Name**. From here you can type in a handle. (All the good ones are taken, so get creative.) The next time you log onto AOL, you can select the new handle from the drop-down list of user names.

Chapter 5 ➤ *Exploring Online Services*

Take Me to the Chatting Rooms

Ready to chat? Click on the **People Connection** button on your AOL button bar (it has two faces on it, one face talking into the other face's ear). You can also get to the chatting areas by clicking on the **People Connection** selection in the main menu window. When you select AOL's chatting feature, you're immediately dumped into a general lobby. Stick around for a minute and you'll soon see conversations scrolling across the window. Stick around even longer, and you may get some Instant Messages, or *IMs* for short. These are one-on-one conversations you can have with another member.

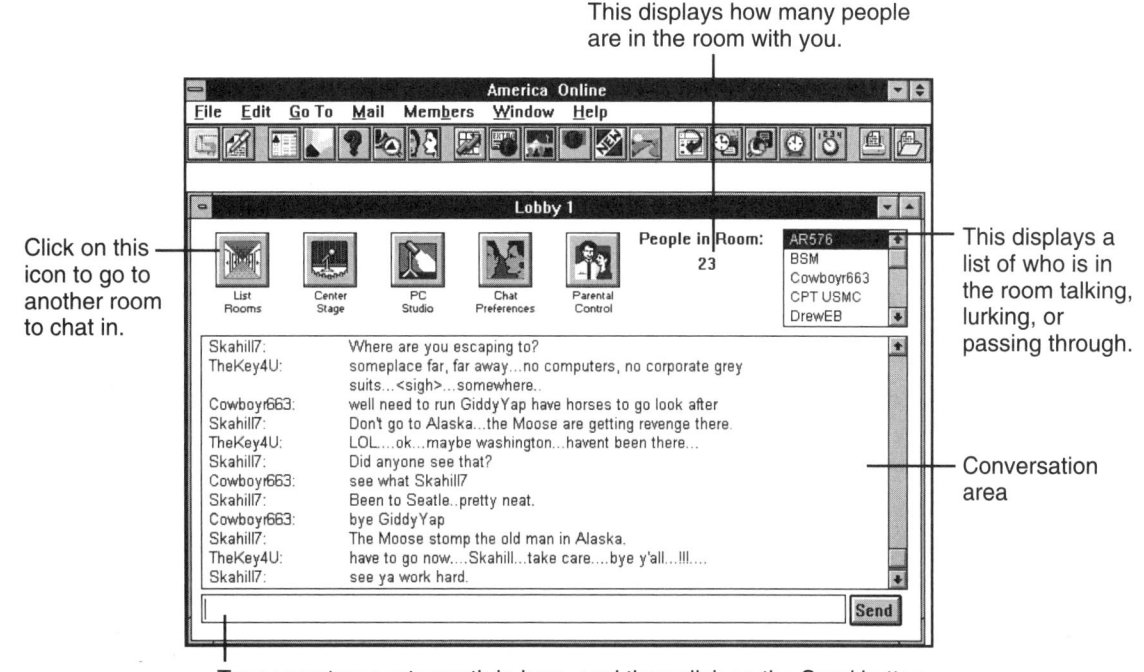

This displays how many people are in the room with you.

Click on this icon to go to another room to chat in.

This displays a list of who is in the room talking, lurking, or passing through.

Conversation area

Type your two cents worth in here, and then click on the Send button.

Here's what chatting looks like on AOL.

55

Part 1 ➤ *Straight Talk About Chatting*

> **What Are Rooms?** AOL's rooms are the same thing as CompuServe's channels. I don't know why they call them rooms instead of channels. Most of the other services call them channels. But hey—I don't own and run AOL, so I can't make them change the name of their various chatting areas.

AOL's chatting feature has an interesting layout. The various places where chatting occurs are called *rooms*. There are dozens of lobby rooms to flit back and forth between, as well as rooms geared to specific topics. At any time, you can access lists of other rooms. All you have to do is click on the **List Rooms** button at the top of your chatting window. This will open a dialog box, where you can continue listing rooms by clicking on the **More** button, or list another set of rooms by clicking on the **Available Rooms** or **Member Rooms** buttons. You can select any room on a list by double-clicking on its name.

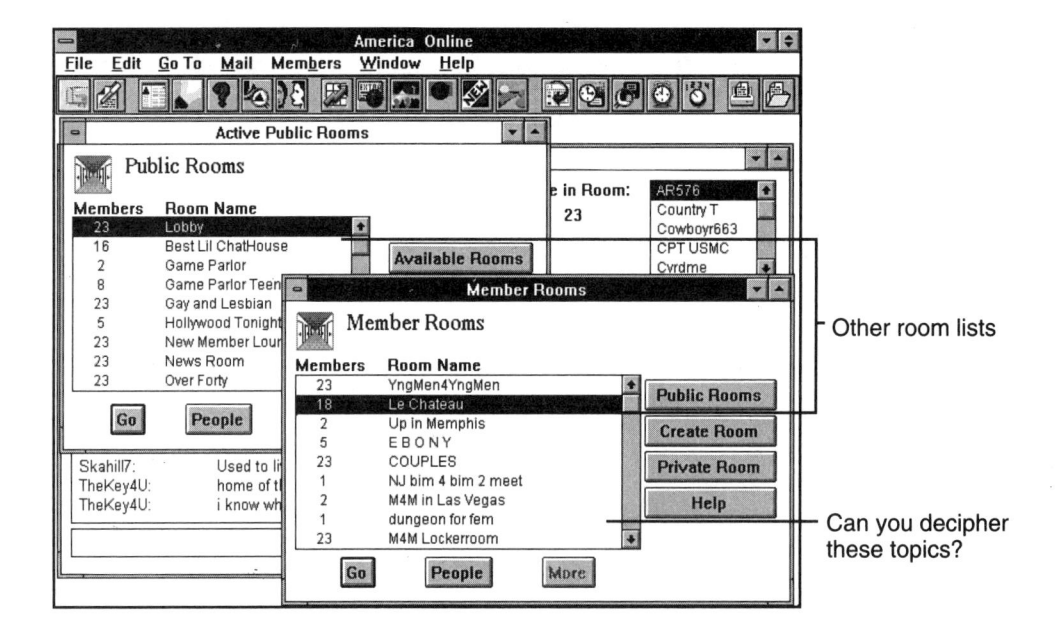

There are dozens and dozens of chat rooms on AOL.

I should stop and tell you about AOL's Member Rooms. When you display this particular list of rooms on your screen, it's rather like looking at classified ads. The majority of these rooms are geared to cybersex, as you can see in the list in the figure. I often have trouble deciphering the codes names for some of these rooms—but that's not surprising—after all, I'm from Indiana.

56

Chapter 5 ➤ *Exploring Online Services*

When you select a room, you're "beamed" into a conversation window. You can simply watch the conversation roll across your screen, or jump in at any time. To add your own text to the screen, simply type it in the bottom box, and then click on the **Send** command or press **Enter**. Your comment immediately appears in the window.

Among the various lobbies, you'll find guides to help with questions. A *guide* is an experienced AOL user. The word **GUIDE** is part of this person's name, so they're easy to spot in a chatting room. Feel free to ask guides any AOL questions; they're there to help you.

> **There Are More AOL Rooms!**
> You'll also find chatting areas among AOL's various features, such as clubs and special interest areas. MTV has a special area, for example, and you can go in and chat about Generation X stuff any old time.

Check, Please!

AOL has a relatively simple billing structure. The basic monthly package costs $9.95. It includes five hours of AOL usage a month. Anything over and above that costs an additional $2.05 an hour. For the past couple of years, AOL's been offering everyone on the planet 10 free hours of service just for signing up. Try to get your hands on this offer. (I hope the postman didn't steal your disk when AOL mailed it to you.)

You can see your bill by pulling down the **Go To** menu and choosing **Keyword**. Type the word **BILLING** in the keyword box and press **Enter**. (You can also click on the **Keyword** icon button on the button bar and then type in your keyword.) Double-click on the **Current Month's Billing Summary** icon to find out how much you've spent and how much time you have left.

PRODIGY

PRODIGY is another popular online service, originally started as a joint effort between Sears Roebuck Company and IBM. It's grown quite a bit, and has more family appeal than the other services. PRODIGY is very consumer-oriented—among other things, this means lots of advertising.

Like AOL, you need service-specific software to use PRODIGY. They make PRODIGY software for Windows, DOS, and Mac. Where do you get this software? You'll find PRODIGY startup kits available in stores, as well as free startup disks inside new computer or modem boxes. (I'm telling you, these big online guys really know how to wheel and deal with hardware manufacturers!) Other PRODIGY members can also get you great sign-up deals. But if you can't find your way onto PRODIGY by any of these methods, then just call them up yourself (1-800-PRODIGY). They'll send you the software to install, give you a user ID and a password, and help you locate two local access numbers. Be sure to write down all this stuff.

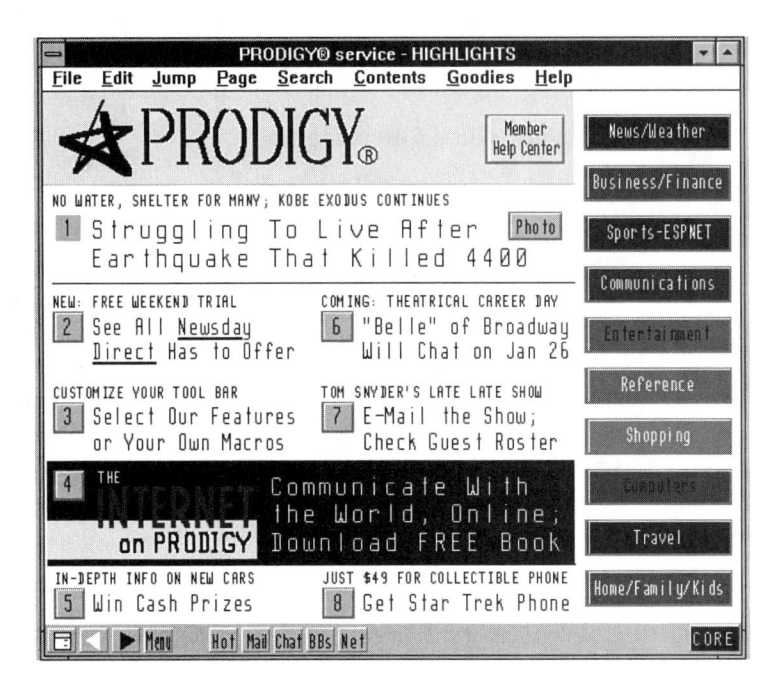

PRODIGY looks a little different from the other online services. It reminds me of a newspaper.

When you get your PRODIGY software, follow the appropriate steps for installing it on your computer system.

Logging On with PRODIGY

Hang on, here we go. Depending on your computer system, there are several ways to get online. If you're using Windows, with the Windows version of the PRODIGY software installed, just open up the PRODIGY program group window and double-click on the **PRODIGY** icon. If you have a Mac, open the PRODIGY folder and select the **Launch the Service** icon. If you're using DOS, switch over to the PRODIGY directory, type **PRODIGY** at the prompt, and then press **Enter**.

Chapter 5 ➤ *Exploring Online Services*

At the logon screen that appears, type in your ID number and password. Press **Enter** and your modem will place the call to PRODIGY. When you're finally online, you'll see PRODIGY's opening screen. From here, you can venture off to explore the service, by clicking on buttons or pulling down menus and making selections.

To log off, select the **Exit** command from the command bar at the bottom of the screen. Depending on your software version, the Exit command can appear in different places—sometimes it's a button. When you start the logoff procedure, an exiting box appears, asking you to confirm whether you really want to exit.

Welcome to Chat

To jump to PRODIGY's chatting area, you can click on the **CHAT** button (located at the very bottom of your Main menu screen), or access it through the Communications area. When the Chat screen appears, you can click on the **Change Nickname** button to set up a handle for yourself. When you're ready to start chatting, click on the **Begin Chat** button.

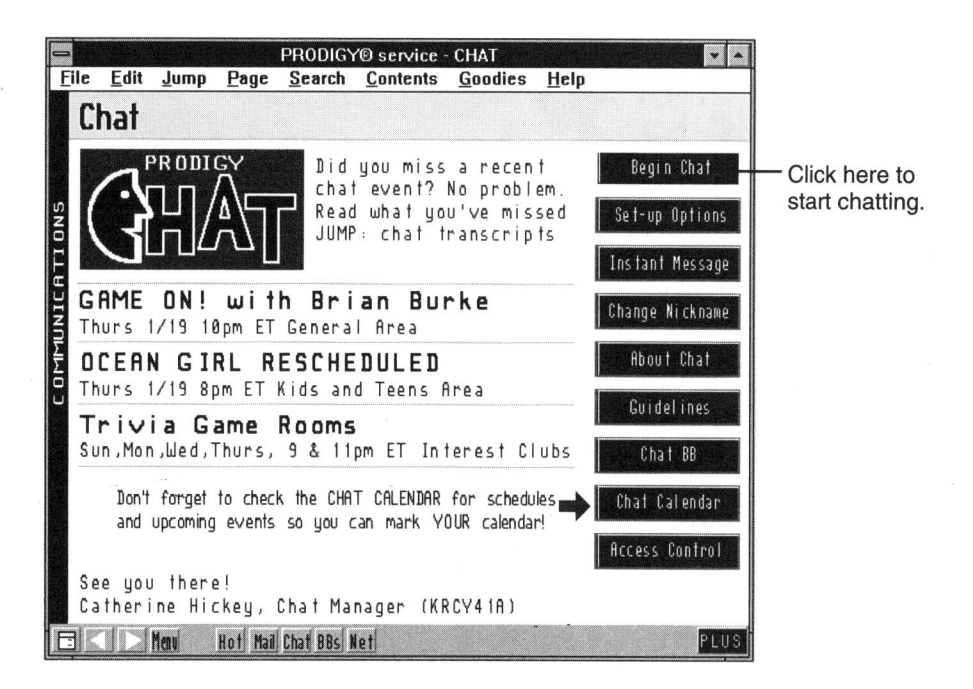

Here's the entrance to PRODIGY's chatting feature.

Click here to start chatting.

59

Part 1 ➤ *Straight Talk About Chatting*

When you enter the chatting area, you're presented with an Area and Room List dialog box. From here, you can choose a chatting room to go into. Like AOL, PRODIGY calls the chat topics "rooms." PRODIGY's chatting area is fairly new, introduced in the summer of '94. They've been doing a lot to improve it and make it more fun for everyone.

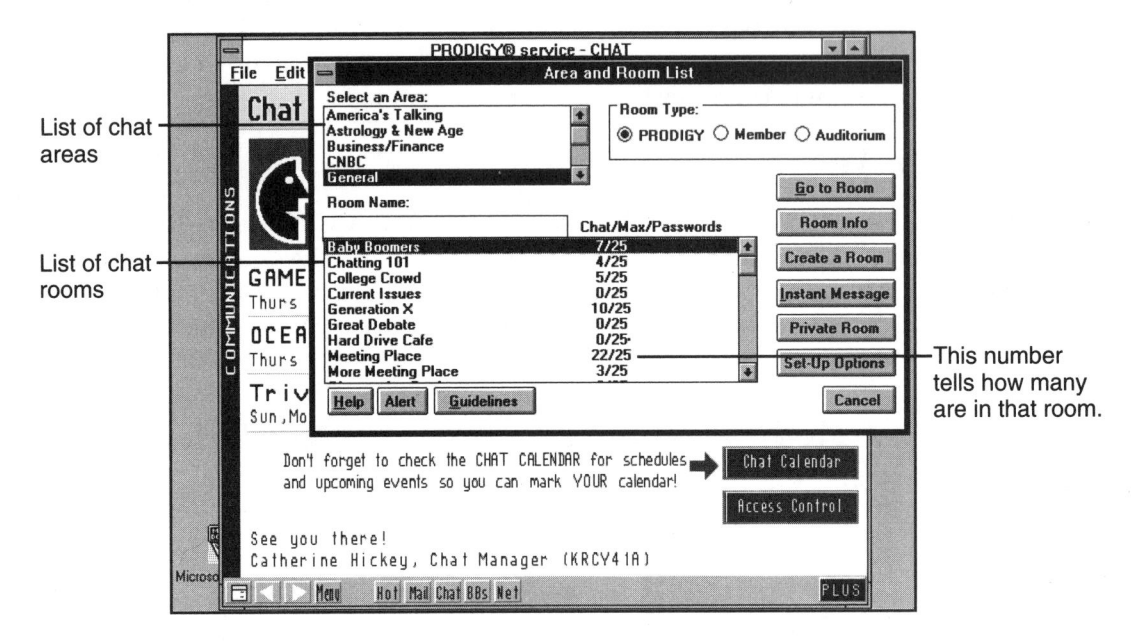

From the Area and Room List box, you can select a chatting room to enter.

To enter a room, highlight the room name and click on the **Go to Room** button, or simply double-click on the room name in the list. You can change rooms by clicking on the **Change Room** button. The various buttons to the right of the conversation window let you send instant messages to other users, find out who's in a room with you, and other such stuff. Like CompuServe and AOL, PRODIGY's instant messages are little windows that contain private conversations between members.

60

Chapter 5 ➤ *Exploring Online Services*

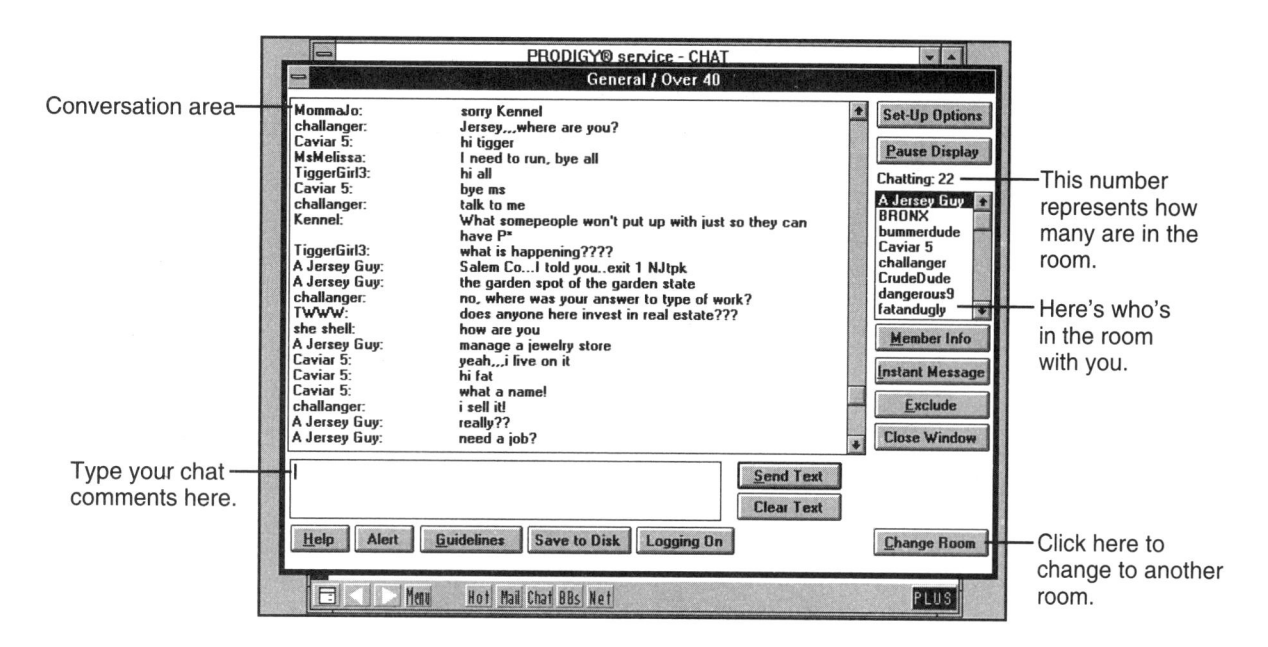

Here's what a conversation looks like on PRODIGY.

And the Grand Total Is?

PRODIGY has several different levels of services. The Free services include member services, the Core services include all the basics (like news and weather), the Plus services include bulletin boards and chatting, and the Extra-fee services include primo stuff (like the Baseball Manager game and Wall St. Edge).

PRODIGY's Basic plan costs $9.95 a month and covers 5 hours of usage. If you go over your allotted time on PRODIGY, they will bill you an additional $2.95 an hour. Cha-ching. The Value plan costs $14.95 a month, and lets you spend as much time as you want using the Core services, plus 5 hours of Plus services.

GEnie

The GEnie online service has been around awhile—since 1985. It's owned by General Electric (get it, GE?). The name itself actually stands for General Electric Network for Information Exchange. Sounds to me like they were pushing it with that one, eh?

Part 1 ▶ *Straight Talk About Chatting*

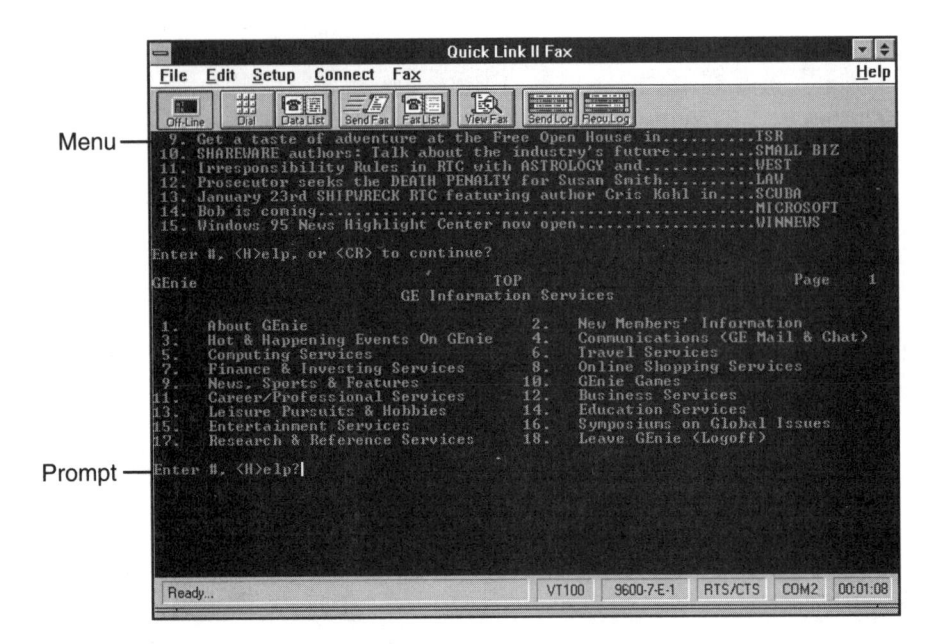

Here's what GEnie looks like, without a graphical user interface.

After reading about the other major services, you may be wondering what makes GEnie any different. It turns out that GEnie is one of the last services left to truly support a variety of computer systems, many of which are extinct now. For example, you can still access GEnie with an Atari computer, or with Commodores, Tandys, Apple IIs, and Amigas, to name a few. Because of this, GEnie still uses the old menu-driven approach. Like CompuServe without CIM, you have to use a numbers-based menu to select items, or memorize commands to type in at a prompt.

GEnie has tried to improve things by offering Windows and Mac users a GUI, called a frontend program. Sure, the GUI makes it a little easier to navigate the service, but it doesn't come close to all the nifty icons, windows, and dialog boxes used by the other big services. Aw, well. You can still chat as much as you want on GEnie, with or without a GUI.

Chapter 5 ➤ *Exploring Online Services*

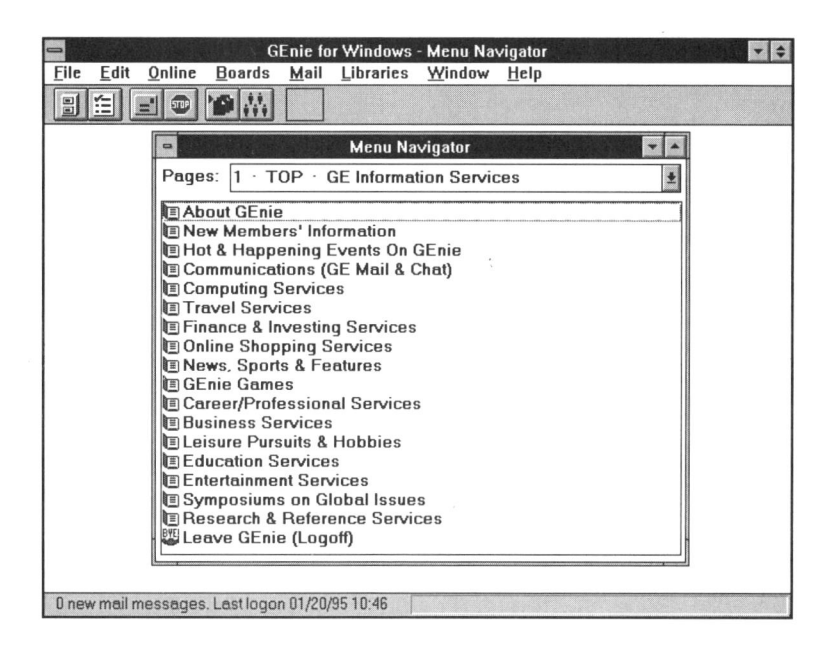

And here's what GEnie's GUI program for Windows looks like.

Summoning the GEnie

First, you have to set up an account. As you read in the discussions about the other online services, you should check your new computer box or modem box for a GEnie flier. GEnie is in on this popular advertising ploy, too. You'll also see ads for GEnie in computer magazines. But why bother with all that when I'm going to give you the number to call? To contact GEnie with a voice call, dial 1-800-638-9636. If you'd rather sign up using your modem, dial 1-800-638-8369.

You'll endure the typical sign-up process: handing over your credit card number and receiving a user ID and a password. You'll also choose a local access number to use to contact GEnie online. After you've been through this process, you're ready to log on for real.

Get Me That GEnie GUI!
Want the GEnie GUI for yourself? Call 1-800-638-9636, or download it right from the GEnie system. Type **FRONTEND** at any prompt and press **Enter**. Follow the menu selections to choose the version your system requires. Once you've downloaded the program, read the directions for installing it in the README file.

63

Logging Onto GEnie

Adjust Your Settings First! Granted, GEnie doesn't require any special software to use it, but, you'll still need to check your communications parameters before making your first call. Make sure the settings are 8-N-1 (8 data bits, parity set to **None**, and **1** stop bit). Also, turn your **Echo** setting to **On** or your **Duplex** setting to **Half**. If you don't, you may not be able to see the characters you type in. And of course, choose an appropriate modem speed to use.

When you're ready to log onto GEnie, have your communications software program call up the local access number. After the connection is made, quickly type **HHH** and press **Enter**. It doesn't matter if you type it all uppercase or lowercase, just type three *H*s as fast as you can. Why? I think the GEnie people get a perverse pleasure in seeing users type a cryptic logon command as fast as they can. Weird, huh? (If you don't type it fast enough, you'll have to go back and dial all over again, which really makes you feel like a loser.)

When you finally reach a prompt, which looks something like **U#=**, type in your assigned user ID and password, both of which are separated by a comma. Press **Enter**, and open sesame—GEnie's online. From GEnie's top menu, you can select menu items by number (typing the number in at the prompt and pressing **Enter**) and explore the service.

To log off, type **BYE** at a prompt and press **Enter**. If you're in the middle of a chatting session, type **/BYE** and press **Enter**.

Chatting with GEnie

To find GEnie's chatting area, type **CHAT** and press **Enter** from any prompt. (You can also access chatting by selecting the **Communications** option from GEnie's top menu.) When you find your way to the chatting area, you get to pick a handle for yourself.

Next, choose a chatting channel to enter, and away you go. To start talking, just type in your text and press **Enter**. To take such radical action as changing channels or exiting the program, you'll need to learn the commands to type. All the commands you issue in a chat session must be preceded by a slash. To see a list of those commands, type **/HELP** and press **Enter**.

Chapter 5 ➤ *Exploring Online Services*

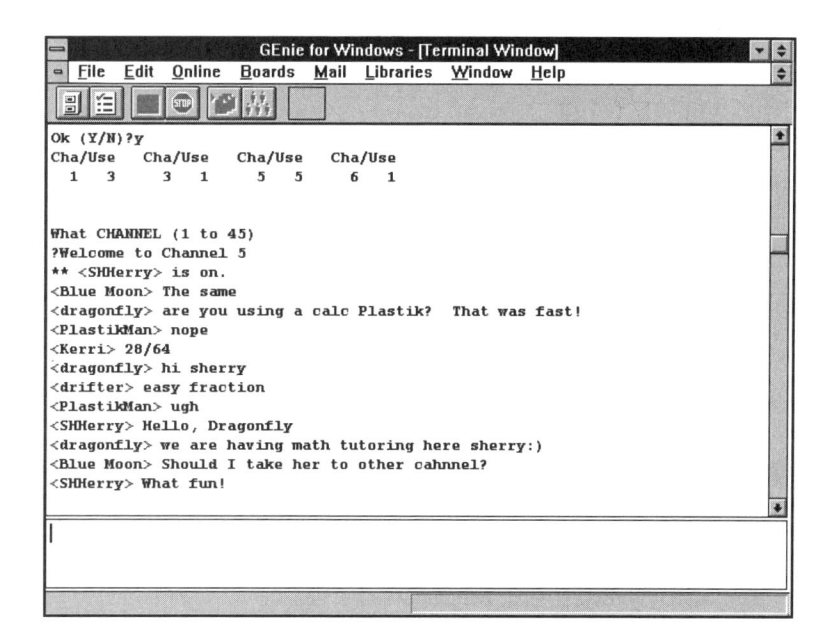

Chatting on GEnie looks a little different from chatting on the other online services.

If you install GEnie's GUI, or *frontend* program, your chatting experience may look a little better.

Send Me a Bill

GEnie is trying to be competitive with the other big online services. In fact, GEnie offers a low monthly rate of $8.95, which includes four hours of GEnie services, but none of the Premium services. If you go over the four hours, it costs $3.00 for each additional hour ($9.50 if you call GEnie between 8:00 a.m. and 6:00 p.m.).

To find out GEnie's current rates, type **RATES** at the prompt and press **Enter**.

The Other Guys

How many more online services can there be? Plenty, pal. It seems like someone starts one up every couple of months. Granted, they may not be as famous or established as the ones I just told you about, but they're still out there to explore. And chatting on them is a natural draw.

DELPHI

DELPHI started up back in 1982 as an online encyclopedia; then it added other features and quickly became a full-fledged network. Today DELPHI offers the typical online features, including live chatting and a passageway onto the Internet. DELPHI uses a menu-and-command system similar to CompuServe (without CIM) and GEnie (without the frontend program).

To get online with DELPHI, call 1-800-695-4005 and have your credit card number ready. You can also sign up via your modem; call 1-800-365-4636. DELPHI currently charges $10.00 a month, which includes four hours of service time. For $20.00 a month, you get 20 hours of service (that's only $1.00 an hour, for crying out loud!).

ImagiNation Network

Those of you who are young at heart (or who just like to play a lot of games) should sign up with the ImagiNation Network. This online service is focused entirely on games. They have games for adults, including an adult Casinoland, and for kids, including Sierraland. This is, by far, the wildest service available. What a perfect marketing concept—a service that has nothing but games. Who wouldn't want to call this up?

The ImagiNation screen looks like an amusement park, and varies depending on which season of the year it is.

The ImagiNation network also has e-mail, bulletin boards, shopping, and real-time chat. In fact, you can chat with other players in the middle of a game. The on-screen graphics are great, and it's easy to explore the service by clicking on buttons and icons. They've set up the service to look like an imaginary town. There's even a feature for setting up a composite graphic "photo" of yourself, putting a face to your name or handle.

You'll need service-specific software in order to use ImagiNation. Call 1-800-IMAGIN-1 to sign up. They'll send you the software, a user ID, and local access numbers to call. There are three cost plans to choose from. The Basic plan is $9.95 a month with five hours of service usage. The Gold plan costs $49.95 for 25 hours of usage. If that's still not enough for the game addict in you, then you can buy the Platinum plan at $99.95 for 50 hours of online play.

eWorld

Apple just introduced a new online service in 1993 called eWorld. It's a GUI-friendly service, complete with icons and windows. In fact, it reminds me a lot of the ImagiNation Network. Everything revolves around a metaphorical town square. However, somewhere in that town square is a gateway to the Internet.

Right now, eWorld is catering to Mac users, but it plans to let Windows users on in 1995. eWorld costs $8.95 a month, which includes 2 hours of services. If you run over this, it costs you $4.95 an hour. You'll need service-specific software to use the service. To get your own eWorld startup kit, call 1-800-775-4556.

There Are More Services Than Even These?

Are you bowled over by all the choices in commercial services? Well, stand back up, there are tons of other online services to try. Pick up *The Complete Idiot's Guide to Modems and Online Services* for a list of names and numbers. You might also check with your computer friends and find out who they like best. Look for new services coming out each year, like The Microsoft Network (due with Windows 95) and AT&T PersonaLink Services.

The Least You Need to Know

So which online service are you going to sign up for? In case your head is spinning, here's what you learned in this chapter:

➤ You don't have to have service-specific software to use CompuServe. Your communications program will suffice, if you reset your parameters. (But you'd be better off with CompuServe's CIM software because it makes it a whole lot easier.)

➤ CompuServe's chatting feature is called CB Simulator.

➤ America Online and PRODIGY require service-specific software in order to use their systems.

➤ Most of the online services charge you extra to use the chatting features. That's because they're run by evil, money-hungry ogres... at least that's what I hear.

➤ GEnie is in the same boat as CompuServe when it comes to interfaces. It uses a menu-based system, but you can also download a GUI for Windows or Mac.

➤ There are dozens of other online services to try; just get out there and look for them!

Chapter 6

Finding Your Way Onto the Internet

In This Chapter

- Tips for finding a service provider
- The pros and cons of connecting to the Internet using your modem
- Steps for logging onto the information superhighway
- See what IRC, the Internet's chatting feature, is all about

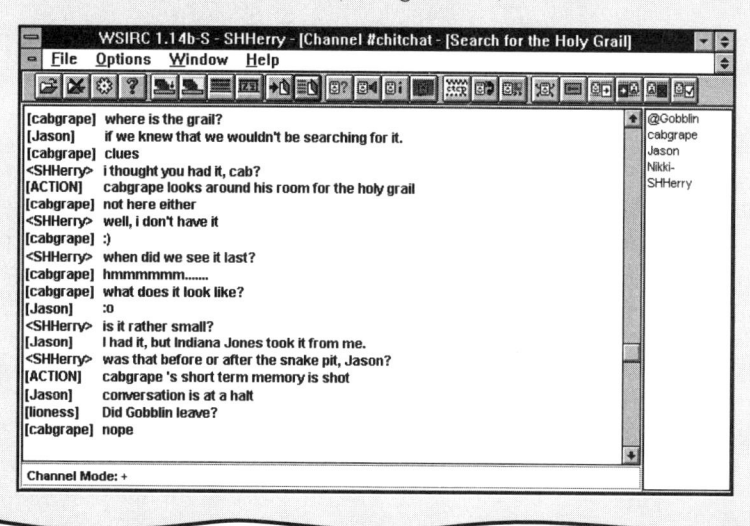

```
WSIRC 1.14b-S - SHHerry - [Channel #chitchat - [Search for the Holy Grail]
File   Options   Window   Help

[cabgrape]   where is the grail?                                          @Gobblin
[Jason]      if we knew that we wouldn't be searching for it.             cabgrape
[cabgrape]   clues                                                        Jason
<SHHerry>    i thought you had it, cab?                                   Nikki-
[ACTION]     cabgrape looks around his room for the holy grail            SHHerry
[cabgrape]   not here either
<SHHerry>    well, i don't have it
[cabgrape]   :)
<SHHerry>    when did we see it last?
[cabgrape]   hmmmmmm......
[cabgrape]   what does it look like?
[Jason]      :o
<SHHerry>    is it rather small?
[Jason]      I had it, but Indiana Jones took it from me.
<SHHerry>    was that before or after the snake pit, Jason?
[ACTION]     cabgrape 's short term memory is shot
[Jason]      conversation is at a halt
[lioness]    Did Gobbllin leave?
[cabgrape]   nope

Channel Mode: +
```

Part 1 ➤ *Straight Talk About Chatting*

As you probably know, unless you've been hiding out in a cave for the past two years, everyone's surfin' the Net (a.k.a. Internet) these days. If you haven't had a surfing lesson yet, now's as good a time as any. In this chapter, I'll tell you about what electronic surfboards to use and show you how to paddle out and catch the big one (cowabunga, cyberdude!). However, I will not be held responsible for any wipeouts or drownings, so make sure you're wearing a life-preserver (cow*abungle*, newbie-dude!).

> ### Where Did the Internet Come From?
>
> What an intelligent question. I'm glad you asked that. The Internet started in the '70s. Many trace its roots to the Department of Defense's computer system, ARPANET. This system was a test network designed to see if they could keep the computer network intact in the event of a large-scale military attack. They set up the network over a huge area, connecting it so that if some computers were damaged in an attack, the others could continue functioning as necessary, especially the communications portion of the network. The system turned out to work quite well, even though there never was an attack.
>
> Time passed, and along came the National Science Foundation (NSF) with ideas for tapping into the network to share scientific information all across the world, especially among the big universities and research centers. It wasn't long before large businesses, educational facilities, and everyone else started getting on board.
>
> Since then, the Internet has continued to grow and grow, mostly without guidance, control, or planning. That's why it seems like such a jumbled mess out there on the superhighway.

How to Look for an On-Ramp

In Chapters 3 and 4, you learned some important details about the Internet—like, for instance, what it is. Obviously, since the Internet is a vast network of many networks, it's not always a simple thing to get online with it. Why's that? Because it's so darned vast. It's like looking at the stars at night, and every star is like an electronic destination point on the great cyberspace roadmap. (Wow, man, that's really heavy.)

I've already explained some possible ways to find an on-ramp. If you don't have a free permanent connection, you need to look for a service provider. Remember what I told you about service providers? (Just nod your head and I'll move right along.) A service provider is hooked up to the Internet and will let you hook up, too, using their computer system—all for a nominal price, of course. To connect to a service provider, you'll need to

Chapter 6 ➤ *Finding Your Way Onto the Internet*

use your computer's modem. (If you've already got a permanent connection to the Internet, such as through a networked office computer at work or something, you can doze off during the next few paragraphs while I talk about modem connections.)

> **About Those Permanent Connections...**
>
> A permanent connection, also called a *dedicated connection* or a *permanent direct connection*, literally connects you directly to the Internet—without the aid of a modem. These types of connections are common among large businesses, universities, and schools. Typically, the organization's computers are connected to a router, which in turn is connected to a service provider through a leased telephone line. With such a network connection, the organization never needs to call up the service provider with a modem. The leased line is their constant link to the Internet.
>
> As you can imagine, such a connection is very expensive—$5000 and above for all the hardware involved, plus hundreds to thousands monthly for the leased telephone line. If you happen to be using a computer linked to the Internet in this way, then more power to you. I just hope you're not the one paying the bills for this newfangled technology. However, the rest of us have to scramble for individual connections, so don't give us any grief over it.

There are hundreds of service providers to choose from. Being the incredibly nice author I am, I'm going to give you the names and phone numbers of some of the better ones. Take a look at this handy chart.

Service Providers	Phone Numbers
Internet Transit	315-453-2912, ext. 230
The Well	415-332-4335
NOVX	800-873-6689
NETCOM	800-501-8649
Portal	408-973-9111
ICNet/Innovative Concepts	313-998-0090
The World	617-739-0202
MV Communications	603-429-2223

continues

Part 1 ➤ *Straight Talk About Chatting*

Continued

Service Providers	Phone Numbers
ANSRemote	800-456-8267
CERFnet—General Atomics/CERFnet	800-876-2373
Gateway to the World	305-670-2930
CICNet, Inc. (Midwest)	313-998-6104

Those are just a few. There are hundreds more out there, you just have to locate them. Look among the advertisements in computer magazines, check with your local computer club, or ask your geeky technical friends. You can also call such organizations as FARNET (1-800-723-2763), InerNIC Information Services Referral Desk (1-800-444-4345), or Network Information Services Center (1-415-859-5318) for help with finding a service provider.

You'll find suggestions for service providers mentioned among the various Internet-focused computer books. You might try Peter Kent's *The Complete Idiot's Guide to the Internet*. It has lots of suggestions for using the Internet, plus coupons for numerous service providers from around the world.

> **Other Internet Connections**
>
> Just about every commercial online service these days offers you some access to the Internet. It may be limited access, but it's still a way to look around and locate information on the Net. In fact, there's a big scramble among all the services right now to offer you the best and most Internet access, and we're not just talking about e-mail. Services like AOL and PRODIGY offer members access to newsgroups (message boards), browser programs (for looking around the Net), and FTP capabilities (downloading files from the Net). Shop around and see what you can find.

Let's Go Over Those Internet Connections Again

In Chapter 4, I told you about the various types of connections you can make to the Internet. Remember? Of course not, that was two chapters ago. You can connect to the Internet via a service provider with a *dial-in terminal* or a *dial-in direct* account. If you set up a dial-in terminal account, you'll be calling up the service provider's computer and

Chapter 6 ➤ *Finding Your Way Onto the Internet*

using it to connect to the Internet. However, your computer won't have any power to think on its own in this scenario. You'll be using all of the service provider's computer's power. (Are you following along with all this?)

With a dial-in terminal account, you'll probably spend as little as $15 to $25 a month, plus connect-time charges. If that's the kind of Internet connection you want, be sure to find out from your chosen service provider what exactly you'll be charged for. Sometimes they charge you different prices based on your modem's speed. There may be an initial first-time setup fee involved, too. Also find out how much access you'll have to the Internet, and whether there are limits to your usage. Ask the provider for full access, including e-mail, FTP (file transfer program), Usenet, telnet, and all the other great Internet stuff.

> **Connect-Time Charges** Hourly-based rates for the amount of time you spend tying up the telephone lines with your modem. Depending on what kind of number you're calling—local, toll-free, or long-distance—connect-time charges will vary. They'll also vary based on your modem's speed and the time of day you're placing the call. (At moments like this, I really wish I had invested in telephone wires.)

The beauty of a dial-in terminal connection is that you don't have to have any special software installed on your computer in order to use the Internet. Instead, you'll be using the service provider's software. Hopefully, they have a nice GUI program you can easily understand. Dial-in terminal connections are best for the casual Internet surfer.

But if you're looking to catch some serious Internet waves, you'll want a dial-in direct account (called a *SLIP*, *CSLIP*, or *PPP* connection). This type of account will get you and your computer connected directly to the Internet, via the service provider. With a dial-in direct account, you're directly linked to the Internet and your computer will need some Internet-savvy software to get around. Such software is called *TCP/IP* software. Translated, that means Transmission Control Protocol/Internet Protocol. You can expect to pay anywhere from $300–$400 for it at a software retailer (or if you purchase it from the service provider). There are also some TCP/IP shareware programs available, which will cost a lot less but are also much more difficult to work with. My advice is to go for the commercial software and find a service provider to help you with it all.

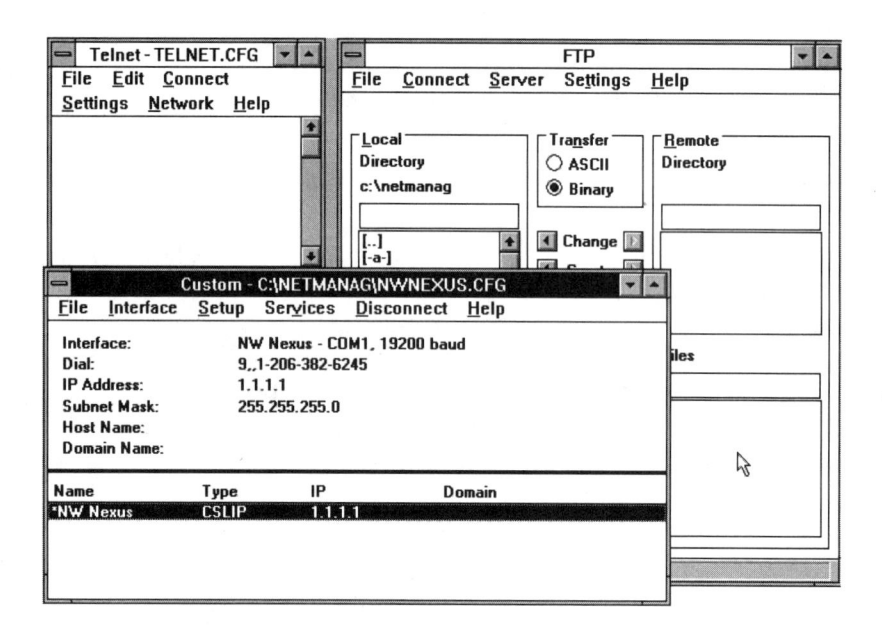

Chameleon is an example of TCP/IP software. It's a suite of Windows programs for using the Internet.

> ### Wait a Minute! What's a SLIP?
>
> Some of you won't be able to read on unless I stop and explain SLIP, CSLIP, and PPP. *SLIP* stands for Serial Line Internet Protocol. *CSLIP* stands for Compressed Serial Line Internet Protocol. *PPP* stands for Point-to-Point Protocol. All of these are TCP/IP connections, designed for telephone wires instead of network wires. These connections are almost as good as a dedicated connection. Okay, now go back to the rest of the chapter.

Once you've managed to sign up with a service provider and open an account (which includes a login name, a password, and a telephone number your modem can call), you're ready to start cruising the information superhighway. Before you speed on out there, I recommend you gas up first. By that, I mean take a look at what steps you need to follow and find out where you're going.

Chapter 6 ➤ *Finding Your Way Onto the Internet*

Going Online with the Internet

At this point, I'm going to tell you how to log on to the Internet. By now, you should have selected a service provider (if applicable), and you should have decided which kind of account type you want to use. Having done so, you should be equipped with the phone number of your service provider's computer, a login name (lovingly referred to as a *handle* in some circles), and a password. Hopefully, your service provider has given you the necessary information for conducting e-mail communications and what settings to adjust on your modem.

So, how do you get online? Try the approach that suits your situation:

➤ If you have a *permanent* connection, there's not a whole lot to worry about when you first go online. All you have to do is type your login name at the appropriate area, type your password, and then press **Enter**. You'll probably have to type a few other commands to get to the Internet, but that's about it.

➤ If you're using a *dial-in terminal* connection, it's very similar to calling up a BBS or online service. You must prompt your modem to make the call connecting you to the service provider's computer. Then you'll have to log in with your assigned ID and type your password.

➤ If you're using a *dial-in direct* account, your steps are a little more complicated. You have to use your special Internet software program to get connected. If your software is installed and running, you can call up your service provider and logon. This usually involves typing your account ID and password.

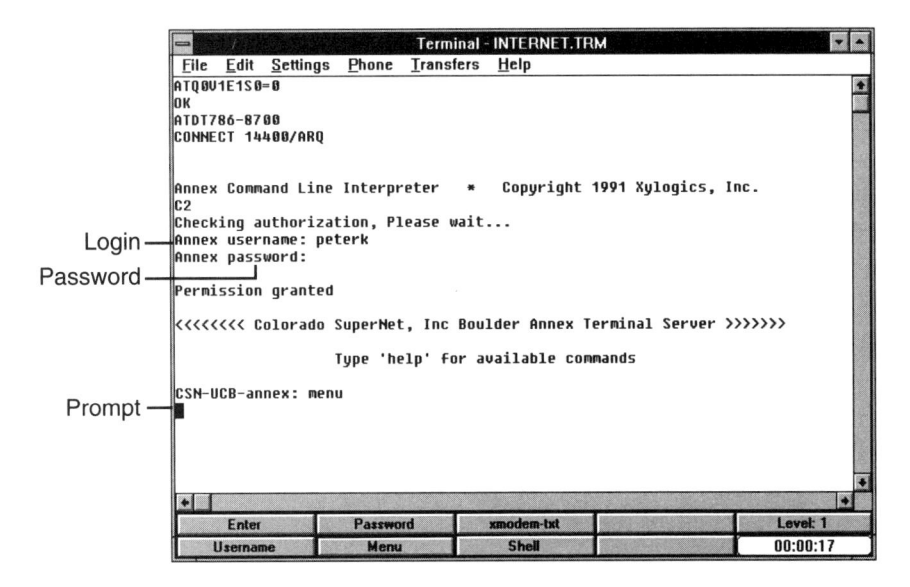

```
Terminal - INTERNET.TRM
File  Edit  Settings  Phone  Transfers  Help
ATQ0V1E1S0=0
OK
ATDT786-8700
CONNECT 14400/ARQ

Annex Command Line Interpreter    *    Copyright 1991 Xylogics, Inc.
C2
Checking authorization, Please wait...
Annex username: peterk
Annex password:

Permission granted

<<<<<<<< Colorado SuperNet, Inc Boulder Annex Terminal Server >>>>>>>

                   Type 'help' for available commands

CSN-UCB-annex: menu
█
```

Login — Annex username: peterk
Password — Annex password:
Prompt — █

This is what a login procedure might look like on your computer.

75

What Happens Next?

So, what happens when I finally make it onto the information superhighway? Are there other users speeding by? Am I going to get run over? Where do I go? What do I do? How do I signal a lane change? Does my service provider come equipped with an air bag? Hold on a minute—you've got to stop asking so many questions or you're going to confuse me and we'll run off the road. Settle back and fasten your seatbelt. I'll explain it all to you.

> **Log Off**
> Be sure to check with your service provider (or system administrator) for the proper steps to follow when logging off the Internet!

Once you've made it online, there are several different scenarios that may present themselves to you. You may see a glaring command line with a UNIX prompt, or you may see a bunch of on-screen instructions prompting you to make some choices. The lucky among you will see a menu shell. A menu shell will definitely make your Internet journey more pleasant. You can use a menu shell to select menu items or commands you want to activate. Just follow the directions provided by your service provider, or follow the on-screen prompts for assistance. If you're super-lucky, your service provider is using a friendly GUI to navigate the Internet.

If you're absolutely *unlucky*, you'll see a wretched UNIX prompt on your screen when you log on. You poor soul, you. Actually, it's not that bad. If you're familiar with DOS, then UNIX won't seem too foreign to you. If you're a Windows or Mac enthusiast, the UNIX prompt may give you some grief. For one thing, you have to know what commands to type in at this prompt in order to get any mileage on the information superhighway.

> **What's a UNIX Prompt?**
> If you're having trouble identifying your UNIX prompt, here's a tip for you. Your UNIX command line with a prompt may look different, depending on your host's computer. For example, your UNIX prompt may include the host computer's name followed by a percent sign or a dollar sign, or something along those lines. Look for such a prompt on your screen. If you find it, that's where you can enter UNIX commands or menu commands.

UNIX is a lot like DOS; for example, everything's arranged in directories. To open a directory, you have to type **cd /directoryname** (you type the real directory's name in place of *directoryname*). There are many more UNIX commands you need to know to navigate the Internet. Make sure your service provider gives you some assistance, or pick up a good book on the subject (try *The Complete Idiot's Guide to UNIX* by John McMullen).

After you've figured out how to get around on the Internet using the techniques appropriate to your situation (menu shell, GUI, or UNIX prompt), you're ready to make your way to the chatting areas.

IRC

Here's the fun part: finding your way to the chat areas of the Internet. Internet's real-time chatting is called *IRC*, which stands for Internet Relay Chat. IRC is arranged into channels. This channel motif should start to seem pretty familiar to you after reading the chapter about online services. Borrowing from the CB craze of the '70s, channels are simply online places where you can talk to other users.

When IRC channels are hoppin', you may find 50 people chatting at a time. During slow periods, there may only be one or two people on a channel. Like online services, IRC channels have names. Since we're talking about the broad spectrum of the Internet, channel names range from the ordinary to the obscure, and beyond. There really is something for everyone, including the good, the bad, and the ugly.

Dying to try out IRC? Here's what you can do:

➤ If you're using a permanent networked connection, follow your site's access instructions. For some users, this may just mean typing the word **irc** at the main menu and pressing **Enter**.

➤ If you're using a dial-in direct account, look for IRC among your GUI icons or among the menu commands (depending on your situation). Follow the guidelines pertaining to your software or service provider.

➤ If you're using a dial-in terminal account, you'll have to look for IRC options among the service provider's Internet menus or features.

Chatting the UNIX Way

After you've logged onto IRC, you probably want to know what to do to start chatting. Well, you have to pick a channel first. Type **/list** at the UNIX prompt, and press **Enter**. This will display a list of available channels, including a description of the channel name and how many fellow online travelers are on the channel.

When you're ready to select a channel, type **/channel #*channelname*** (substitute the real channel's name after the number sign), and then press **Enter**. For example, to enter the Chatzone channel, type /**channel #chatzone**, then press **Enter**. To start adding your own comments to the conversation, just type your text. To change channels, use the slash command that I just showed you. To exit IRC, type /**quit** and press **Enter**.

Any commands you'd like to activate while in IRC chat have to be preceded by the slash. If you don't type a slash first, your command is entered into the on-screen conversation, making you look a little foolish for not remembering to type the slash in the first place. To see a list of commands, type /**help** and press **Enter**.

```
[Ariela2-MODE] Has changed Snugglez's mode to -o
[leena]       pretty good DONO how about you?
[Gaul]        newgrl: second/third
[SERVER]      rk has left this channel
[CptDanger]   Snugglez! Hiya
[SERVER]      starboro has left this channel
[DONO]        leena...not that bad...got a class in 15 min :(
[newgrl]      gaul: what's your major?
[SERVER]      indica!dkaplan@acad.bryant.edu has joined this channel
[SERVER]      Duke44!~duke@barton.spring.com has joined this channel
[GAMER]       newgrl hows life??
[Gaul]        newgrl: comp.sci
[SERVER]      Duke44 has left this channel
[Snugglez]    re duke...
[leena]       DONO : :( I'm sorry to hear that..I have one class left today..at 2:30
[newgrl]      gamer, not bad, u?
[Uncloud]     *sigh*
[SERVER]      DONO has left this channel
[indica]      hi newgrl....I major in Management...soon Law.
[Tozai]       'lo Sungglez
```

Here's what chatting looks like on the Internet.

GUI Chatting on IRC

Real-time conversations look a little better using a GUI program for the Internet. In fact, chatting in this manner looks very similar to the chat rooms found on AOL or PRODIGY. Instead of a black screen with scrolling text, you get lovely little window boxes with special places for typing in your comments, reading what the others say, and seeing who else is on the channel with you.

Chapter 6 ➤ *Finding Your Way Onto the Internet*

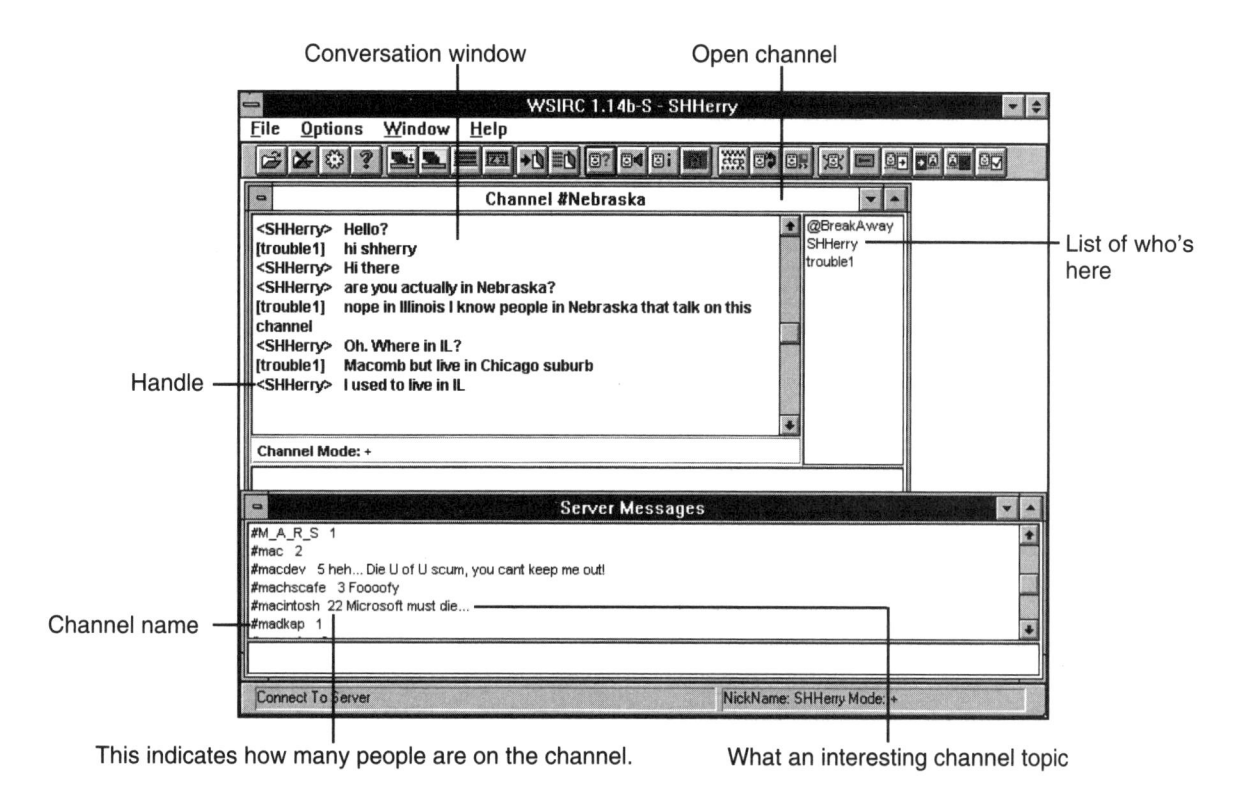

Chatting looks a little prettier in a GUI setup.

When working with GUIs, there are usually icon buttons and menus you can select from to change channels, send private messages, identify others, and so on. If you're a visual person by nature, then this format will seem simpler to use and much easier to follow. In case you couldn't tell, I'm a big advocate of GUI programs—after all, seeing is believing.

Other Chat Areas

Is there anyplace else on the Internet for chatting? Yup. If you prefer one-on-one conversations with an Internet friend, you might want to try your hand at *YTalk*, *ntalk*, or just plain *talk*. All of these are variations of real-time private conversations.

Just Plain talk

To access *talk*, which is the simplest one to try, type **talk** *username* at the prompt, and then press **Enter**. (Substitute your Internet friend's name for *username*.) If your friend isn't

79

using the same service provider as you, you have to type the name of his/her location. For example, you'd type in **talk jsmith@swestern.edu** using the @ sign and typing the location of the other person.

This greeting immediately shows up on your friend's screen. To respond, your friend types **talk** and your name and address. Naturally, you and your friend have to be logged onto the Internet at the same time to get this to work. It won't work if your friend is in the middle of running a program and the paging feature is turned off. As you've probably figured out by now, this method of conversation works best when it's arranged in advance between both parties. One more thing: your service provider has to have talk available as a feature for you to use, or all of this is pointless.

How About YTalk?

YTalk is another chatting option, but unlike simple *talk*, YTalk lets more than two people get together for a private chat. To use YTalk, type **ytalk *username username username***, and then press **Enter**. The *usernames* are the names of all the people you want to talk to in a conference setting. YTalk will contact each person and invite them into the conversation. In order to use YTalk, it must be loaded onto your service provider's computer or your own computer depending on your scenario.

Windows Talking

Windows users can chat with WinTalk or WSIRC. WinTalk is a GUI-based one-on-one chatting feature. If your Internet software or service provider has WinTalk, it's easy to find. Its icon looks like a smiley face. When selected, it brings up a window from which you can select someone to talk to. You can also try chatting with WSIRC, which stands for Windows Sockets Internet Relay Chat, a Windows-based version of IRC.

The Dirt on MUDs

Ever play in the MUD? The Internet has a very strange group of games called *MUDs*. MUD stands for Multiple User Dimensions, but some people prefer Multiple User Dialogue. Basically, MUDs are text-based games played by multiple players. You can create your own character and wander around a virtual environment filled with other players. As you wander about, you'll meet other people, fight monsters, solve puzzles, and chat.

I wouldn't have even mentioned this odd concept at all, except that it involves a lot of chatting. If you're into this kind of thing (adventure playing while socializing at the same time), you can *telnet* (an Internet feature that lets you access other Internet computers—kind of like beaming around cyberspace onto other "ships") to a MUD site.

Chapter 6 ➤ *Finding Your Way Onto the Internet*

Check your service provider; they might even be running a MUD game you can play. You can also use Internet's seek and find tools, like *Gopher*, to locate other MUDs to try.

The Least You Need to Know

Now you know what it takes to surf the Net and chat on IRC. Hopefully, you've found a suitable electronic surfboard to use, and you're wearing plenty of sun-block. Just remember to wait 30 minutes before going into the cyber-water after eating, okay?

- ➤ A permanent connection is a direct link to the Internet via a leased telephone line or dedicated wiring—no modem is required.

- ➤ A dial-in terminal connection lets you use a service provider's computer and surf the Net from the host computer. You get to use the host's Internet programs without having to worry about buying any software of your own.

- ➤ A dial-in direct connection hooks up your computer directly to the Internet via a service provider. You have to have special software to do this.

- ➤ Depending on your service provider connection, you may see a UNIX prompt, a menu shell, or a friendly GUI when you log onto the Internet.

- ➤ To access Internet's chat feature, look for IRC (Internet Relay Chat). IRC is set up into many channels. Each channel has a different name or topic.

- ➤ You can carry on private conversations with talk, YTalk, and other similar programs.

Chapter 7

BBSs: Small Group Chatting

In This Chapter

- Tips for finding a good BBS for chatting
- Steps for logging onto a BBS
- Details about how to answer the questions during the sign-on procedure

```
          Channel #x-files -  UFO's, Abductions, Sightings

[Sisyphus]  SHHerry : The gov't is the government dudes who are doing the coverups
<SHHerry>   Which dudes in particular, that's my point
[DeLIrluM]  Experimental Dudes R Us Inc. probably ;)
<SHHerry>   We always say "they" but who are "they" exactly?
[Medea]     well, higher officials excluding the president who is really a puppet, Shherry
[prancer]   They (always spelled w/a capital T) rearrange your furniture when you're not
            home & then put it back.
[System]    nutcase has joined this channel
[GGA]       hi nutcase
[nutcase]   hi gca
[DeLIrluM]  hi nutcase. They also take your socks, but only one of each pair!!
[Medea]     hi nutcase
[nutcase]   hi medea
[DeLIrluM]  i HATE that - i've got 12 black socks without pairs!!!
<SHHerry>   I think I have the other 12, DeLirlum
[prancer]   hey, i really do. they're all different shades of black...
[DeLIrluM]  shh & prancer - i guess we make a club called Mystery socks
[Medea]     yes
[DeLIrluM]  i think i've seen UFo's and i don't take drugs - so know one can say i was on them
            when i saw them..
```

If commercial online services and the Internet seem too big for you, try your hand at chatting on your local BBS. BBSs offer you a smaller "group" setting in terms of the number of users. In this chapter, I'll tell you how to find a BBS and what to expect when you log onto one.

How to Find a Chatty BBS

The very first time I heard the word BBS mentioned, I thought it referred to television. Obviously, I was confusing a BBS with the BBC (British Broadcasting Company). But that was a long time ago. Once I figured out what BBSs were and how to use them, I stopped watching a lot of TV and spent more time dialing around the globe with my modem and computer. This new electronic hobby can be rather entertaining in and of itself.

> **Sysop:** Short for systems operator. A sysop manages everything involved with the upkeep of a BBS or message board. Sysops keep things organized and updated. Sysops also have the power to boot people off the system, especially if they anger the sysop in any way. Some sysops are nicer than others; try to keep on the good side of your system's sysop.

Compared to the commercial services which are designed for the masses, BBSs are flavorful little communities, each with its own distinctive personality. Run by a variety of people from a variety of places, BBSs can take on many forms. For example, some BBSs you call up are governed by committee; a select group of people determine how it's run. These types of BBSs can be sort of clique-ish, or snobby at times. Others BBSs are operated by a lone *sysop* (systems operator), who may choose to run the BBS like a dictator. Still other BBSs are incredibly friendly and welcoming, treating you like a long-lost brother or sister. My point is, you'll find all kinds of BBSs—you just have to be willing to search for the one you want to join.

BBSs, or bulletin board systems, aren't for everyone. New users might find them intimidating and difficult to navigate. Why? Because BBSs aren't as slick-looking and user-friendly as the big online services. But that doesn't mean you shouldn't check them out. There are thousands of BBSs out there, hundreds if you live in a large city. You may even have a local BBS in your own town. BBSs range in topics and focus, you'll find anything from technical support BBSs to fun-and-games BBSs. But most of all, you'll find plenty of chatting on the BBS circuit too.

Chapter 7 ➤ *BBBs: Small Group Chatting*

What's a BBS?

Flashback to Chapter 3 for the gory details about what a BBS is, who runs it, and the different kinds of BBSs available.

Look Ma, No Software

Unlike many of the commercial services and parts of the Internet, you don't need any special software to call up a BBS. Your communications program will work just fine. You may have to adjust a few settings first, such as your communications parameters, but for the most part, your modem software will suffice. Isn't that a relief? That means you don't have to buy anything else, or download and install software—you can use the communications program already installed on your computer.

The software you'll encounter running the various BBSs will vary greatly, which explains why every BBS out there looks different. Most BBSs use a menu-based system that lets users select from a variety of menu commands. You can type corresponding menu letters or numbers at a prompt, and then press **Enter** to make your selection. PCBoard, Wildcat!, TBBS, Major BBS, First Class BBS, and Galacticom are some of the more popular BBS software programs. These programs let the BBS operator set up how the screens look and how the menus appear. If you ever start up your own BBS, you'll need to use one of these BBS software packages.

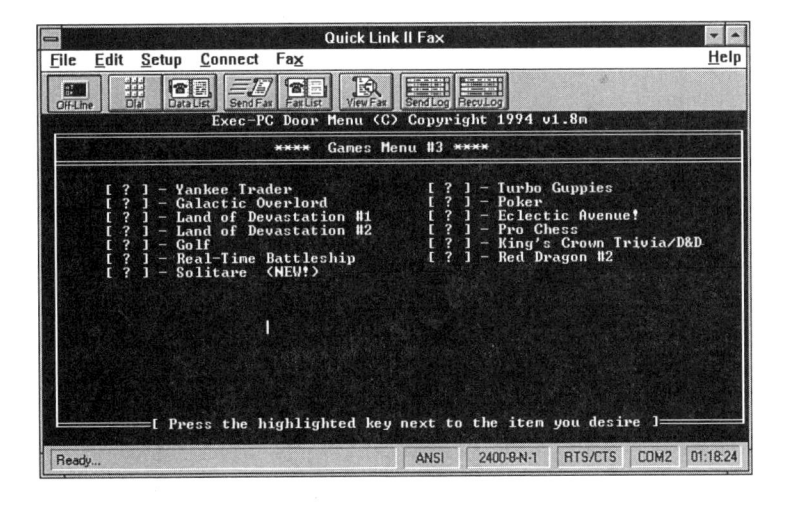

BBS menus will have many different looks, but they invariably involve menus.

Part 1 ➤ *Straight Talk About Chatting*

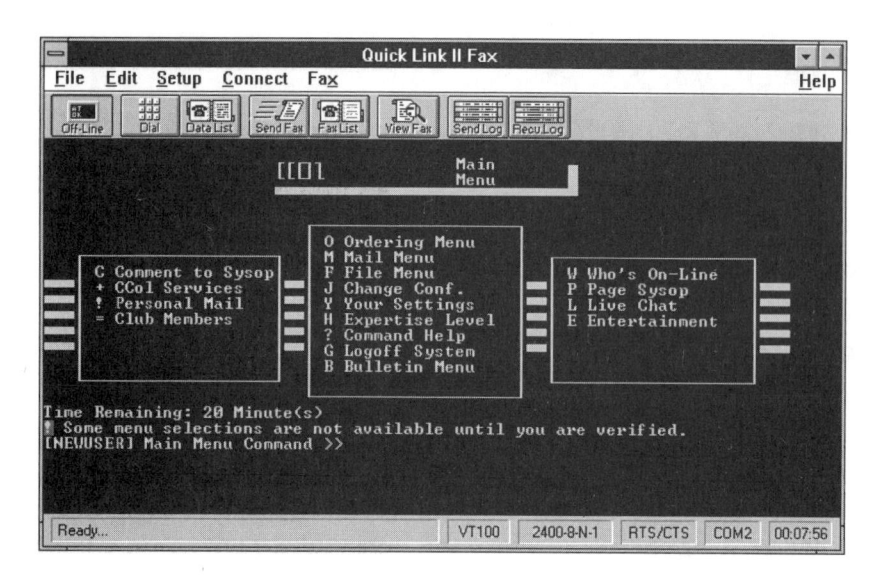

A menu from a Wildcat! board.

Who You Gonna Call?

Maybe you're wondering where to begin looking for a good BBS. There are many places to check. Start by asking computer friends; they usually know some cool BBSs to try. Consult with your local computer club; you'll probably run across some members who run their own BBSs. Your local computer stores also post BBSs you can call. One of the best resources for finding a BBS is *Boardwatch Magazine*. It lists popular BBS numbers. *Computer Shopper* magazine also has a column that gives out BBS numbers from around the world.

To get you started on your BBS journey, however, I'm going to give you a list of BBSs you and your modem can call. They vary in location and interests, but they all offer online chatting.

BBS Name	Number	Location	Description
Monterey Gaming System	408-655-5555	Monterey, CA	Lots of online games and plenty of real-time conferencing
The INDEX System	404-924-8472	Woodstock, GA	Good place for finding BBS listings, Internet e-mail, and chat

Chapter 7 ➤ *BBBs: Small Group Chatting*

BBS Name	Number	Location	Description
The File Bank, Inc.	303-534-4646	Denver, CO	Shareware files, e-mail, and lots of chat
Ultimate BBS	217-792-3663	Mt. Pulaski, IL	Big on chat, as well as files to download
The Rock Garden	602-220-0001	Phoenix, AZ	Games and chat
Compass Rose	916-447-0292	Davis, CA	Very social chat system, plus e-mail and message-posting
Tampa Connection	813-961-8665	Tampa, FL	A romance-focused group, access to Internet
Micro Message Service	919-779-6674	Raleigh, NC	Shareware files, chat, and Internet connections
Top City	612-225-1003	St. Paul, MN	Lots of chat and info
Capital City Online	206-956-1123	Olympia, WA	Files, games, and chat
Tech Talk	407-635-8833	Titusville, FL	Tons of files, Internet e-mail, and Ultrachat
Point Blank	516-755-3000	Plainview, NY	Internet e-mail, entertainment and business info, chat
Possibilities	619-748-5264	Poway, CA	Games, message boards, Ultrachat
Synergy Online	201-331-1797	Parsippany, NJ	Online games and large chat system
24th Street Exchange	916-448-2483	Sacramento, CA	Over 100,000 shareware files, Internet e-mail, and chat
Infinite Space BBS	407-856-0021	Orlando, FL	General interest, Internet connections, chat
PC-Ohio	216-381-3320	Cleveland, OH	One of the biggest BBSs, lots of chat

There's no way I could list every BBS in cyberspace. It would take more than one book to list them all. I tried to pick out some of the chattier BBSs you can try. Some of the BBSs you stumble across will cost a fee to join. The amount varies greatly. If you decide just to tour the BBS first, your access to certain features among the menu lists may be limited, as will your time online (yes, there's a clock ticking away the moments that you're on the line). You should always take a tour of the BBS before joining up and paying a fee. That's the only way to tell if you like the services.

To find a BBS user group near you, call the User Group Locator at 914-876-6678 (that's a voice number, not a modem number). They'll help you locate a BBS where you live.

How Do I Log On?

Just dial up your chosen BBS's modem number. The first time you call, you may have to adjust your modem's speed (not all BBSs handle all modem speeds) or a few other settings. In the other settings category, you might have to fiddle with your echo or duplex settings. Those control how you see characters on your computer screen. Your settings will have to match the BBS. If not, you won't be able to communicate.

In most cases, your communications parameters will be set to 8-N-1 (8 data bits, parity set to None, and 1 stop bit). Another setting you may have to mess with is your terminal emulation. Since you're dialing onto the BBS's host computer, your computer's thinking power is put on the back burner, so to speak. When it comes to settings, you'll definitely know if they're correct the first time you call; if they're not, your screen may reflect some strange-looking characters. If this happens, call the BBS again with new settings. Once you've got the settings correct, write them down so you don't have to go through the procedure again.

Another problem you may encounter when contacting a BBS is a busy signal. If you picked a popular BBS with only a few phone lines, you may often get a busy signal. Keep trying, or call back during non-peak hours (peak hours are in the evenings or on the weekends).

Chapter 7 ➤ *BBBs: Small Group Chatting*

> **Tricky ANSI Graphics**
>
> If you're dealing with a BBS that has ANSI graphics, you may have to adjust your computer's CONFIG.SYS file. Most programs have built-in ANSI support, but if you run into any problems, check your CONFIG.SYS file to see if it contains a line that says **DEVICE=ANSI.SYS**. If it does, you're in luck; it will let you view ANSI graphics. If not, you can change it so that it does say DEVICE=ANSI.SYS. If all of this sounds confusing, check out your DOS manual or ask an experienced computer friend for help.

Jumping Through Membership Hoops

When you finally connect to the BBS, you have to go through a sign-up procedure. This usually involves answering a lot of questions about you and your computer. The questions may range from your name and address to details about your modem speed, protocols, nearest living relative, favorite color, and so forth. All the information you enter is saved into a BBS registry, so the BBS will recognize you the next time you call.

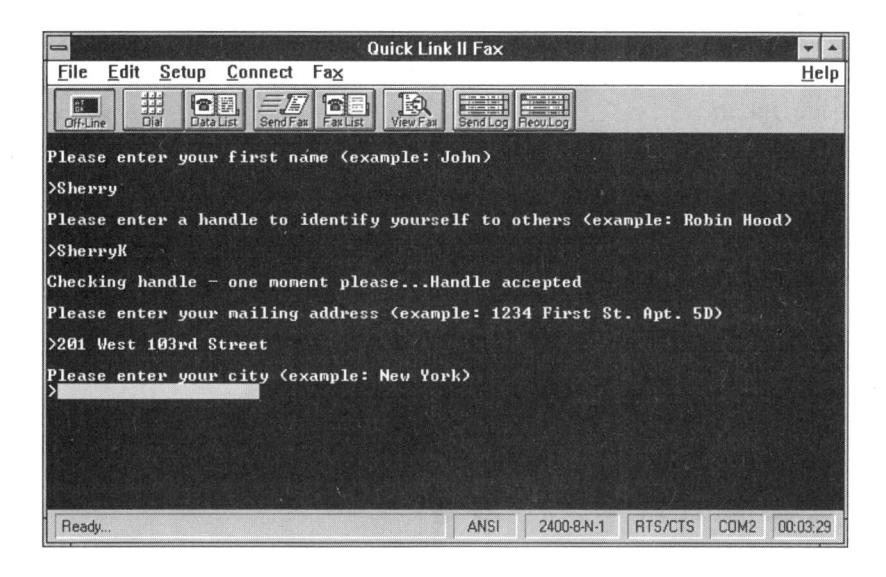

This illustrates a typical question and answer scenario you'll encounter when calling up a BBS for the first time.

Part 1 ➤ *Straight Talk About Chatting*

> ### The Old Callback Verification Procedure
>
> Many of today's BBSs use a *callback verification*. This practice lets BBS operators verify that you are who you say you are. The systems operator calls you back to double-check the information you gave during the sign-on procedure.

The BBS may ask how many characters can appear on a line on your screen. Try answering with 80. That's the average number. If the BBS asks how many lines are on your screen, try answering 24, another average. When the BBS asks what type of terminal connection you're using, try ANSI. If it's wrong, you can change it later. The BBS may ask some other technical questions. Just do your best to answer them based on your computer's setup.

If you're signing up with a fee-based BBS, you may also have to have your credit card handy. Most BBSs let you take a free tour to decide if you want to join or not. If you join, you'll be given a password, or a user ID.

A lot of BBSs make you come up with a handle before you finish the sign-on procedure. Be careful, don't give yourself a name that's not appropriate for the BBS you're calling. Try to avoid names like "Love Meister" or "Macho Man" until you know who you're dealing with.

It's typical for BBSs to scroll you through an update area after you log on or complete the sign-up procedure. The update area is where they display announcements about upcoming events or features on the BBS, news about specific areas to check out, or even advertisements. After the update area is done scrolling across your screen, you'll usually find yourself at a *main menu* (sometimes called a *top menu*). From there you can enter the numerous topics or areas. You should look for the exiting command too, so you'll know how to log off the BBS when the time comes.

Once you log on and jump through the membership hoops, take time to wander around the BBS and familiarize yourself with its features.

Finding Your Way to the Chat Area

The first place to look for your BBS's chat area is on the main menu list, or top menu. See if there's a selection for conferencing or real-time chat (it may also appear on a submenu). If so, make the menu selection and proceed to the chat area. If you get confused by anything, try to access the help menu, or look for a way to contact the sysop.

Chapter 7 ➢ *BBBs: Small Group Chatting*

Every BBS's chatting feature differs. Most, however, resemble what CompuServe and GEnie (commercial services covered in Chapter 5) look like without GUI software. It also looks a lot like the chatting on the Internet.

```
You are in the Main public channel!
Channel Topic: "FREE ACCESS NO FEES!! 217-792-3663"
Liver, Cynful, Hercules, Crazy Wife, Angela, Lustful, and Dave B.R. are here
with you.
Just enter "?" if you need any assistance.
:***
From Dave B.R.: hi sherry
:Hello.
-- Message sent --
:***
From Cynful: hi sherry...
:Hi, Cynful.
***
From Liver: hi sk!
:-- Message sent --
:***
From Liver: !
:***
From Liver: !
:***
From Liver: !
:***
From Liver: i enjoy scrolling
:Hello, everyone.
```

BBS chatting in action.

Chatting on BBSs is sometimes known as *conferencing*, or *teleconferencing*. Basically, it means you can communicate with other BBS users who are logged on at the same time as you. Like the big online services, BBSs often call the different chat areas that you enter "channels" or "rooms." The most popular chatting times are in the evenings and on the weekends. Chatting on a BBS is even more fun when you can get your friends to sign on too.

There are quite a few adult-oriented BBSs out there in cyberspace. You have to be over 21 to sign on with them (how do they know you're telling the truth?) and have a *very* open mind (if you know what I mean). Because BBSs in general are smaller-scale and not as much in the spotlight as the commercial services, they tend to push the envelope more readily when it comes to online activities, such as cybersex (more on this subject in Part 3). Watch out for BBSs that are involved in illegal activities, such as allowing members to download commercial software (like a Microsoft word processing program). People are going to jail for this crime.

Now that I've shown you what BBSs look like and how to sign up with one, I hope you'll try some out. Granted, they're not as easy to use or visually appealing as the commercial services, but they still have a lot to offer. There's no telling what hidden treasures you'll find from the thousands of BBSs that exist. Go—call—chat with the universe.

> **What Other Features Does a BBS Have?**
>
> A good BBS will offer you a wide variety of files (pertaining to the interest of the BBS) that you can download onto your own computer. You should also look for a BBS with message boards where you can post notes to other members. Internet connections are a real plus these days, so if you'd rather go Net-surfing through the safety of a BBS, then look for one offering the kind of Internet access you desire. Other features include the standard e-mail, information areas, and help system.

The Least You Need to Know

Hopefully, you're feeling a little braver about calling up a BBS after reading this chapter. This concludes the last chapter on the various online options available, and the steps for locating and logging onto each of them. I don't know about you, but it's been an exhausting seven chapters since the start of the book. I could use a little nap about now. I'll meet back up with you in Chapter 8.

- ➤ You can find BBSs by asking computer friends, computer clubs, and computer stores. Also check out computer magazines for listings.

- ➤ You don't need service-specific software to hook up to a BBS. Your own communications program will work fine.

- ➤ You'll probably have to make a few adjustments to your modem settings before or after calling a BBS. You may have to change things like baud rate, terminal emulation, and echo or duplex settings.

- ➤ When you call a BBS for the first time, you'll have to go through a sign-on procedure. This usually involves answering questions about yourself, your modem, and your computer.

- ➤ Once online with a BBS, it's best to take a tour before committing to joining. Find out if the BBS has all the features you're looking for.

Part 2
Rules and Regulations

Before you jump online and start chatting away, you might want to stop and review the rules of the road (so to speak). Believe it or not, there are some guidelines to adhere to, and that's what the next three chapters are about. Read them to learn what's proper and what's not when it comes to online communications. You'll also learn about the strange symbols and cryptic words that these online natives speak. This information can save you a lot of embarrassment later on, and keep you from making some newbie mistakes—after all, there's nothing worse than committing a terrible faux pas in front of the entire electronic universe.

THE HONESTY OF INTERNET

Chapter 8

A Word About Cybermanners

In This Chapter

➤ Learn the intricacies of online etiquette

➤ Find out how the online world expects you to behave—and what happens when you don't

➤ Discover the secrets of lurking and flaming

Quazy 15:	what is lol
SHHHerry:	laughing out loud
JamesD7406:	Lauging Out Loug
SHHHerry:	what's loug, James?
Lucy2613:	SHHHERRY WHO ARE YOU TALKING ABOUT
JamesD7406:	trying to beat Sherry
Roxxxi:	I hate it when I laugh out those Lougs!
JamesD7406:	<---loug lizard
Quazy 15:	lucy take off caps please
SHHHerry:	they're painful
SHHHerry:	not the caps, the lougs
Gerry 27:	S, you seem like an intelligent woman. any colledge?
SHHHerry:	Yes, and I majored in spelling. How about you?
Gerry 27:	Good one
JamesD7406:	My typing is going downhill
JamesD7406:	I am a shell of my former spelling slff
JamesD7406:	self
Stevejaw:	hi
SHHHerry:	Fresh meat!
Gerry 27:	go get him!!
SHHHerry:	lets see how HE types

Part 2 ➤ *Rules and Regulations*

The expansion of communications technology, including computer modems and networks, has spawned a brand new subculture we now call the online world, or *cyberspace*. When you enter this world, there are boundaries to be aware of, and proprieties in place. In this chapter, you'll learn what behavior is acceptable and what is not.

Minding Your Manners in Cyberspace

When entering any new culture, it's always good to stop and find out what language the natives speak—and how they conduct themselves—before venturing very far. This new online subculture warrants a similar approach. As you begin exploring the world of BBSs, online services, and the Internet, you'll quickly discover that there aren't many rules or regulations posted. Don't take that as a sign that "anything goes." It's not. There's an unspoken etiquette that applies to online communications. It's called *netiquette*. You may also see it referred to as *cybermanners*.

The online world is all about communicating. Whether it's e-mail or chatting in a forum or group, how you communicate via your modem or network connection is important. There are certain standards that apply, just as in face-to-face communication. Netiquette is how you "talk" to people in this electronic medium. Of course, you're not really "talking"—you're typing—but the manners still apply.

The Rule-Makers

Until recently, the online world consisted mainly of professionals, such as researchers, scientists, educators, and government officials, so the online world was a venue for serious information exchange. These people follow certain guidelines in their communications. Today, online usage has increased phenomenally, with up to 2 million people hooking up to the Internet and cyberspace every month. Everybody with a computer and a modem can go online these days. Needless to say, this has created some interesting interpretations of what information exchange is all about.

The founding fathers of the online world still rule. That is to say, violating their communication codes can result in being kicked off. For example, blatant misuse of a commercial online service, a BBS, or the Internet can cause you to lose your account and good standing. They can literally shut you out if you conduct yourself in an unworthy manner. Is that fair? Hey—all's fair in love and online communications, pal. All successful societies have codes of conduct—that's how you can tell the good guys from the bad guys. A culture without guidelines cannot function, so roll with it and learn what it takes to get along.

Chapter 8 ➤ *A Word About Cybermanners*

You Are Not Alone

There are thousands upon thousands of people logged onto the various BBSs, commercial services, and the Internet every day. Information exchange is free-flowing and plentiful. Even your private e-mail isn't so private. This is also the case in the chat areas. As you enter the various chat channels or rooms, be aware that other users can see everything you type in the group conversations. Because everyone is, in a sense, watching you, it's probably a good idea to behave yourself. Don't do anything warped that you'll live to regret later.

The same standards that apply to face-to-face communications apply to online communications. For example, you normally wouldn't meet someone on the street and start yelling at him/her or making lewd remarks. Other passersby might hear you and think you're a moron. If you are indeed a moron, and you're happy with that diagnosis, then I guess you gotta be who you gotta be. But this typically means you're not incredibly popular or well-liked. It's the same thing when chatting online. If you're nice to people, they're usually nice to you. If you're friendly, they're friendly. If you ever want to make friends online, then you have to apply the good old Golden Rule.

Be careful what you say in group conversations. You never know who is online with you. Don't forget, children wander around in cyberspace too. There are some people who stop by the chat channels or rooms and just listen, never adding their own thoughts to the conversations. These people are called *lurkers*. Just because only a few people seem to be chatting doesn't mean that there aren't more people tuning in just to see what's being said. Try not to be offensive or insulting in the group conversation areas.

> **Lurker(s)**
> Typically, the online world is full of people who like to chat and people who don't. The chatty ones are easy to recognize. You'll find them chatting a mile a minute in the online forums and real-time conference rooms. However, in these same areas, you'll also find people who just listen. *Lurkers* are people who observe online conversations but never participate.

The chat areas are also frequently monitored by the people in charge of the service or area. System operators, called *sysops* for short, make sure everything is in order. If there's trouble, they have the power to kick people off the channel. That's why you ought to mind your Ps and Qs.

There are also criminals out cruising the cyberstreets looking to scam other users. That's another reason to be careful about what you say. You've probably heard news reports of online harassment and stalkers, as well as stories about online police officers tracking down pedophiles and such. I just finished reading an article about some computer hackers, people who break into computer systems to wreak havoc or steal information. The FBI was able to track them down through computer communications and send them to jail.

The point is, you're never alone in the online world. Try to be a good citizen or you'll wind up in trouble. If you apply what is socially acceptable in real life to your conduct online, the chances of an untimely cyber-demise are pretty slim.

The Rules of the Road

Netiquette is a hot topic right now because so many people are trying out the various online services and the Internet. Something rather mysterious happens to people when communicating through their computers. They tend to let down walls, get a little bold, and say things online they wouldn't ordinarily say in person. This really brings out the extrovert, pervert, and all-around jerk in some of us. Because of that, you'll find plenty of dialog and message-posting of questionable taste going on. People even go so far as to make up online personas—hiding behind fictional character creations in a sort of weird online drama.

> **SYSOP:** Short for systems operator, a **sysop** is someone who oversees a BBS or an online area. They make sure everything is in order, especially uploaded files. They also monitor online activities and make sure everything is on the up and up. New users will find Sysops very helpful in finding their way around a new online service or BBS. They answer questions and help out with problems, too.

Why is this? Very simple—no one can really see or hear you in cyberspace; it's all electronic. There's a saying, "On the Net, no one knows you're a dog." (Or a gerbil, or a raging psychopath, or a space alien for that matter.) It's absolutely true for all the online areas. You may be a certified jerk or a complete angel in real life, but no one will ever really know if you are who you say you are in cyberspace. This seems to be one of the main attractions of chatting online. You can be whoever you want to be. Before you get carried away, however, you still need to adhere to some guidelines.

The Guidelines

Most online services, BBSs, and even the Internet encourage users to follow certain guidelines for online behavior. These guidelines encompass such etiquette as language, sexual innuendo, and overall politeness. Much of this is dictated by where you are online and what you're talking about. For example, if you're in the Gardening Forum on CompuServe, chances are the other members won't appreciate a lot of profane or sexually explicit

Chapter 8 ➤ *A Word About Cybermanners*

language in the message-posting area or within any of the live conferencing. This is a rather obvious common-sense kind of thing, but bears repeating.

Basically, you can sum up the guidelines as follows:

➤ Avoid using profane, abusive, or sexually offensive language, or language that is considered inappropriate to the average person. (You can save all of that stuff for your private one-on-one discussions.) Some discussion groups allow such language, but always make sure it's acceptable before trying it yourself.

➤ Do not engage in personal attacks against other users.

➤ Business advertising and selling is not allowed. Don't try peddling your wares to the other online members; this isn't a showroom. Online business practices are changing, but unless you're sure you've logged onto a Buy & Sell channel, I'd suggest you hold your sales pitch until you know what's allowed.

➤ Follow the Golden Rule—treat others as you would like to be treated.

Online Etiquette Tips

Just so you won't make a fool of yourself online (unless you really want to), let me give you some other online etiquette tips:

➤ Never type in all caps. IT'S CONSIDERED SHOUTING. It's not so easy to read after awhile, either. Certainly, there are some moments that will arise that require an occasional uppercase word. However, the norm is to type in a combination of upper- and lowercase letters. To do otherwise is most impolite.

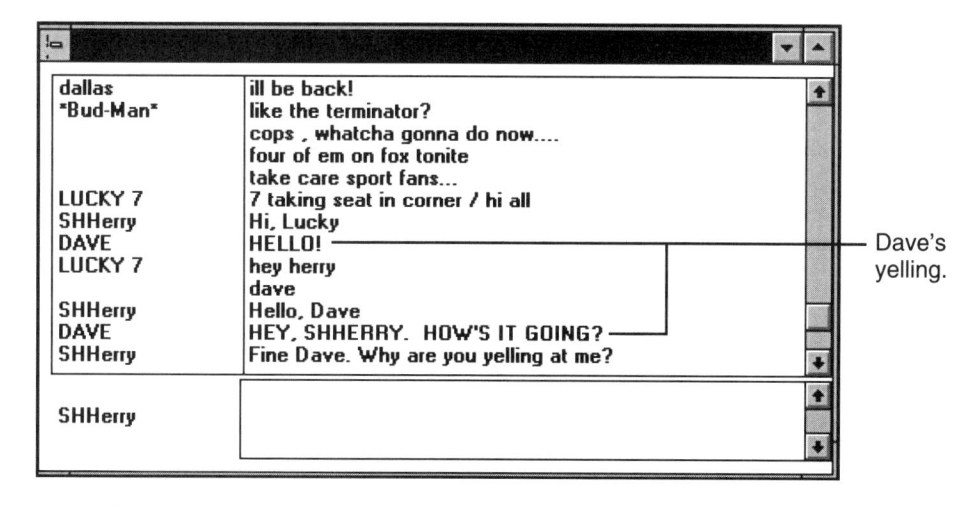

An example of a newbie shouting on CompuServe. If he had read this book first, he wouldn't have committed this faux pas.

Part 2 ➤ *Rules and Regulations*

➤ You don't always have to follow the rules of punctuation and sentence structure. Avid chatterers rarely start sentences with capital letters, for example. That's because they're typing so fast, there's no time for it. It's the same thing with punctuation. You won't see a lot of proper punctuation among online conversations, unless you're dealing with a seasoned writer or a really fast and efficient typist. No one seems to mind that the normal text structure rules are missing. The message still comes across.

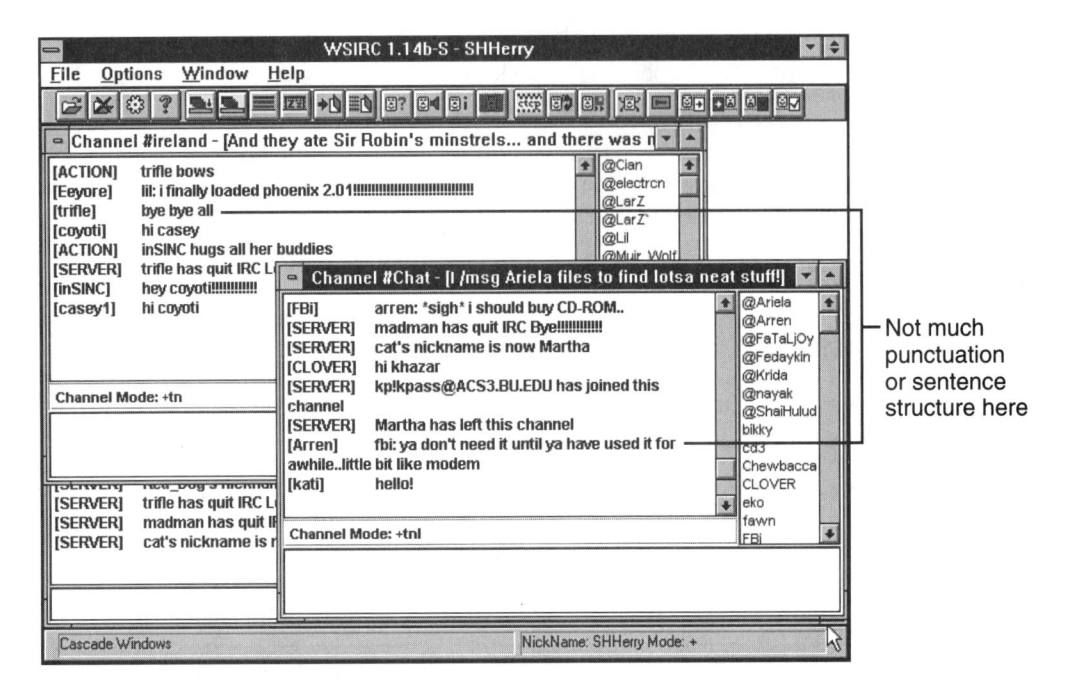

An example of the varying degrees of punctuation found on the Internet.

Flame: To lash out at another user by sending an angry, insulting, rude, or disparaging message or comment. Flaming usually occurs when someone's offended someone else or done something stupid.

➤ Don't succumb to online name-calling or *flaming*. Online conversations never get far when one calls the others names. Resorting to name-calling is never a noble act, and it stumbles far from the art of conversation. In fact, it's quite barbaric (but often entertaining). Sysops monitor most conference rooms to watch for that kind of behavior.

Chapter 8 ➤ *A Word About Cybermanners*

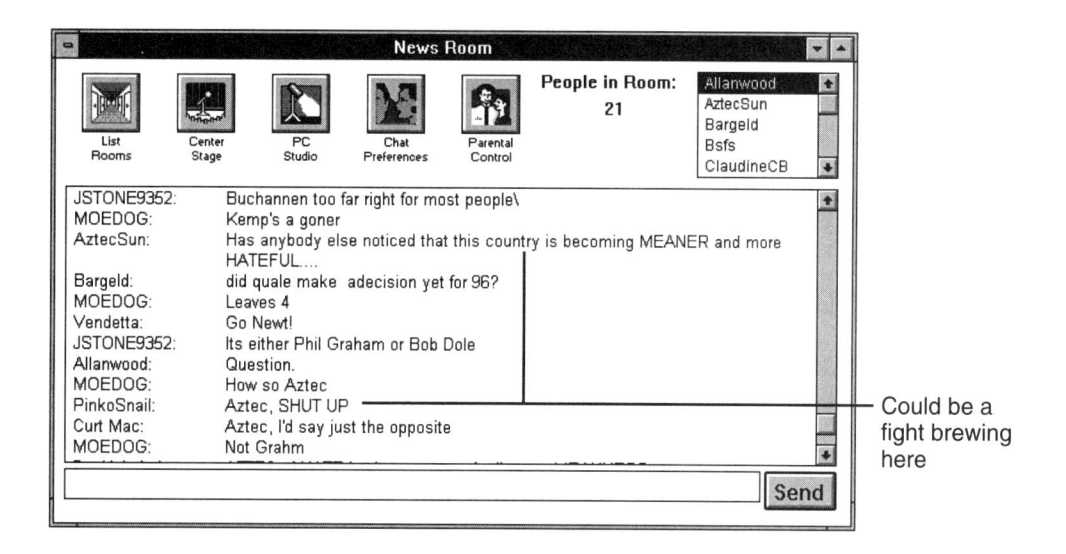

— Could be a fight brewing here

Some chatting areas are more prone to flaming than others. Such is the case in America Online's News Room.

➤ Try not to type so fast as to sprinkle your messages with misspelled words. Incorrect spelling is often a great source of misunderstanding, unintentional humor, and downright confusion. Plus it makes you look silly at times. On the other hand, most everybody online makes this type of mistake sometime; they are usually forgiving when it occurs.

➤ There are some online services that are more family-oriented than others. Be aware of this. In more adult-inclined services, you may encounter conversations and file contents that are very, very adult in nature. This is something to watch out for if your children will be using your modem too.

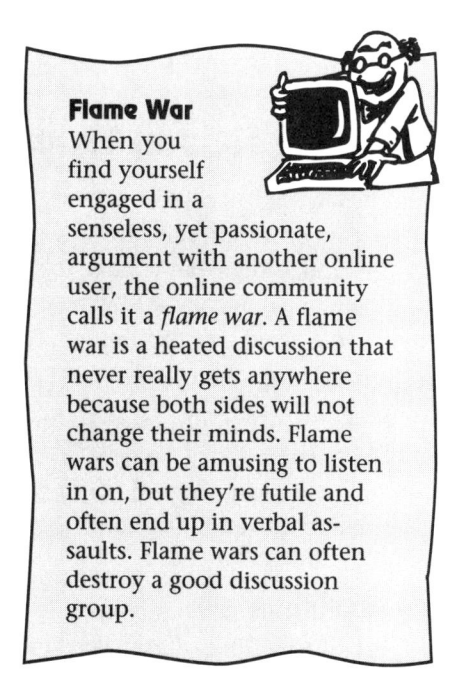

Flame War
When you find yourself engaged in a senseless, yet passionate, argument with another online user, the online community calls it a *flame war*. A flame war is a heated discussion that never really gets anywhere because both sides will not change their minds. Flame wars can be amusing to listen in on, but they're futile and often end up in verbal assaults. Flame wars can often destroy a good discussion group.

101

Part 2 ➤ *Rules and Regulations*

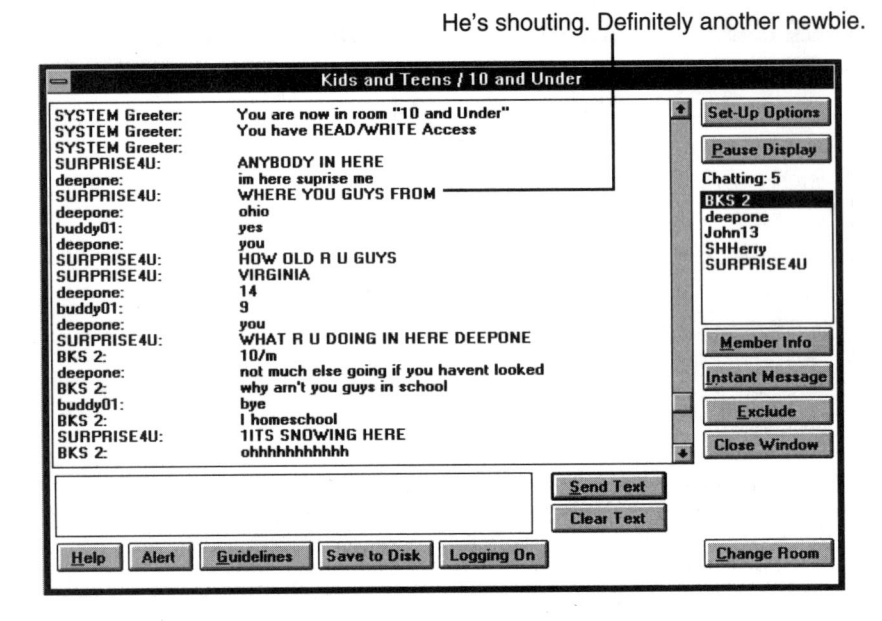

He's shouting. Definitely another newbie.

```
                    Kids and Teens / 10 and Under
SYSTEM Greeter:    You are now in room "10 and Under"     Set-Up Options
SYSTEM Greeter:    You have READ/WRITE Access
SYSTEM Greeter:                                           Pause Display
SURPRISE4U:        ANYBODY IN HERE
deepone:           im here suprise me                     Chatting: 5
SURPRISE4U:        WHERE YOU GUYS FROM                    BKS 2
deepone:           ohio                                   deepone
buddy01:           yes                                    John13
deepone:           you                                    SHHerry
SURPRISE4U:        HOW OLD R U GUYS                       SURPRISE4U
SURPRISE4U:        VIRGINIA
deepone:           14
buddy01:           9
deepone:           you                                    Member Info
SURPRISE4U:        WHAT R U DOING IN HERE DEEPONE
BKS 2:             10/m                                   Instant Message
deepone:           not much else going if you havent looked
BKS 2:             why arn't you guys in school           Exclude
buddy01:           bye
BKS 2:             I homeschool                           Close Window
SURPRISE4U:        1ITS SNOWING HERE
BKS 2:             ohhhhhhhhhhh

                                                 Send Text
                                                 Clear Text
 Help   Alert   Guidelines   Save to Disk   Logging On    Change Room
```

A typical conversation in a kids' chat room in PRODIGY. Brevity is a staple of chatting here.

Newbie Help in Times of Trouble

One of the neatest aspects of using BBSs and online services is the overwhelming helpfulness you'll receive from experienced users. We've all been new at something sometime, and know what it's like to stumble through everything. Most online users I've met have lent a helping hand whenever possible. I encourage you to do the same once you've mastered this technology. By the way, new online people are called *newbies*. If someone asks you if you're a newbie, don't take offense or anything. It's an innocent question.

If you run into netiquette issues that you need some help with, don't be afraid to contact the sysop or ask those around you (online, that is). You'll be surprised at how kind most BBS and commercial service users are. When it comes to online guidelines, just about everybody is willing to give you some advice.

But I need to warn you, the Internet people aren't quite as helpful as the people using other online services. In fact, sometimes they're downright mean to newbies. One of the things that makes Internet geezers the maddest is the continual repetition of *FAQs* (which stands for *frequently asked questions*). Most of the Internet's *newsgroups* (another name for online forums or clubs) have a bulletin board area full of FAQs. When new users log on, they're encouraged to read all the questions and answers posted there before ever attempting to ask a question themselves. This way, the newbie saves himself the embarrassment of appearing stupid and the Internet-grinch doesn't have to waste time telling that person what to do. However, this doesn't always stop a new person from asking a FAQ anyway. And when he does, it's very likely that he'll get flamed by other users (everyone sends them angry messages telling them what an idiot they are). Of course, this won't happen to you because I warned you about it ahead of time. Right?

Hopefully you're getting the gist of what I mean by *netiquette*. When you talk to someone via your modem or network connection, be polite, just as if you were talking to them in person. Of course, there are people who deviate from this guideline in the real world, but try to keep your own typing in the cyberworld civil.

> **FAQ:** Stands for *frequently asked question*. Many message boards or forums set aside answers to frequently asked newbie questions in a special file or area called FAQs. Look at FAQs before posting your own message or chatting in a topic-oriented discussion area (when applicable).

When Cybermanners Go Bad

As with any area in the social arena, there are good people and there are bad people. You will encounter users that are complete jerks. They may call you names or flame you or your ideas and thoughts. However, you'll also meet people who are absolute saints, helping you out with modem woes and more. For those times when you meet up with the bad people, there are some actions you can take.

One thing you can do, although it's usually futile, is tell the person that you don't appreciate their behavior, especially if they're flaming you for no good reason or bothering everyone else as well. Another recourse is to flame them right back. This route won't go anywhere, but you might feel better.

Don't be surprised to find a lot of unwanted attention in some of the chat venues. There's a lot of raunchy stuff going on, so be prepared. It's not uncommon to get an occasional uninvited private message (one-on-one message) containing questionable content. If it offends you, look for a command for squelching or ignoring repeated messages from that person. Some software features let you turn off (or *kill*, in online-ese) correspondence from certain users. Most online services and the Internet have specific buttons or commands for doing this.

If someone bothers you to the point of harassment, check your online service or sysop for steps to follow. You may have to file a report. If someone harasses you repeatedly, definitely report the person (and his/her ID) to the online service administrators. People exhibiting bad online manners can be kicked off the system. On the other hand, don't *you* become a candidate for online detention!

The Least You Need to Know

Does it feel like you've just attended online charm school? Here's what you learned:

- Be polite and sit up straight, people are watching you... or at least watching what you type.
- Don't type in all caps; it looks like you're shouting.
- Don't try selling stuff unless it's okay with the service or board you're using.
- Don't be a jerk online. Nobody likes jerks.
- Avoid offending people, and stay out of flame wars.
- If someone harasses you online and you can't make that person stop, see the sysop or contact those in charge of the service.

Chapter 9

Getting Emotional with Emoticons

In This Chapter

➤ Find out why everybody online sprinkles strange symbols throughout their conversations

➤ See a handy chart of smileys that you can use yourself

➤ Learn how to depict an action on-screen

```
JESSE JAMES5:        hi matt
JESSE JAMES5:        hi herb
SpeedMcKills:        <tapping foot>
SHHerry:             oh..you still waiting for an answer?
SpeedMcKills:        lol
bbcakes1a:           got it
SpeedMcKills:        u got it
SpeedMcKills:        ??
bbcakes1a:           that one took a while..<s>
bbcakes1a:           ok..try it
bbcakes1a:           <s>
SpeedMcKills:        {s vh-gnr}
Max Kansas 2:        00000--------->>>{{{{{ HEIDI }}}}}<<<---------00000
bbcakes1a:           ((((((((((((((( Maxie )))))))))))))
Max Kansas 2:        Xx¤Xx¤Xx¤Xx¤Xx BB Cakes xXx¤xXx¤Xx¤Xx¤xX
bbcakes1a:           lol LOVE IT! heh
It's Heidi:          {{{{{{{{{{{{{{{{{{{{{{(Max)}}}}}}}}}}}}}}}}}}}}}}}}}}
Max Kansas 2:        {[])x{[])x{[])x{[]} BBCakes {[]}x{[]}x{[]}x{[]}
OOPS 95:             Hiya BB:>
bbcakes1a:           ooo Max....new ones? cooool   my fav.
OOPS 95:             Hi Heidi:>
Max Kansas 2:        bb<.....HAS MULTIPLE HUGS...LOL....
```

When dealing with a text-based world, which you are when chatting online, it's often difficult to express emotions in the words you type. This difficulty can lead to misunderstandings, arguments, and lots of confusion. The problem stems from the fact that you can't see the facial expressions of the people you're chatting with. This means you can't always tell whether someone is joking or not, or a number of other conversational nuances.

Thankfully, the online culture has found a way to deal with this. You can turn certain keys on your keyboard into expressions of emotion. Sound interesting? Then read this chapter.

What's with the Weird Symbols?

If you're new to online chatting, it won't be long before you begin to notice strange symbols sprinkled amid the conversations. You know you've entered into another world when you start seeing things like :(or <=====. All these symbols have meaning online. Take a look at this figure to see some more examples:

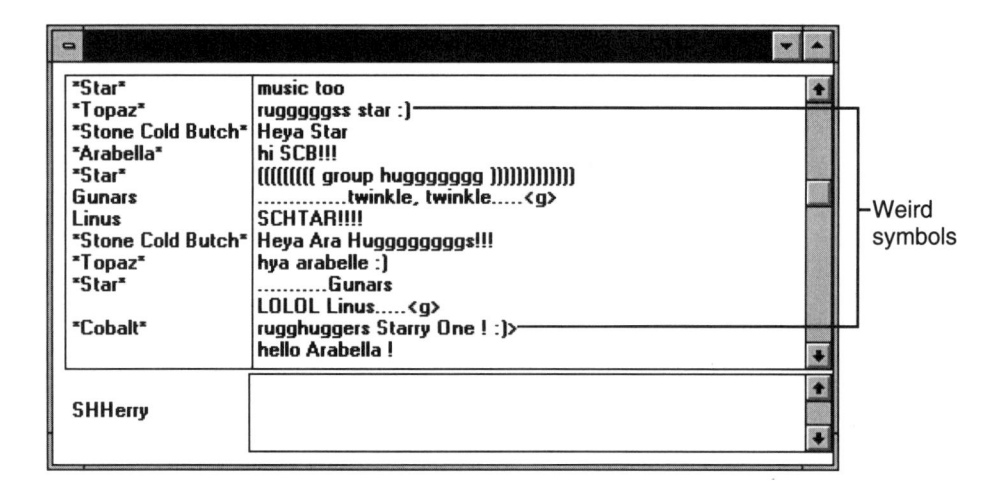

Here is a prime example of emoticons in an online chatting situation (from CompuServe).

These symbols are called *emoticons* (short for *emotional icons*). Another name for them is *smileys*. They are used to express emotion. To read them properly, turn your head to the left and look at them sideways. (Careful, this can put a kink in your neck. I guess if that bothered you, you could always pick up your monitor and turn it sideways. But then that might put a kink in your arms. Gee, this computer stuff can be a hazard to your health.)

Composed of a variety of combined keystrokes, emoticons express facial expressions in your online conversations. For example, the :) is a smiley face, which means you're smiling. ;-) is a winking smiley face, meaning that you're winking. Get it? Sadly, one cannot always tell if you're being serious, sarcastic, or funny in your online communications, but these symbols help get the true meaning of your text across.

> **Emoticons:** Symbols used to express emotions in online conversations. Also called smileys, these symbols are comprised of a variety of combined keystrokes that look like faces when you stare at them sideways :).

The Smiley Table

The following smiley table will help you recognize and use common smileys in your online conversations and e-mail messages. The dash-nose is optional, but widely accepted.

Symbols to type	What it means
:)	Smiling
:-)	Smiling, with a nose
:.)	Small-skewed-button-nosed smiley
:->	Ironic or devious smile
:-(	Frowning
:-<	Really sad
>:-(	Someone mad or annoyed
:-c	Bummed out
:-I	Grim
:-D	Laughing
:-o	Shouting
:-O	Shouting loudly
:-p	Sticking out my tongue
:-*	Puckering for a kiss
:-x	My lips are sealed

continues

Part 2 ➤ *Rules and Regulations*

Continued

Symbols to type	What it means
:-{}	I have a moustache
:-()	Big mouth (when you feel you rambled on)
;-)	Winking
8-)	Wearing glasses
B-)	Wearing cool shades
{(:-)	Wearing a toupee
I-o	Yawning
I^o	Snoring
X-(	Dead
C=:-)	I'm a chef
*<:-){	I'm Santa Claus
@>—,—'-	A rose
xxooxxoo	Love (or hugs) & kisses

How Do I Use Them?

It's easy to use these symbols. Just type them into your own text. For example, when you want to show someone you're just kidding after you've written a sarcastic statement, type in a colon and then type a right parenthesis :). You'd be surprised at all the interesting symbols you can come up with on your own.

In fact, there's all kinds of artwork that people have created out of keyboard symbols. Allow me to show you some:

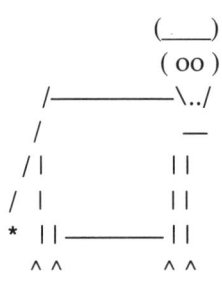

```
                     (___)
                     ( oo )
              /-------\../
             /         —
            / |        | |
           /  |        | |
          *  ||--------| |
             ^ ^        ^ ^
```

That's a cow. What do you think? Pretty avant garde, eh?

108

Chapter 9 ➤ *Getting Emotional with Emoticons*

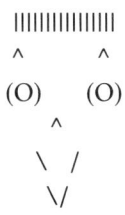

```
         ||||||||||||||
          ^         ^
         (O)       (O)
              ^
              \ /
              \/
```

Does that look like a boy with a buzz cut to you? Well, use your imagination.

Pretty clever stuff, eh? If you like that, take a gander at what you can create online in the chat channels. Look at the two examples coming up.

Deton8:	no, they come and go so fast
Deton8:	never stopping to say hello
DimJJ:	[laughing]
Deton8:	on their way to teen chat
DimJJ:	thats where i about to gooooooooooooooooooooo
Deton8:	have fun
Kelly214U:	hello
Deton8:	Hi, kelly
Kelly214U:	\\\\\\\\\\\\\////////
Kelly214U:	(o o)
Kelly214U:	--oOOo------U------oOOo---
Deton8:	nice
Sarah119d:	hi kelly
Deton8:	hello, sarah

— Is this inspiring, or what?

Now this takes talent, I'm telling you.

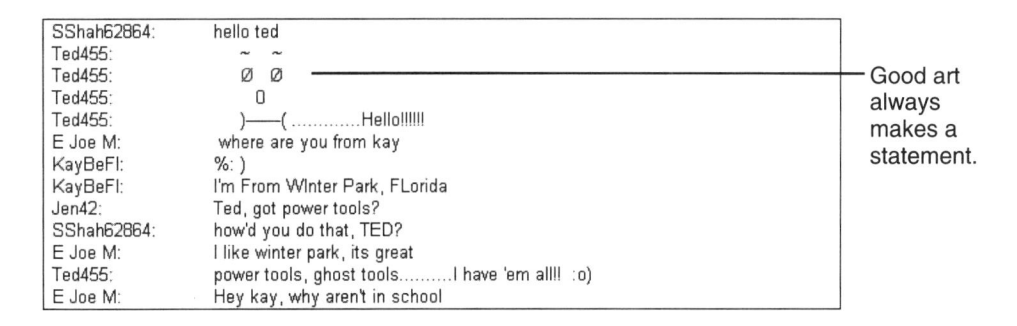

SShah62864:	hello ted
Ted455:	~ ~
Ted455:	Ø Ø
Ted455:	o
Ted455:	)——(............Hello!!!!!!
E Joe M:	where are you from kay
KayBeFl:	%:)
KayBeFl:	I'm From Winter Park, FLorida
Jen42:	Ted, got power tools?
SShah62864:	how'd you do that, TED?
E Joe M:	I like winter park, its great
Ted455:	power tools, ghost tools...........I have 'em all!! :o)
E Joe M:	Hey kay, why aren't in school

— Good art always makes a statement.

Most folks store their keyboard art as macros (pre-recorded keystrokes) and then whip them out to dazzle the audience.

109

I think you get the idea by now. You can use the keyboard keys to make all kinds of artwork. Some people even use the artwork in *taglines*. (Taglines are kind of like electronic bumper stickers. You'll find them used in message posting areas and among the Internet's newsgroups.) Anyway, feel free to use emoticons in your own online conversations. However, I caution you about emoticon overkill. You shouldn't use too many emoticons at a time.

Other Online Actions

I'm sure it's obvious by now, but without the use of your voice or facial expressions, it's hard to communicate whether you're joking, expressing sarcasm or depression, or just making a play on words. (This happens in book writing too, in case you hadn't noticed.) Emoticons can solve this problem. Aside from smiley symbols, you can also express physical actions.

Actions are typed in brackets, such as {blushing}, <grin>, or [very big grin]. You'll see action brackets almost as much as smileys in online conversations. In fact, some channels are dedicated to fictional environments where everything is expressed in this manner. Take a look at this PRODIGY chat room, called Peaceful Warrior Inn:

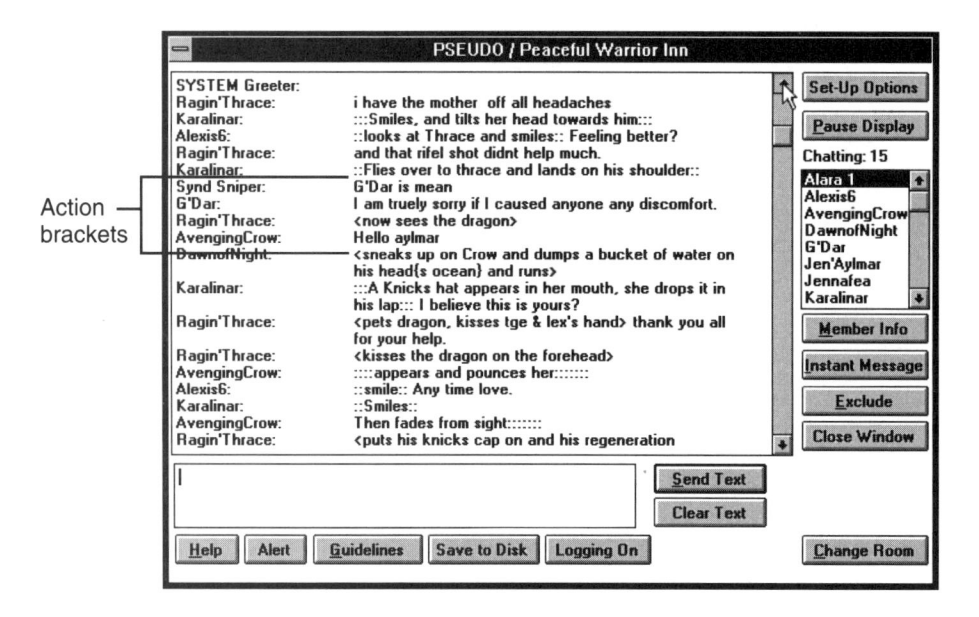

Action brackets are used a lot in online chat rooms (like this one from PRODIGY).

110

Chapter 9 ➤ *Getting Emotional with Emoticons*

Wild, huh? It's like reading a fiction book at the same time it's being written. America Online has a room like this too, called the Red Dragon Inn. Pop in some time and see what's going on. I think you'll find it very interesting.

Anyway, the action brackets really come in handy when you want to write something, but it's not part of your conversation. Use the brackets to convey an action. For example, <g> is another way of indicating that you're grinning, similar to :).

Here's another example, if you ever see this {{{{{{Sherry}}}}}} with your name in the middle, that's an online hug. You can also use the asterisk symbols to emphasize words, such as *really*. The colon symbol can do this too, :::**rattle papers**::::. So, try your hand at online actions as well as smileys. It can be loads of fun, as you'll soon see.

> **Taglines:**
> Sayings, phrases, quotes, or pictures used as signature lines or electronic bumper stickers among online messages. Watch out for the prank taglines that tell you to do something like press **Ctrl+Alt+Del** or **Alt+H**. Prank taglines can dump you off the system if you follow the instructions.

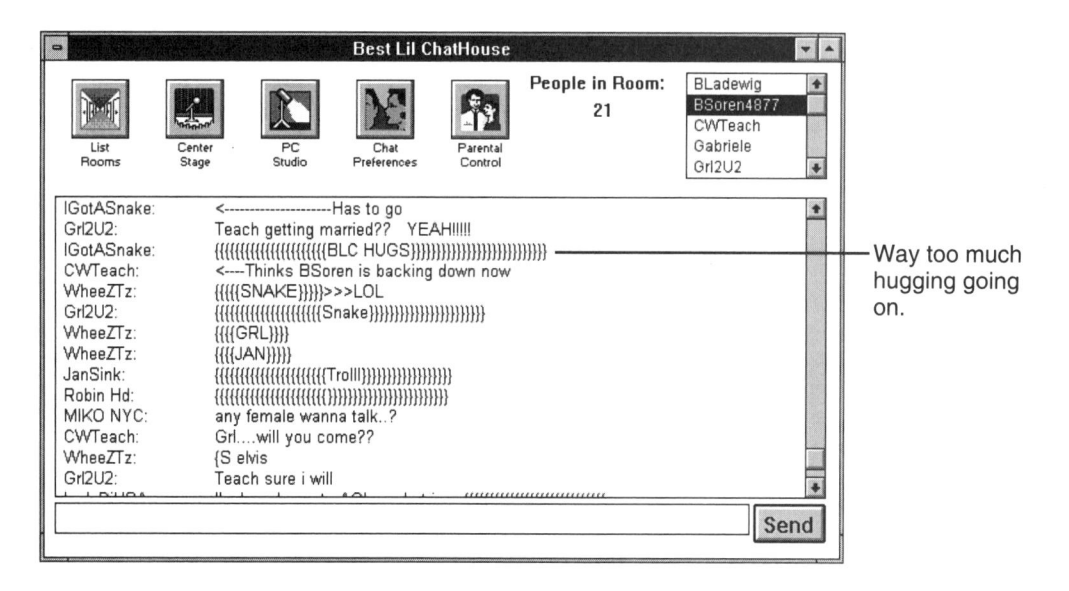

An example of on-screen hugs on America Online. Sometimes it's a little nauseating.

— Way too much hugging going on.

111

Part 2 ➤ *Rules and Regulations*

There's more to communicating than just smileys and action brackets; there are also bizarre abbreviations to learn. Turn to the next chapter to see what that's all about.

The Least You Need to Know

Congratulations :). You're mastering the art of online conversations and you've not even broken out in a sweat yet. That's pretty good, for a newbie ;).

➤ Emoticons are used to express emotions and facial expressions in your online chat.

➤ You can create all kinds of interesting artwork with the symbols on your keyboard.

➤ Use action brackets for times when you want to show an action on-screen, like [going to get a cup of coffee].

Chapter 10

Deciphering Cryptic Online Codes

In This Chapter

➤ Finally, an explanation for all the strange words found in online chat!

➤ Learn how to use acronyms in your own communications.

➤ Check out the exhaustive chart of common online abbreviations.

"SYSTEM"	Switching to Adult
"Lady Gracie"	ok....PLEASE FASTEN YOUR SEAT BELTS
"Mr. DJ"	‹fastening seat belt for Gracie›
"SANDI"	mr dj@@!!huggggles
~Ms.WildChild~	BRB
"SANDI"	puckster@@!huggggles
"R.W"	please fasten your seat belts and return your flight attendant to her normal upright position....
"Mr. DJ"	LOL
"SANDI"	good one RW
¥¿PÜÇKŠTËR¿¥	roflol
Putsch	Someone say something intelligent please.... The information super hi-way is really great but most people out there don't have anything to say worth reading....
"Lady Gracie"	‹--back
~Ms. Ima Nut~	PEPSI?
"Pepper Lady"	Nutsi?
Mr DJ	Hey Pepper Lady, Sug! ‹G,D,R›

When you're online, you don't want to waste precious time when you're running up a bill that includes an hourly connect-time charge. For this reason, a lot of online conversants have adopted abbreviations for frequently used words or phrases. In this chapter, I'll introduce you to the lingo known as online *acronyms*.

What's with the Weird Words?

The first time I entered an online chat channel, I kept noticing these strange words being tossed about in the conversation. It was only when I asked and the other users explained them that it dawned on me—there's a whole new lingo to learn with online communications. As if I hadn't already had my fill of geeky hardware and software terms! Fortunately, my despair was for naught. There isn't much to this jargon once you know what it's about. It's certainly not as hard as learning to speak a new language.

Abbreviations are quite common among online chatterers. They pop up throughout real-time conversations as well as in the message-posting areas. This particular form of online jargon mainly consists of interesting acronyms for commonly used words or phrases. I guess you could consider it online communications shorthand. In the early years of online services, it was very expensive to place a call with your modem and send files or live messages. People practically counted every character they sent. So this shorthand sort of evolved to save time communicating. In an effort to speed up communication, the online community developed a common jargon that includes things like LOL (laughing out loud), IMHO (in my humble opinion), and WTH (what the heck). GTP? (Get the picture?)

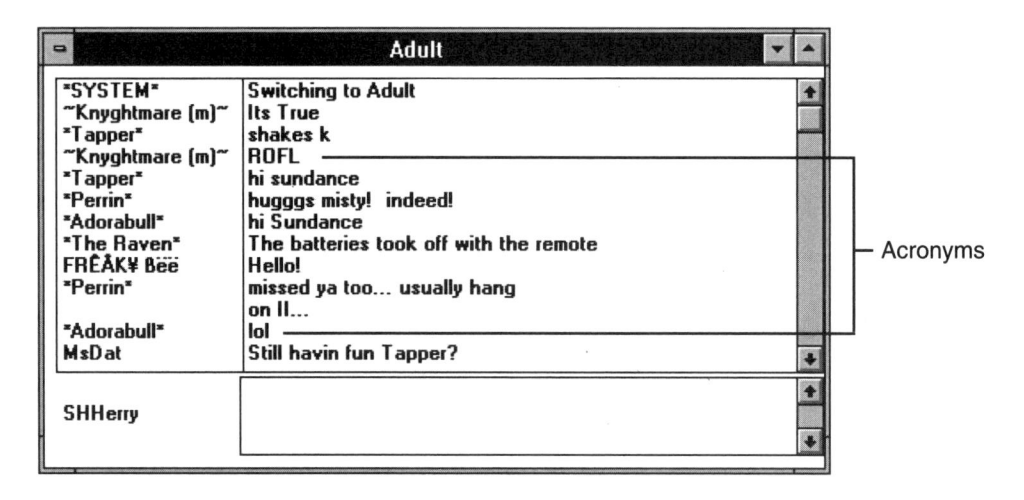

The online chatting feature of AOL (America Online) is often filled with acronyms.

Chapter 10 ➤ *Deciphering Cryptic Online Codes*

If an acronym confuses you, ask the person to spell it out. You'll learn something and your online friend will feel better for helping you understand online shorthand.

The Acronym Table

Today you can find these acronyms in all areas of modem and network communications—but predominantly in live conferencing, messaging, online forums, or electronic gathering places. To keep you hip when you're online, I've compiled a table of acronyms you'll frequently run across. Feel free to use them yourself. You'll sound like an old online pro.

Online Acronyms to Use and Abuse	
AKA	Also known as
AOL	America Online
AFK	Away from keyboard
BAK	Back at keyboard
BIF	Basis in fact
BRB	Be right back
BTW	By the way
CIS or CI$	CompuServe
CU	See you
CUL	See you later
FAQ	Frequently asked question(s)
FWIW	For what it's worth
FYA	For your amusement
FYI	For your information
GMTA	Great minds think alike
GR&D	Grinning, running, and ducking
HHOK	Ha ha, only kidding
HHOS	Ha ha, only serious
IAC	In any case

continues

115

Part 2 ➤ *Rules and Regulations*

Continued

Online Acronyms to Use and Abuse

IMO	In my opinion
IMHO	In my humble opinion
IMNSHO	In my not-so-humble opinion
IMAO	In my arrogant opinion
IOW	In other words
LOL	Laughing out loud
MOTD	Message of the day
NBIF	No basis in fact
NRN	No response necessary
OTOH	On the other hand
PITA	Pain in the a**
PMJI	Pardon my jumping in
PC	Politically Correct (or Personal Computer, depending on context)
PI or PIC	Politically Incorrect
POV	Point of view
RL	Real life
ROFL	Rolling on the floor laughing
ROFLOLPIMP	Rolling on the floor, laughing out loud, peeing in my pants
RSN	Real soon now
RTM	Read the manual (or message)
SIFOTCN	Sitting in front of the computer naked
TANSTAAFL	There ain't no such thing as a free lunch
TIA	Thanks in advance
TIC	Tongue in cheek
[TM]	Trademark

Chapter 10 ➤ *Deciphering Cryptic Online Codes*

Online Acronyms to Use and Abuse	
TTFN	Ta-ta for now
TTYL	Talk to you later
WB	Welcome back
WTG	Way to go
WTH	What the h*** (or heck)
YMMV	Your mileage may vary
unPC	A cute way of saying the same thing as PI

How Do I Use Them?

It's easy. During your online conversations, use an acronym any time you want to use a common phrase. For example, if you're in a discussion about politics, throw in a POV (point of view) or a PMJI (pardon my jumping in).

By far, the most popular acronym you'll see used is LOL (laughing out loud). It's probably the best way to express the fact that you're literally laughing out loud.

As I warned you about emoticons in Chapter 9, it's not a good idea to use too many acronyms at once. That would be overkill. Also, you can come up with your own acronyms, but you'll probably have to explain them to everyone else.

The Least You Need to Know

This completes your course in the rules and regulations of online communications. I'll quiz you later on all this stuff, so you'd better be prepared.

➤ Acronyms save time and effort in your online communications.

➤ If you're ever confused by the use of an acronym, be sure to ask the person using it what it means.

➤ Don't use too many acronyms at once; it's confusing.

Part 3
What's Going On Out There?

It's absolutely amazing out there. People are meeting, chatting, laughing, crying, and raising lots of eyebrows. It's fast and furious or slow and mind-numbing. Online chat is full of adventure, romance, and danger. Basically, it's like a revolving plot from your favorite novel. Sometimes it's your own life story, other times it's someone else's story. Want to find out what the heck I'm talking about? Then read this section!

In this Part of the book, I'll give you a first-hand account of what going on in the online world, including cybersex, flaming, gender issues, and more. I'll also tell you about the grimy underbelly of online chat and how you can deal with it, including online crime and troubleshooting tips.

Chapter 11

Sex, Lies, and Other Online Motivations

HELLO, MY DEAR...

In This Chapter

➤ Find out the secret motivations that bring people online

➤ Learn what cybersex is all about, without a drawn-out discussion of the cyberbirds and cyberbees

➤ Discover the challenges to living an online lie

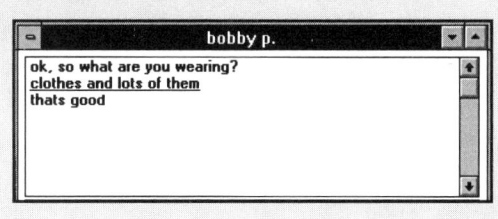

```
bobby p.
ok, so what are you wearing?
clothes and lots of them
thats good
```

Let's summarize the plot thus far. In the first section of this book, you learned about a burgeoning online subculture in which all kinds of communication are taking place. Soon after, you discovered that the only way to join this radical new world was through a modem or a network connection with your computer. You explored three distinct paths to access this subculture: through commercial online services, BBSs, and the awesome Internet. In no time at all, you learned the secrets of each, including how much they cost, how to sign up for an account, and how to actually log onto them.

Fully armed with this new knowledge, you proceeded to the second section of this book, where you found out how the online natives behave in the cyberspace world. You received a thorough grounding in online etiquette and you were introduced to symbols and acronyms to help you express yourself in your own written dialog.

Now, the plot thickens. In this third part of the book, you're going to get the lowdown on what's really going on out there, find out what you can expect when you finally go online yourself, and learn how you can jump in and participate. This is the part where you see the seedy elements of the online world as well as the good stuff—or in novelist's terms, this is where things get juicy.

What Really IS Going On Out There?

Well... everything. You name it, it's happening online, especially when it comes to the dynamics of real-time chat. Sometimes it's like a soap opera, sometimes it's like a bad movie, sometimes it's hilarious, and sometimes it's boring. Every time you log on, it can be a different experience. Perhaps that's what draws people into the chat areas to begin with. There are always open-ended possibilities to every new conversation you start.

In the dynamics of real-time chat, anything can happen. You never know who you're really talking to online or what's going to be said. It's spontaneous and very unpredictable. Why's that? I can answer that with two words—*traffic flow*. People log on and off with amazing frequency. Sometimes, just watching from afar (lurking), it seems as if the chat channels are online intersections. People drive in, chat a bit, and move on. Some of the higher traffic areas, such as AOL's lobby rooms, are like busy interstate exchanges—jumping off points to reach other destinations (conversations). Because of the traffic flow of online users, there's a constant mix of people and personalities. There are literally hundreds of people online chatting at any given moment.

What compels people to log on and make their way to the chat areas? To really understand, you need to stop and examine the different motives that bring people online to talk to absolute strangers. This will give you a feeling of what's going on out there in cyberspace chat.

Just Shootin' the Breeze

Lots of people go online just to indulge in idle chitchat. Imagine this... you're at work or at home, feeling a little bored, so you call up your favorite online service (such as CompuServe or PRODIGY). You check out the news reports, read your e-mail—but you're still bored. So you navigate over to the chat feature and strike up conversations with everyone else who's logged on there. What about? Anything—the weather, daily events, last night's game, tonight's episode of *Seinfeld*, whatever. Before you know it, an hour has passed.

In this scenario, you're just shootin' the cyberbreeze, kind of like hanging out at the office water cooler or coffeemaker. Other users wander by—some jump into the conversation, others don't. You're all just goofing off, joking around, and taking it easy.

Chapter 11 ➤ *Sex, Lies, and Other Online Motivations*

You'll find plenty of online action just like this in all the common communal chat areas among BBSs, commercial services, and the Internet. It's very relaxing, and there's not a lot of pressure to be witty or profound. This type of online conversing is very casual and laid back. If you're consistent about pursuing this level of online conversation, such as logging on at a certain time each day or on a regular basis, you'll meet others who are doing the same thing. After awhile, you'll find yourself with a set of online friends and establish a cyber-camaraderie that's very enjoyable.

> ### Another Great Tip!
>
> Let me clue you in on another enjoyable aspect of online chat. There's nothing nicer than logging onto the chat areas and finding someone you've met before, especially if you had a nice conversation with them. It's like running into a familiar face at the grocery store. Each time you meet, you get to know each other better. Never underestimate the camaraderie of chat and its benefits.

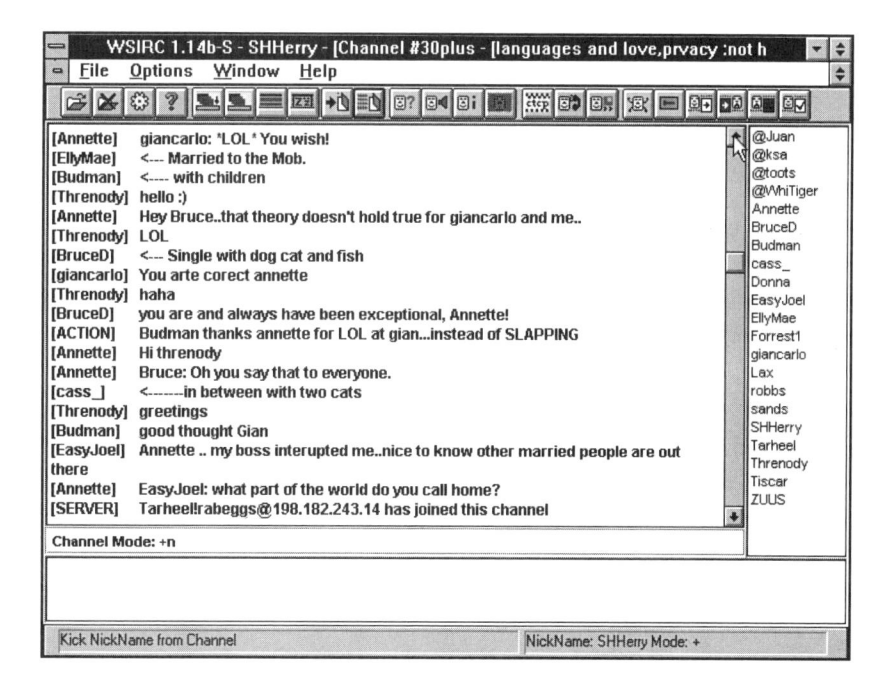

Idle chitchat is a staple among many of the group conversation areas online. Here's an example of meaningless chatter on IRC.

This particular mode of conversation, plain and simple chitchat, is probably the best way to start your online chat adventure. There's no commitment, no stress. You can just log on and go with the flow. You may have to try different channels or rooms to accomplish such chatting. Some may be too cliquish for newbies. Just be patient, however, and you'll eventually be able to find a neutral area for a simple shootin'-the-breeze kind of talk.

> **Finding Idle Chitchat**
>
> Want to know where the most popular areas for idle chitchat are found? If you're using CompuServe, the CB-1 band has a Welcome Newcomers channel where lots of banter goes on. If you switch to CB-2, the adult band, channel 1 has all the idle talk. If you're using AOL, any of the lobbies are for general talk. If you're using PRODIGY, you'll find lots of dialog in the Meeting Place room on the General channel. If you're using the Internet, look for general-topic channels with lots of users on them. That's where you'll find loads of chitchat. If you're using a BBS, you may have to ask where the best place for generalized conversations is.

Winning Friends and Influencing People

Some people are very good at making friends. If you're one of those people, you'll find that online chat presents a whole new way to do this. To really make friends online, you have to be willing to stop and spend some time talking and asking questions. If you have the patience it takes to build relationships, glue yourself (figuratively, not literally) to one chat channel or room and start talking. Greet everyone else who enters the room and take an avid interest in who they are. It won't be long before everyone else strikes up a dialog with you.

How do you begin talking to people? Start off by saying hello. Seek out things that you have in common with the other users, whether it's location, background, modem or computer woes, whatever. It also helps to treat everybody nicely. If you hope to make online friends, then it's probably not a good idea to flame them (that is, to insult them and pick a fight).

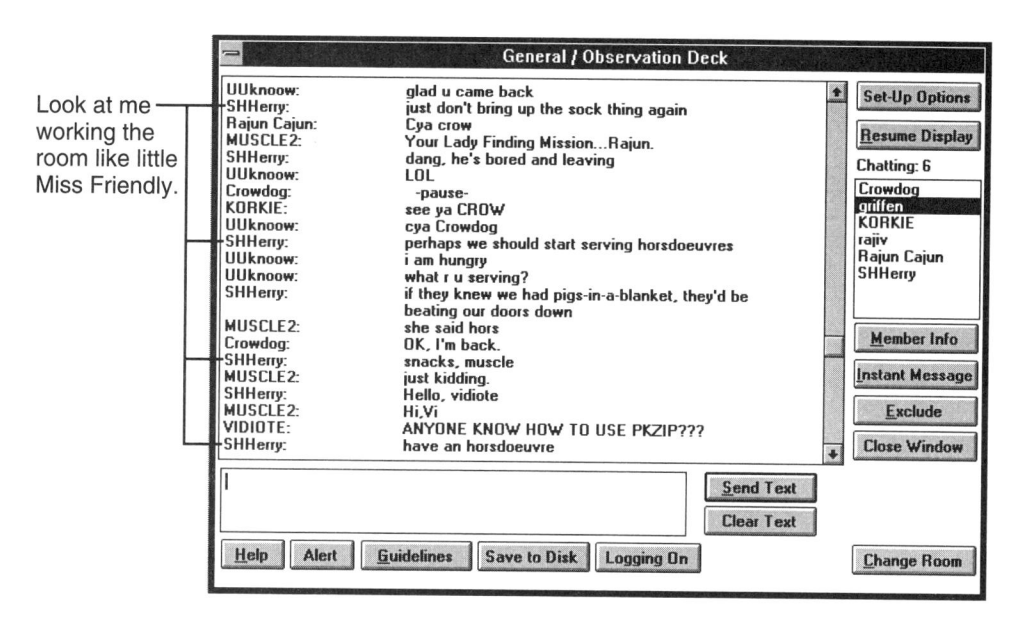

Chapter 11 ➤ *Sex, Lies, and Other Online Motivations*

```
                General / Observation Deck
UUknoow:       glad u came back
SHHerry:       just don't bring up the sock thing again
Rajun Cajun:   Cya crow
MUSCLE2:       Your Lady Finding Mission...Rajun.
SHHerry:       dang, he's bored and leaving
UUknoow:       LOL
Crowdog:         -pause-
KORKIE:        see ya CROW
UUknoow:       cya Crowdog
SHHerry:       perhaps we should start serving horsdoeuvres
UUknoow:       i am hungry
UUknoow:       what r u serving?
SHHerry:       if they knew we had pigs-in-a-blanket, they'd be
               beating our doors down
MUSCLE2:       she said hors
Crowdog:       OK, I'm back.
SHHerry:       snacks, muscle
MUSCLE2:       just kidding.
SHHerry:       Hello, vidiote
MUSCLE2:       Hi,Vi
VIDIOTE:       ANYONE KNOW HOW TO USE PKZIP???
SHHerry:       have an horsdoeuvre
```

Look at me working the room like little Miss Friendly.

One way to make friends is to greet others who enter into the same chat channel.

It's not uncommon to see people in an online channel pretend they're at a party. One person circulates around the electronic room serving funny-looking drinks made out of parentheses c(_), another greets everybody who comes into the room, while everyone else mixes and mingles. Sometimes the party gets a little wild—one person dances around with a lampshade, another passes out in a corner of the "room." I personally was in charge of hors d'oeuvres at such a party. It's not easy making hors d'oeuvres out of keyboard keys, you know. Anyway, I think you get the picture. Such an electronic party is kind of loopy, but it's also fun if you can get into the spirit of the thing. Socializing is one of the primary reasons why people log on and chat.

It's really neat when you start running into the same people over and over again. Unique bonds exist in the I've-seen-you-here-before encounters. Online chat definitely offers you some great opportunities for making new friends, and sometimes they even become flesh-and-blood friends.

It's also important to keep a sense of humor in your online conversations. If you add a little humor to your own chat, you'll attract more friends.

Neighborhood Bar If you log onto PRODIGY, seek out the Pseudo area and dive into the Neighborhood Bar room. Everyone pretends they're hanging out at the local pub on this chat channel. There's even a bartender on duty to serve cyber-drinks! Check it out.

125

Part 3 ➤ *What's Going On Out There?*

Everybody likes a good laugh now and then. Don't be afraid to try out jokes, play on words, or toss out one-liners. It's lots of fun when you run into other online users willing to participate in your humorous ramblings.

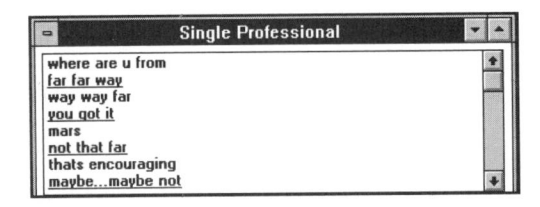

Mr. Single Professional was more than happy to engage in some amusing banter.

Don't Mind Me, I'm Just Browsing

There are those among us who possess very short attention spans. Rather than settle down in a chat room or channel to get to know people, they flit about from channel to channel like a moth at a light, looking for something to catch their attention. *Flitters* are a lot different from lurkers (you learned about those in Chapter 8). Flitters just jump around; lurkers stay and watch what's going on.

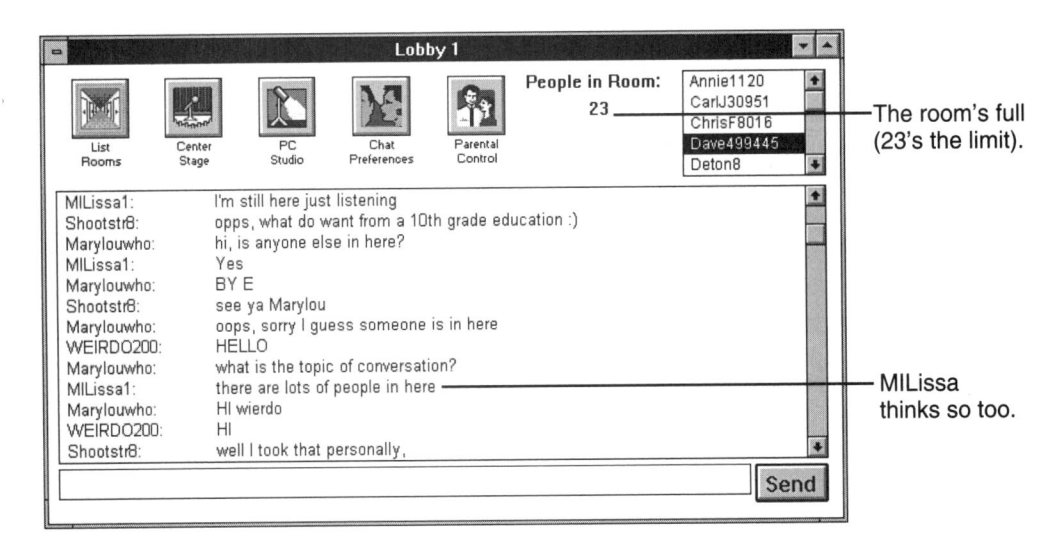

The number in the corner says there are 23 people in this chat room, but only a few are talking. The others are flitting around, simply passing through.

126

If you're a flitter, I'm going to have to be honest with you—you're not going to make many online connections unless you slow down and stick with a channel or discussion. You'll never get a true sense of what's going on unless you spend some serious time observing and participating. That goes double for those of you who expect to log on once and say you've experienced online chat, then proceed to tell everyone that it's overrated. You've got the wrong idea if this is your attitude.

Even if something bad happens to you online, like you get some unwanted attention or something offends you, that doesn't mean the whole system is screwy. There are lots of nice people out there, but you've got to have patience.

My, I was on a little soapbox, wasn't I? It's okay to flit, as long as you're aware that you won't get much out of it.

> **Keep in Touch** It helps to keep the friendships going by sending e-mail back and forth during those times that you're not online at the same time as your cyber-friends. If you say you're going to e-mail someone, you'd better do it. If you don't, you'll lose a friend.

Get a Hobby

Another reason to seek people out online is hobbies and interests. No matter what your hobby is, there's a place to talk about it somewhere online. For example, CompuServe has all kinds of hobby-related and interest-related forums, which in turn have conference rooms in which to converse with live-banter. I happen to like pets, and joined the Pets Forum. Every time I entered the Pets Forum to read posted messages, I ended up in the conference room or a live group discussion talking about pets and things.

You'll find plenty of hobby-related BBSs, and channels on the Internet's IRC. Most of these areas come alive in the evening and weekend hours, when most people are at home with their hobby or computer. For some people, computers are a hobby, so going online every night is all part of pursuing their hobby.

Part 3 ➤ *What's Going On Out There?*

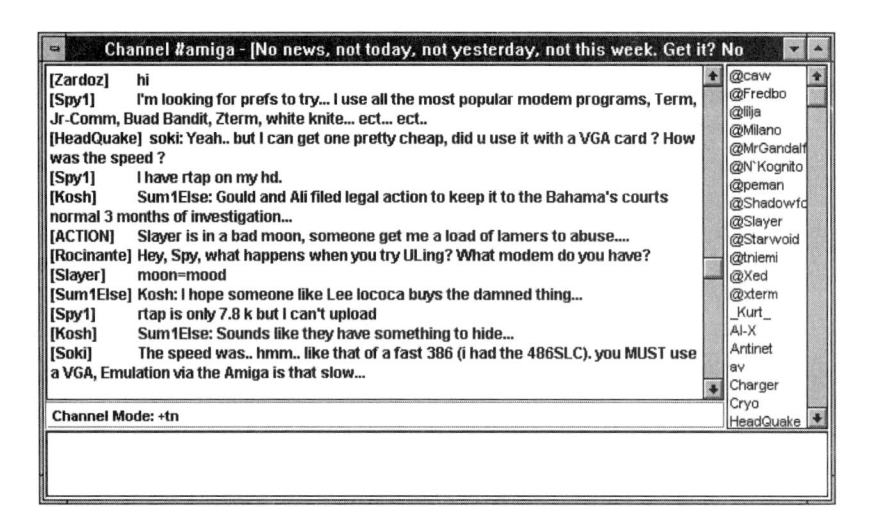

```
Channel #amiga - [No news, not today, not yesterday, not this week. Get it? No
[Zardoz]    hi                                                              @caw
[Spy1]      I'm looking for prefs to try... I use all the most popular modem programs, Term,   @Fredbo
Jr-Comm, Buad Bandit, Zterm, white knite... ect... ect..                    @IIija
[HeadQuake] soki: Yeah.. but I can get one pretty cheap, did u use it with a VGA card ? How   @Milano
was the speed ?                                                             @MrGandalf
[Spy1]      I have rtap on my hd.                                           @N'Kognito
[Kosh]      Sum1Else: Gould and Ali filed legal action to keep it to the Bahama's courts   @peman
normal 3 months of investigation...                                         @Shadowfd
[ACTION]    Slayer is in a bad moon, someone get me a load of lamers to abuse....   @Slayer
[Rocinante] Hey, Spy, what happens when you try ULing? What modem do you have?   @Starwoid
[Slayer]    moon=mood                                                       @tniemi
[Sum1Else]  Kosh: I hope someone like Lee Iococa buys the damned thing...   @Xed
[Spy1]      rtap is only 7.8 k but I can't upload                           @xterm
[Kosh]      Sum1Else: Sounds like they have something to hide...            _Kurt_
[Soki]      The speed was.. hmm.. like that of a fast 386 (i had the 486SLC). you MUST use   Al-X
a VGA, Emulation via the Amiga is that slow...                              Antinet
                                                                            av
Channel Mode: +tn                                                           Charger
                                                                            Cryo
                                                                            HeadQuake
```

Here's a stimulating discussion about the Amiga computer system and other such electronic wonders.

There are also online channels geared to specific topics, like various types of abuse, illnesses, support groups, and other such things. A lot of people find these chat areas very therapeutic. For one thing, you're anonymous; these people have never met you before. But it's also helpful to meet others who are going through whatever you're experiencing. You can get a lot of good advice this way.

So when it comes to interests and hobbies, online chat can really expand your horizons. You can meet with like-minded people from around the world and share ideas about a specific topic. Cool, huh?

Sending Out an S.O.S.

Having trouble with your computer? You probably need to talk to a computer geek. What better place to find such a person than online with your computer? There are plenty of experienced computer users wondering around the cyberspace chat channels. There are even BBSs and forums dedicated just to the topic of computers and software. All you have to do is log on and look for them.

To find a computer expert in the chat areas, just start asking around. Ask if anyone knows about whatever you're having trouble with. You can also consult with online guides and sysops (people in charge of monitoring things). Some online services even offer "live" technical help. You can also dial up technical-support BBSs, those devoted exclusively to answering questions about hardware and software, and talk live with an expert.

Chapter 11 ➤ *Sex, Lies, and Other Online Motivations*

Flirting

Since the online world is inhabited by both males and females, it's inevitable that a lot of flirting occurs in the chat areas. Some people log on just to do this, whether they're married or single, old or young. Why? Because it's fun. The exchange of clever repartee makes for an entertaining online session. It recalls the youthfulness of discovering the opposite sex, and the playful banter that goes along with dating and other such things. Ever dream of being a Cary Grant type, or a Mae West? Online flirting gives you a chance to exchange your best lines.

You'll find plenty of flirting in the open conversation areas, as well as in private messaging. Online flirting is typically harmless. If anything goes in the wrong direction, you can always change channels, squelch the person (turn off their messages), or simply log off the system.

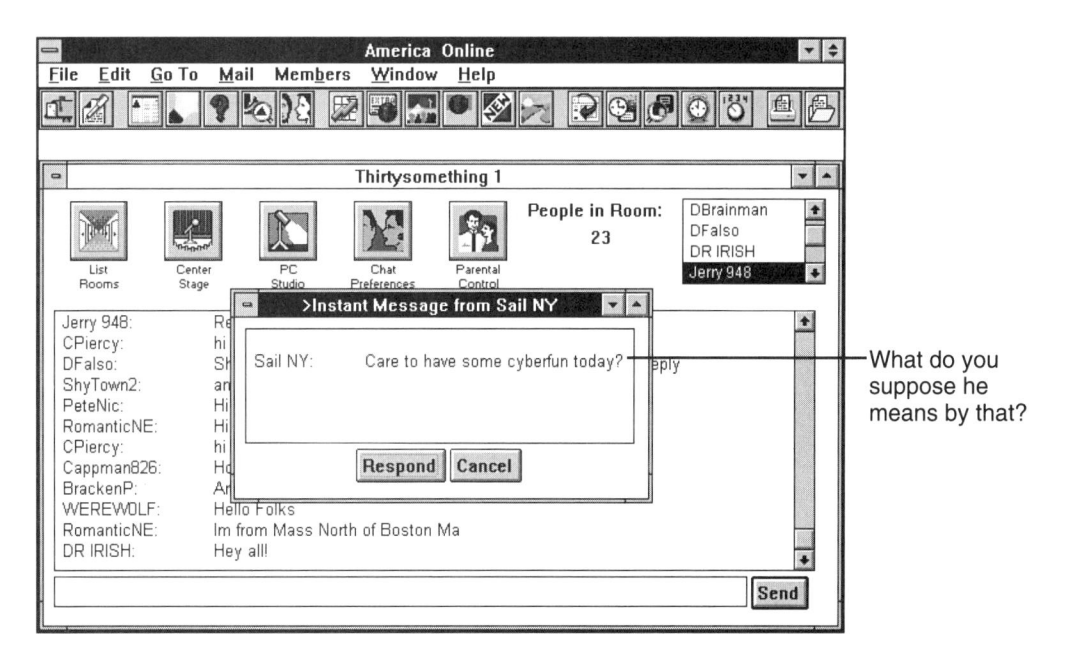

What do you suppose he means by that?

Here's an instant message that popped up on my screen while I was in AOL's Thirtysomething chat room.

Part 3 ➤ *What's Going On Out There?*

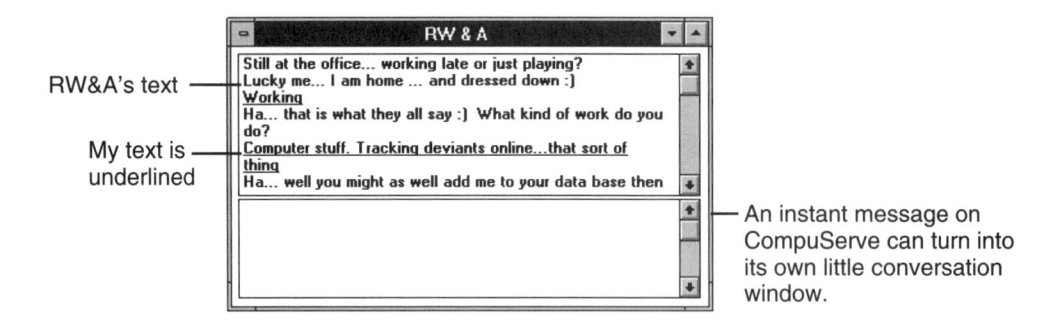

RW&A's text — [points to text in window]
My text is underlined — [points to text in window]

Window contents (RW & A):
- Still at the office... working late or just playing?
- Lucky me... I am home ... and dressed down :)
- Working
- Ha... that is what they all say :) What kind of work do you do?
- Computer stuff. Tracking deviants online...that sort of thing
- Ha... well you might as well add me to your data base then

An instant message on CompuServe can turn into its own little conversation window.

And here's a little flirting I did with RW&A. I never pass up a chance to type in a clever line, and as you can see, neither does RW&A.

Much of the flirting that occurs in group conversation areas is easily identified by the usage of emoticons and brackets that express hugs and kisses, and other goofy nuances of romance. There are quite a few online Romeos (and Juliets) out there, so be forewarned. Some online flirting leads to other online activities, which I'll explain in the next few paragraphs.

Looking for Love

You've probably read about online romances. It seems like every time I pick up a *People* magazine or a newspaper these days, there's an article about some couple who met online, fell in love, met each other in person, and then got married. Online chat has become the new matchmaking service of the '90s.

Well, if Rush Limbaugh did it, so can you. Online romance is quite a popular pastime in cyberspace. Apparently there are a lot of lonely people out there looking for relationships. Why's that? Good grief, I could give you a whole dissertation on the state of our culture and its eroding pillars, but that would be another book.

When it comes to online love, you don't have to worry about the superficiality of looks. Instead, the spark comes from falling in love with the other person's mind. It's either that or their great typing skills. Anyway, you can really get to know someone through their written dialogue.

There's also a goofy side to all this. There are actually online members who get married "electronically" online. This is one of the activities that online teenagers do. Yeah, it's a little weird, and the relationship doesn't usually last long, but I guess it's the thought that counts. If you ever find yourself involved in an online "wedding," don't forget to splurge for a "cyber-gift."

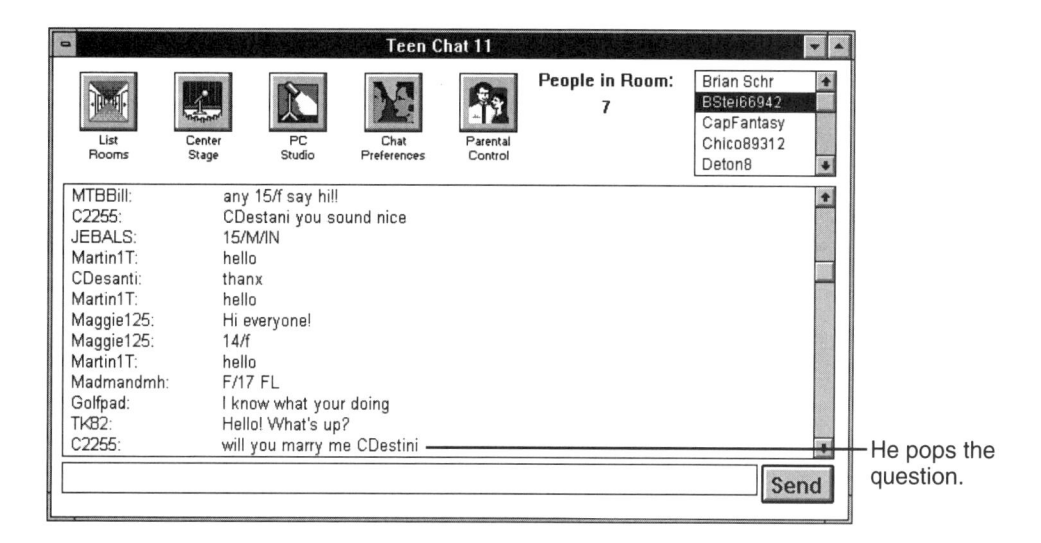

Chapter 11 ➤ *Sex, Lies, and Other Online Motivations*

It's not uncommon to see online "marriages" take place, especially in the teen chat areas.

Then There's Cybersex

Okay, you knew we'd come to this sooner or later. In fact, it's probably foremost on your mind, isn't it? Be honest! Now, about cybersex… what is it and who's doing it? Cybersex, also known as *hotchat*, is not your typical concept of sex. Basically, it's sex with (I mean *through*) your computer—but it's not physical sex, it's mind sex. Everything's typed out in words, like an erotic novel. I'm not sure why this still counts as sex, but that's what they call it. Before you get all fired up about trying this, you ought to keep in mind that not everybody out there writes like Jackie Collins or Sydney Sheldon—in other words, not everybody can write the stuff of erotic novels. In fact, a lot of cybersex chat is written like a song and dance routine—step one, I do this to you… step two, you do this to me… step three, I do this to you… step four, you do this to me, and so on. Mambo, everyone!

As far as who's doing it—generally speaking, it's people with raging hormones and way too much free time, or those just looking for some cheap electronic thrills. There are some days online when it's like a veritable meat market. If you log on as a female, you'll definitely be wearing a "fresh meat" sign over your head. It doesn't take long before at least one or two hot-blooded males approach you, usually in a private message, and attempt to lead you away for an intimate discussion. During peak hours (evenings) it's not uncommon for a female member of an online service to be inundated with private messages. Sure, at first it's kind of flattering, but then it becomes downright annoying.

Part 3 ➤ *What's Going On Out There?*

To give you an example of how other onliners think about cybersex, here's a conversation I had with someone named Long Gone (who turned out to be a very nice person).

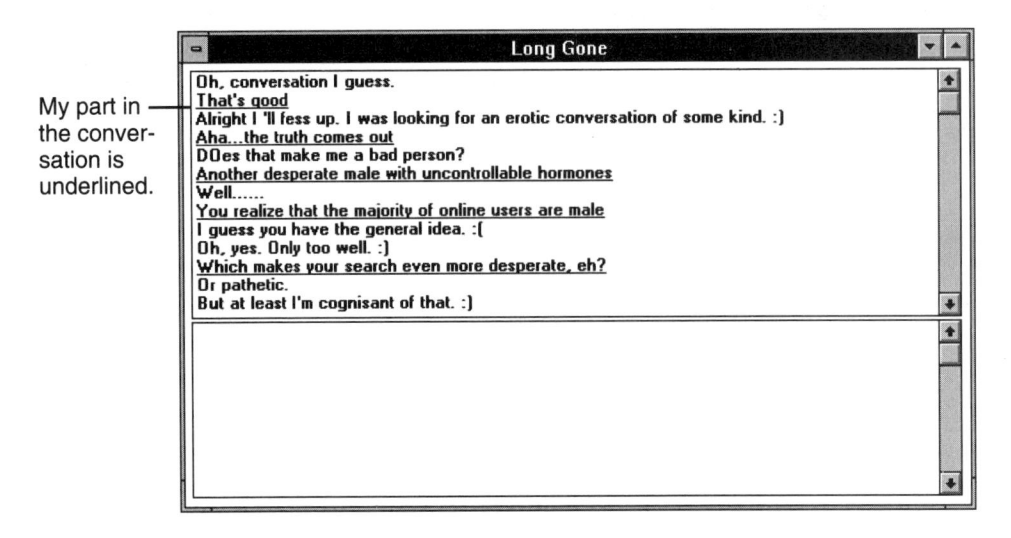

```
                            Long Gone
Oh, conversation I guess.
That's good
Alright I'll fess up. I was looking for an erotic conversation of some kind. :)
Aha...the truth comes out
DOes that make me a bad person?
Another desperate male with uncontrollable hormones
Well......
You realize that the majority of online users are male
I guess you have the general idea. :(
Oh, yes. Only too well. :)
Which makes your search even more desperate, eh?
Or pathetic.
But at least I'm cognisant of that. :)
```

My part in the conversation is underlined.

In the text before this, I had asked Long Gone what exactly brought him online to chat. He responded by saying conversation, then the truth came out in his next line.

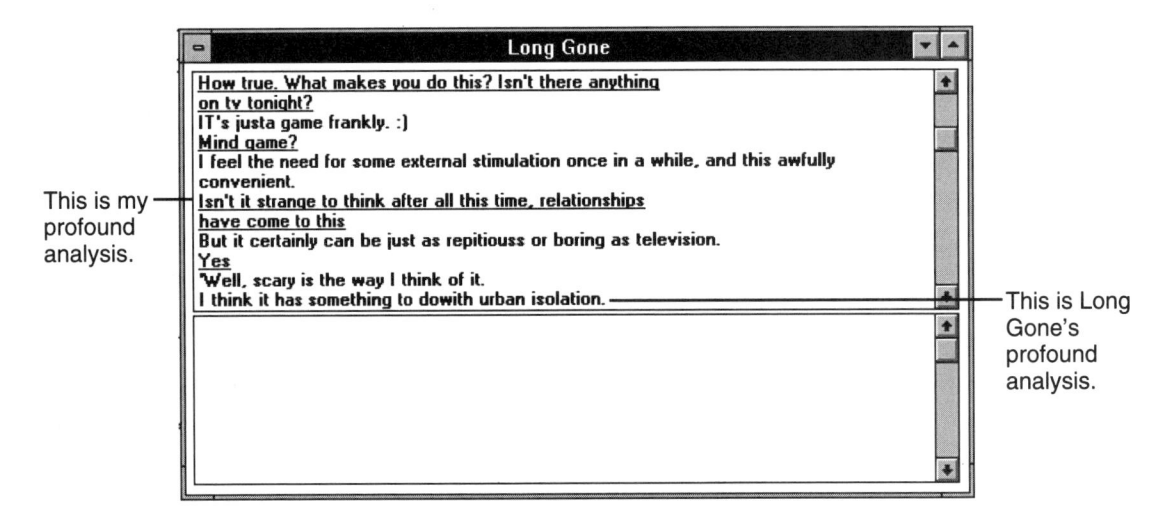

```
                            Long Gone
How true. What makes you do this? Isn't there anything
on tv tonight?
IT's justa game frankly. :)
Mind game?
I feel the need for some external stimulation once in a while, and this awfully
convenient.
Isn't it strange to think after all this time, relationships
have come to this
But it certainly can be just as repitiouss or boring as television.
Yes
Well, scary is the way I think of it.
I think it has something to dowith urban isolation.
```

This is my profound analysis.

This is Long Gone's profound analysis.

A great deal can be learned from these online interrogations, as revealed in this conversation. Psychologists really should be studying this phenomenon.

Chapter 11 ➤ *Sex, Lies, and Other Online Motivations*

Remember, I told you early on in this book that the majority of online users are male. Can you imagine what it's like with a bunch of electronic gigolos fighting for the attention of every female who logs on? It's a jungle out there. If you're not into this much attention, you shouldn't choose a female handle or nickname. That's good advice based on personal experience.

If you're using a guy's handle, you're not going to attract nearly as much attention when it comes to cybersex. But hey, that's life in the big online city. The concept of cybersex also explains some of the lurid handles you'll encounter while online, even in the group conversation rooms. For example, you may run across such individuals as BuxomOne, HairyGuy, CyberVixen, and BuckNaked. If a handle gets too risqué, the user might get kicked off the system, so beware.

As you can see from this next figure, someone going by the name of HOTnHEAVY has made it pretty clear about what he's after. You will run into lots of these kinds of queries online, especially if you've given yourself a female-oriented handle. I have found, however, that the majority of these overt advances occur on the larger commercial services. Why? Larger population of online users.

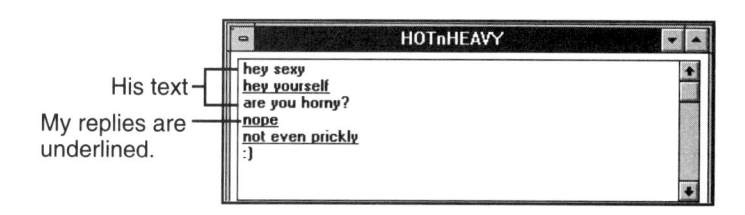

```
                    HOTnHEAVY
           hey sexy
His text    hey yourself
           are you horny?
My replies are   nope
underlined.  not even prickly
           :)
```

As you can see, HOTnHEAVY isn't holding anything back.

For the most part, cybersex takes place between two people privately, in a separate area from the group conversation channels, or in private messaging. If the behavior spills into the group area, you're just asking to be booted, so behave yourself. Cybersex occurs between two consenting parties, so you're never obligated to continue the conversation if it starts. You'll encounter aspects of cybersex among every online area, including BBSs, commercial services, and the Internet.

Some of the more ill-mannered online get their kicks out of sending users obscene private messages or trying to shock you with their lewdness. Most of these types are just trolling for attention, but you need to be aware of what to expect. (See Chapters 8 and 13 for ways you can fight back if this becomes a problem for you.)

Speaking of the darker side of cybersex, a small percentage of online users are seeking to turn an online connection into an actual phone call, or phone sex, or even an actual physical encounter. You need to be aware that this goes on too. Take a look at this figure to see what I mean:

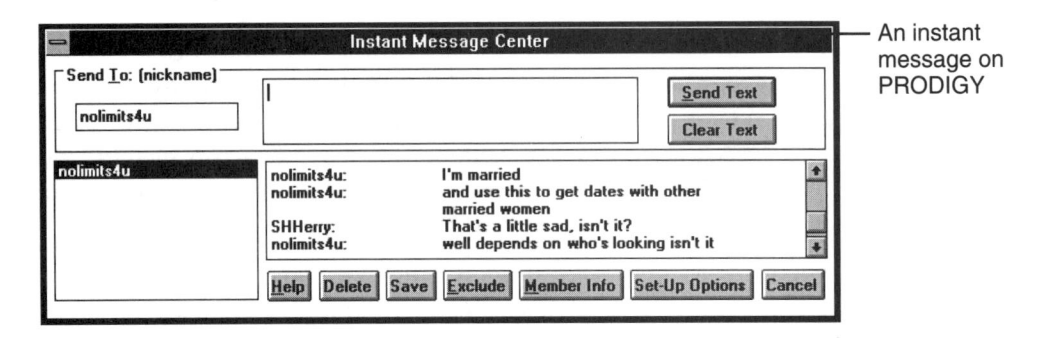

An instant message on PRODIGY

This guy's using an online service to cheat on his wife, for real (not just electronically). After I insulted him with my question, he wouldn't talk to me anymore. No great loss.

There are uglier sides that include cyberstalking, pedophiles seducing children who use the family computer, and online scams. (Read Chapters 14 and 16 for more information about handling these topics.)

So, will cybersex replace real relationships? Well, it's only words, but if that's your cup of tea… As for me, I'm not replacing my husband with my computer. However, in the world of sexual relationships and rampant diseases, cybersex is an electronic alternative for some people. For those who are immersed in the world of erotic writing and pornography, cybersex is just one more way to get some kicks. I'm sure there will be studies done about the downside of cybersex and its effects on online users. Don't be surprised if you start seeing this topic on *Geraldo*, or *Oprah*, or other such talk shows. In the meantime, you at least now know what cybersex is all about. Hey, you're not blushing, are you? ;)

Living an Online Lie

A surprisingly popular thing to do online is pretend you're someone else. Why not? It's not like anyone can really see you or anything. With online chat, you can pretend to be someone or something else, change your personality, or take on another gender. Why would anyone want to do this? There are several reasons.

Chapter 11 ➤ *Sex, Lies, and Other Online Motivations*

One reason you might want to assume another identity is if you're trying to avoid your own personality. Remember that saying I told you about earlier: "On the Internet, no one knows your a dog"? Well, if you're an absolute jerk in real life, assuming another identity online is your chance to be a more likable person. Or, if you're a wallflower in real life, becoming an obnoxious and aggressive person online can really give you another image. This may turn out to be a real self-esteem booster for you.

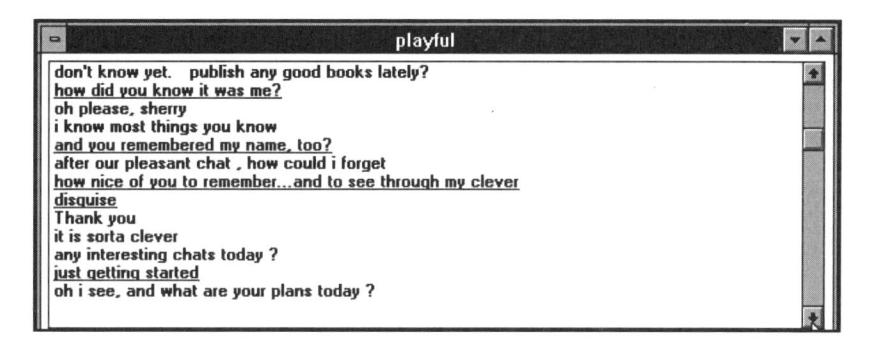

```
playful
don't know yet.   publish any good books lately?
how did you know it was me?
oh please, sherry
i know most things you know
and you remembered my name, too?
after our pleasant chat , how could i forget
how nice of you to remember...and to see through my clever
disguise
Thank you
it is sorta clever
any interesting chats today ?
just getting started
oh i see, and what are your plans today ?
```

Here's what happened to me when I logged on as a new person—someone I met the day before figured out it was me and foiled my plans. Don't you hate when that happens?

For some people, living an online lie is big challenge. As you can guess, it takes a lot of energy to keep up a charade. For example, let's say you're a guy pretending to be a 13-year-old girl. As you converse in a room, you may be asked your age and gender. You have to stop and remember to type the same thing each time you're asked. You also have to try and chat like a 13-year-old would chat, using the appropriate lingo and talking about appropriate experiences. It's not easy keeping this up, plus you're always wondering if someone else can see through your charade. Gender-changing is a popular online lie to try.

Another reason you might hide behind an assumed identity is if you're a famous celebrity. You may have to disguise yourself to avoid attention that naturally comes from your fame. On the other hand, pretending to be a celebrity is another way to live an online lie. Hey, I try to look at all angles.

Part 3 ➤ *What's Going On Out There?*

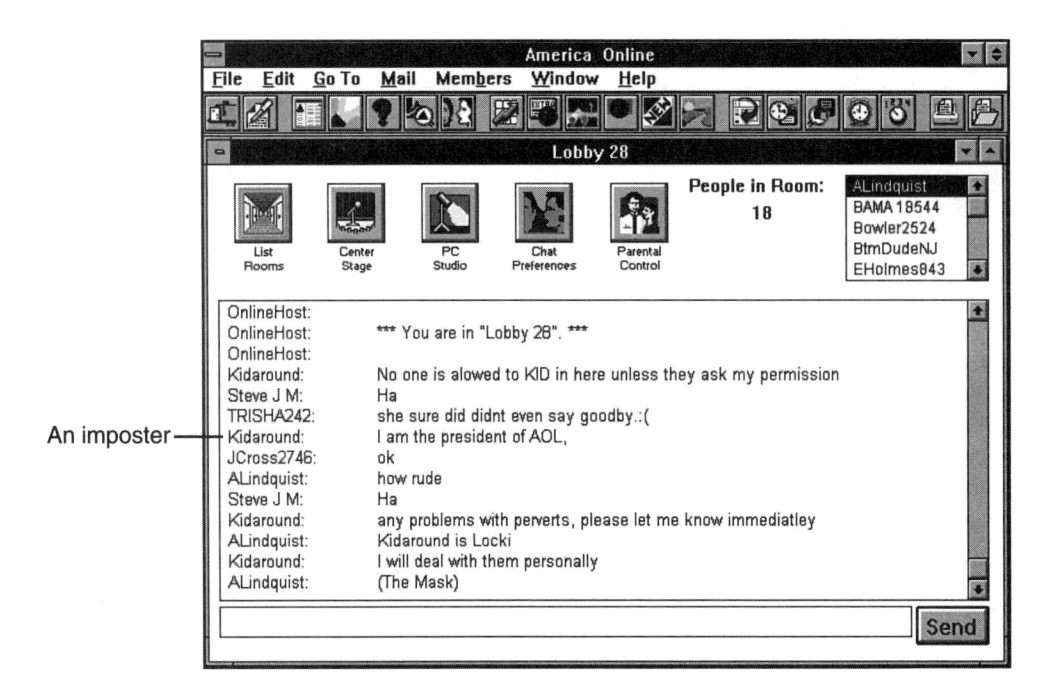

```
                    America Online
File  Edit  Go To  Mail  Members  Window  Help

                         Lobby 28

                                    People in Room:   ALindquist
  [List    Center   PC      Chat        Parental        18       BAMA 18544
   Rooms]  Stage    Studio  Preferences Control                  Bowler2524
                                                                 BtmDudeNJ
                                                                 EHolmes843

OnlineHost:
OnlineHost:    *** You are in "Lobby 28". ***
OnlineHost:
Kidaround:     No one is alowed to KID in here unless they ask my permission
Steve J M:     Ha
TRISHA242:     she sure did didnt even say goodby.:(
Kidaround:     I am the president of AOL,
JCross2746:    ok
ALindquist:    how rude
Steve J M:     Ha
Kidaround:     any problems with perverts, please let me know immediatley
ALindquist:    Kidaround is Locki
Kidaround:     I will deal with them personally
ALindquist:    (The Mask)

                                                          [ Send ]
```

An imposter — (pointing to Kidaround: I am the president of AOL,)

> *Here's someone pretending to be the president of AOL. Needless to say, the other members were not convinced.*

If you get found out in an online lie, expect to get flamed. It usually makes other users mad to know you've been fooling them, especially when playing around with gender identification. Be careful that your role-playing doesn't backfire on you. If you've been up to no good, you can get kicked off the system.

There's one more thing to remember. If you can pretend to be somebody else, then who's to say that the person you're chatting with isn't engaging in the same deception? The bottom line is this: you never really know who you're dealing with. Just because it walks like a duck and talks like a duck, doesn't mean it's really a duck in cyberspace.

You're Dealing with Other People's Feelings

One thing to remember when assuming an online persona is that your encounters with others are not always innocent. Feelings are often at stake. For example, if you're a guy who likes pretending he's a girl and leading other online guys on... expect some major emotional response (re: flaming) when your cover is blown. It really makes people mad when you play with their minds like that. Be careful out there.

Chapter 11 ➤ *Sex, Lies, and Other Online Motivations*

Flaming for Fun

It seems a lot of my friends (real friends, not electronic friends) like to log on and pick on people, start fights, and generally commit random acts of flaming. Why's that? They're just mean. Or maybe they just need an outlet for their aggression or frustration. Disappointed to find this out? You shouldn't be—the online world mirrors reality.

Because of the anonymity, however, online flaming can be more aggressive than in real life. Think about it—why would an ordinary person log on just to pick on the other users? A sadistic streak? A childhood trauma that hasn't been dealt with? Or just seeking attention fast? Perhaps it's all simply for the sake of entertainment? It could be any of these things. For example, I introduced my sister to PRODIGY the other day. In every chat room she entered, she tried stirring up controversy by talking about a heated topic or demeaning the other people in the room. Why did she do this? She obviously needs help developing her friend-making skills—though it probably didn't help that I used to ridicule her when we were little. Yes, it's probably all my fault.

You can get flamed just for showing up at the wrong place at the wrong time, or for spurning someone else's advances. When I was logged onto CompuServe pretending to be a teenage boy (I *had* to for my research on Chapters 11 and 15! Really!), I refused to flirt with a girl. She went ballistic. She kept bothering me, cursing me, following me into every channel. It was horrible. I guess that went beyond flaming for fun.

I have to admit, there have been days when I've logged on in a bad mood and snapped at a few people... but they deserved it, I'm sure. Flaming isn't very productive, however—it hurts, and it never goes anywhere. So be careful... even if you do think it's fun.

Believe it or not, there is an upside to flaming. When you're part of a good discussion group, or participating in a really great online conversation with others, flaming can occur if outsiders enter and try and violate netiquette or stir up trouble. In my personal experience, I've found that people tend to stick together during such intrusions. For example, I was logged onto an AOL lobby with four other people and having a wonderful time chatting. We were joking around, talking about all kinds of stuff... then along comes a pesky teenager. She began telling people to shut up, typing in caps, saying rude things to each of us—typical teenage behavior. But we all stuck together, defending each other, and generally flaming back at the pesky teenager, almost like a tight military fighting unit. It was fun. Soon the teen was defeated and left the channel, probably wandering off to annoy some other unsuspecting members. We celebrated our victory.

The moral of the story is this—online camaraderie is an important part of the online social structure. It's nice to see some acts of chivalry and honor in the course of online dialogue. It's satisfying to see people defend each other, even though they've never met before. There are infinitely more benefits to making friends than making enemies, but if you insist on being the bad guy, then go ahead… you're going to be awfully lonely, though.

Group Discussions

Cyberspace has all kinds of large conferences going on. Most of these involve guest appearances by experts, celebrities, authors, and other well-known personalities. Celebrities are all the rage on the big commercial services. They schedule all kinds of chat events where you can log on and ask questions of your favorite actor, author, or even game show host. (As I'm writing about this, I have an opportunity to chat with Alex Trebek on PRODIGY. Neato.) Services like PRODIGY and AOL sponsor weekly guests in a variety of professions focusing on a variety of interests. Look for similar events on all the big commercial services.

How's it work? There's usually a big gathering place, called an arena or coliseum, where you go to hear a speaker "chat." Sometimes only a certain number of people can attend these events, so it pays to find a "seat" before the action starts. Conferences are often governed by a moderator who takes questions and sends them to the celebrity. It's not a free-for-all—most conferences are very organized. If you ever get a chance to attend a live online conference, do so; you'll learn a lot about group discussions when you do.

Some of the services or BBSs offer users a conference feature that lets you invite a select group of people into a private channel for chatting. The Internet even has such a feature (see Chapter 6). Time for another personal experience story: While I was logged onto CompuServe one night, I struck up a wonderful conversation with about five or six people in Channel 2 on CB-2. One of the users was experimenting with the chat buttons, and ended up forming a private group window. He proceeded to invite everyone from Channel 2 into the group window. The invite is literally an invitation message that pops up on your screen, asking you if you want to join so-and-so in a group conversation. You can select yes or no. Most of us ended up in the private window, but periodically, due to technical difficulties, would drop out of the window and back into Channel 2. The same five or six people must have spent 20 minutes going back and forth from the channel into the group window, trying to hook up with each other again. It was like watching a slapstick routine in word form.

Anyway, organized group discussions and large conferences are another aspect of chat that brings people online.

Putting It All in Perspective

After reading about all the motives for chatting, some of you may still be wondering exactly why it is that people enter cyberspace and practice the many forms of conversation. Well, I've given this a lot of thought. Just what does compel people to call up an online service or the Internet, seek out the real-time chat area and then engage in an hour or more of ceaseless chatter? I think it's loneliness, a desire for attention, the challenge of connecting to others, and the response you get when you do—that's what brings people online to chat. Plus a good connection (or an exceptionally large credit limit on your favorite VISA card) can bring you online too. With hundreds of users logged on at the same time, there's always somebody you can talk to... even if it is just to insult them.

Our society has grown cold in many ways: it's grown colder in terms of relationships and in the ability to get involved with each other's lives. Cyberchat fills a gap in this area, allowing you to reach out and meet other people in a way our world has never been able to do before. However, I strongly caution you against relying on online chat as your only answer to communication fulfillment. It's not a substitute for reality, so be careful about plunging off the deep end (unless you've got an emergency therapist standing by). After all, it's still just a computer and some wires.

In the next chapter, I'll give you a first-hand account of what it's like to go online and chat. I'll bet you can't wait.

The Least You Need to Know

After reading this chapter, you should have a fairly good idea about the reasons behind online chat. Now you can determine what's compelling you to go chat too.

- ➤ You can find friendships through chat, focusing on your hobbies or interests, or focusing on romance.
- ➤ Cybersex is "mind sex" through words typed onto your computer, or something like that. ;)
- ➤ Live chat is helpful when you've got a computer problem and need immediate advice or help.
- ➤ Chat gives you a chance to switch identities or genders.
- ➤ Flaming isn't a good way to make friends, but it can vent some hostility.
- ➤ Many of the commercial services sponsor "live" chat with celebrities and established experts.
- ➤ Basically, people log on to chat in order to reach out and communicate with the rest of humanity... in one way or another.

Chapter 12

Pick a Sex, Any Sex

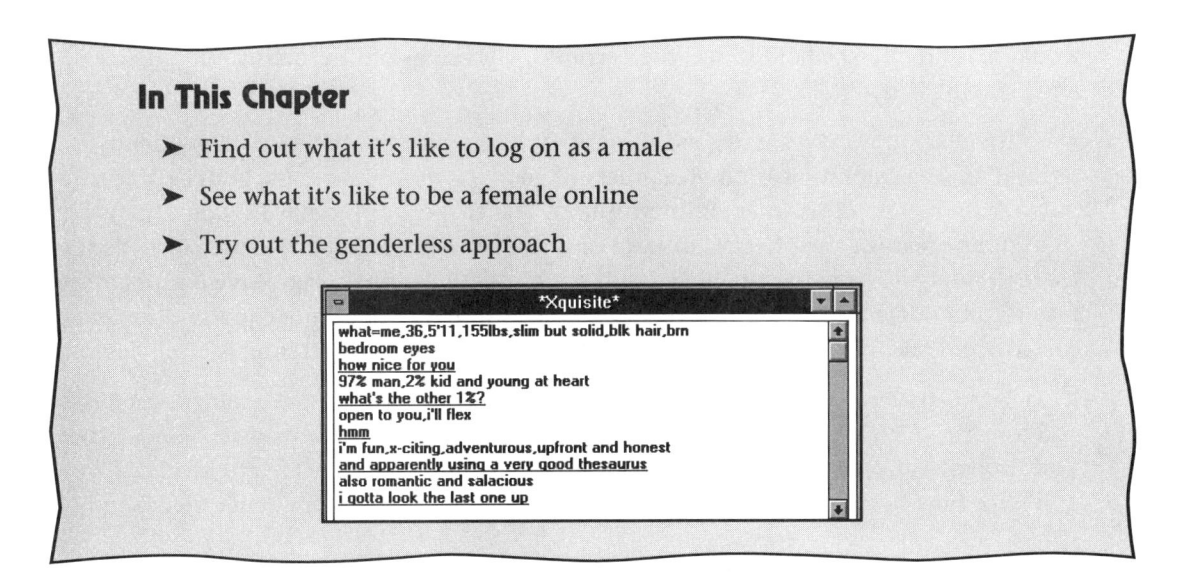

In This Chapter

➤ Find out what it's like to log on as a male
➤ See what it's like to be a female online
➤ Try out the genderless approach

```
*Xquisite*
what=me,36,5'11,155lbs,slim but solid,blk hair,brn
bedroom eyes
how nice for you
97% man,2% kid and young at heart
what's the other 1%?
open to you,i'll flex
hmm
i'm fun,x-citing,adventurous,upfront and honest
and apparently using a very good thesaurus
also romantic and salacious
i gotta look the last one up
```

Believe it or not, but the gender you choose as your user ID or handle plays an important part in how you're treated online, the attention you receive (sexual or otherwise), and in the friendships you make. This is true for BBSs, commercial services, and the Internet. To show you what I mean, I'm going to give you a first-hand account of what it's like to go online as a male, a female, or a genderless person.

Is Gender Even an Issue Online?

What an intelligent question. The answer is—it depends. In many cases, gender isn't an issue because, when it comes right down to it, you never really know who you're talking to anyway. Not everyone is who they say they are, male or female. On the other hand, you'll never really be able to escape the subtleties of the sexes online. Women will communicate differently than men and men will focus on different issues than women. It's life, so deal with it.

> **Cybersex:** Simulated sex online using text you type in at your keyboard—mind-sex. Cybersex most resembles the stuff you'd find in erotic novels. Sometimes it's sweet and mushy, other times it's graphic and deviant.

As far as the battle of the sexes goes online, not a lot has changed from the battle offline. In fact, some say it's even worse. For example, certain normally shy fellows become overbearing macho-men under the guise of online anonymity. This anonymity factor contributes greatly to the constant search for cybersex, too. Dozens and dozens of male users, safe in the guise of their online handles or nicknames, patrol the online channels looking for cheap thrills and cybersex. Yet, this also works in the other direction. Women who would never dare to be bold in real life become cybervixens online, acting out alter egos and breaking barriers.

There are, however, some good things that come with the "iffiness" of gender in terms of online communication. Regardless of your sex, you're more likely to be able to put your thoughts across without interruption. You're more apt to have serious discussions online because the physical distractions, such as looks and facial expressions, aren't there to stop you. Even personality traits, such as domineering or aggressive personalities, play second fiddle in online communications. The very root of online communication is the give-and-take, the ask-and-answer, the "you say I say" teeter-tottering we call *dialogue*.

So, to answer your question, is gender really an issue online? Well, sometimes it is and sometimes it isn't. You have to decide for yourself what kind of issue it's going to be. You also have at your fingertips the power to deal with the issues related to gender. If you don't like how things are going, you can switch channels, log off, or change your handle.

Setting Up Your Profile

Before I give you an account of my own online adventures, I ought to stop and tell you how to set up an online profile. Most of the bigger BBSs and online services let users set up a special information box or list that tells others who you are, what kind of computer you're using, what your interests are, and so on. These info areas are called *profiles*.

Chapter 12 ➤ *Pick a Sex, Any Sex*

For example, here's a profile from America Online:

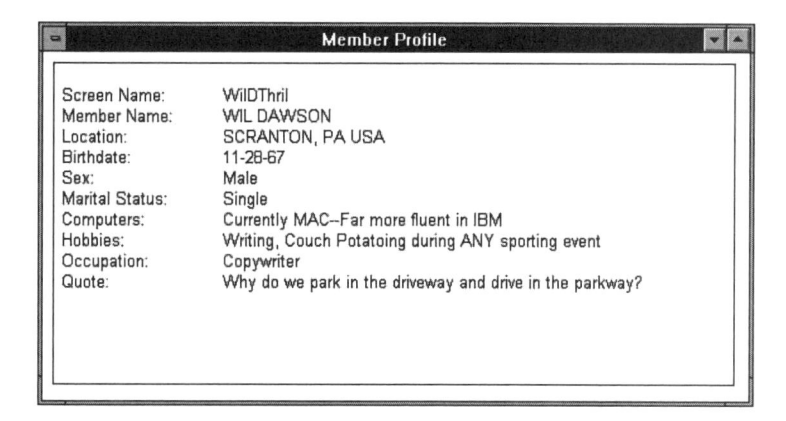

A profile from America Online.

Now, here's a profile from CompuServe:

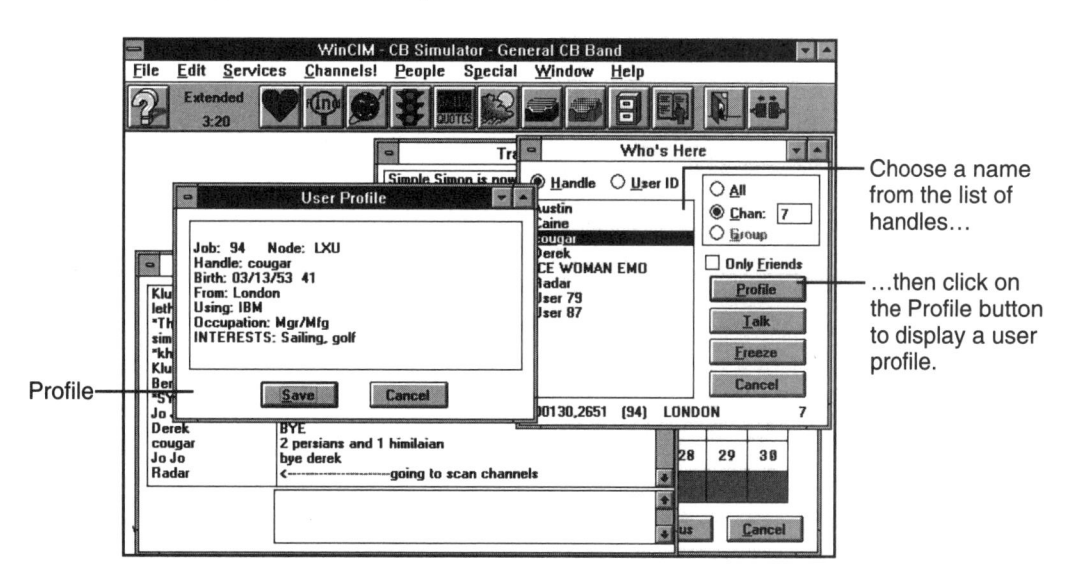

A profile found on CompuServe.

Profiles are a great way of putting commonly asked information about yourself into one place. That way, instead of having to answer the same questions over and over again, you can refer them to your profile instead. Most profiles include names, locations, birthdays, hobbies, and quotes. You can pretty much decide what information you want to include, and it can be funny stuff or serious stuff.

To read a member's profile on AOL or PRODIGY, you can double-click on the member's name in the list of people in the room. If you're in CompuServe, click on the **Who's Here** button on the toolbar, then select the user's name and click on **Profile**. You can also pull down the **People** menu and choose **Who's Here**.

To set up your own profile online, check out the member profile options or commands. It only takes a second to whip up a profile, and you can always go back and change it any time.

Lots of online members check out other people's profiles before even talking to them. On some channels, they get mad if you don't have a profile. To remain anonymous, I don't have a profile on any of the services I use. Because of that, I'm constantly being asked, "Where's your profile?"—to which I usually respond that I'm trying to be mysterious. Just remember, profiles are optional; you don't need one to chat.

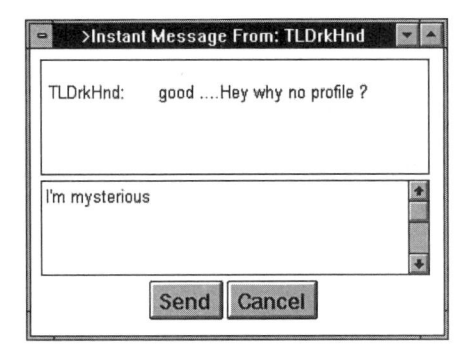

People without profiles get a lot of flak sometimes.

Logging On as a Male

I've already told you this several times, but you might as well hear it again. The majority of the online population is male. This is changing somewhat as modems and computers continue to proliferate, but for now you should know that online the male population is greater than the female population. So what does that mean? It simply means that you'll encounter more males than females.

Being female myself, it took a little attitude adjustment on my part to log on as a male. I had to rethink how I phrased even the simple things, like saying "hello." I thought an outright "hello" should be replaced with a "hey" instead. "Hey" sounded more masculine to me. So "hey" became part of my disguise.

Chapter 12 ➤ *Pick a Sex, Any Sex*

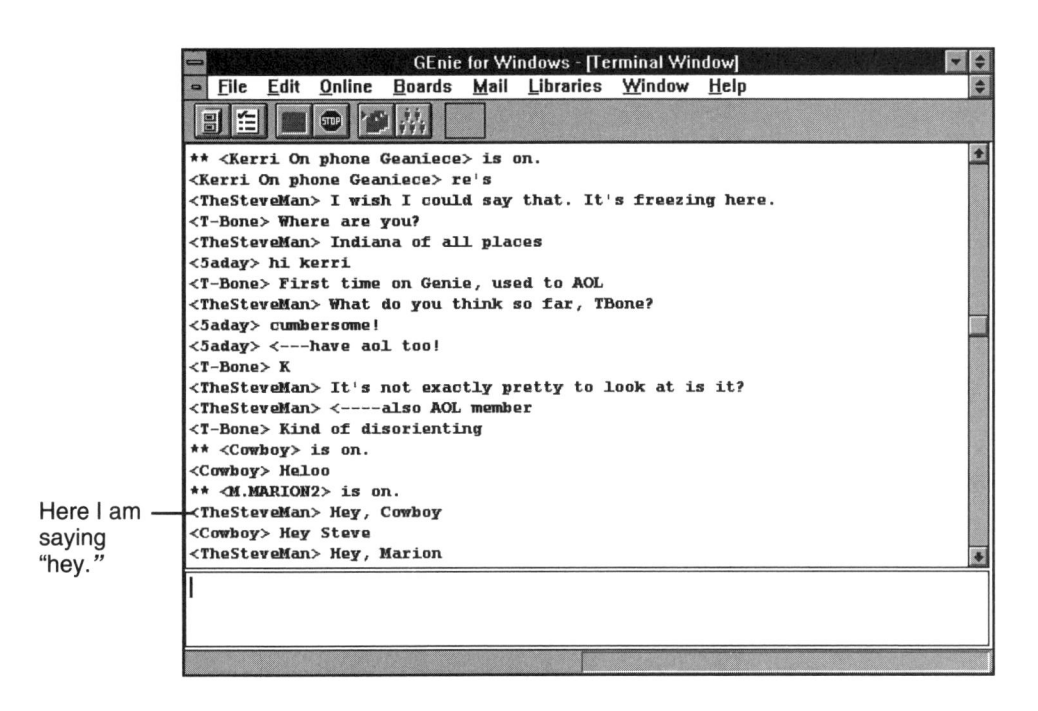

```
** <Kerri On phone Geaniece> is on.
<Kerri On phone Geaniece> re's
<TheSteveMan> I wish I could say that. It's freezing here.
<T-Bone> Where are you?
<TheSteveMan> Indiana of all places
<5aday> hi kerri
<T-Bone> First time on Genie, used to AOL
<TheSteveMan> What do you think so far, TBone?
<5aday> cumbersome!
<5aday> <---have aol too!
<T-Bone> K
<TheSteveMan> It's not exactly pretty to look at is it?
<TheSteveMan> <----also AOL member
<T-Bone> Kind of disorienting
** <Cowboy> is on.
<Cowboy> Heloo
** <M.MARION2> is on.
<TheSteveMan> Hey, Cowboy
<Cowboy> Hey Steve
<TheSteveMan> Hey, Marion
```

Here I am saying "hey."

I'm on GEnie as TheSteveMan.

When I logged on under a male handle or nickname and entered some of the chat channels, it seemed as if I was thrown into an immediate state of competitiveness. There's a lot of competition for attention, and much of it revolves around flirting and cybersex (not all, just in some areas). It's kind of like watching male birds in a strange mating dance, displaying their fine feathered plumage in order to catch the eye of the female bird.

I didn't get a lot of immediate attention as a male online. If I wanted attention, I had to get it myself. (It's a dog-eat-dog world!) I became more assertive, and sometimes aggressive in my rush to communicate with everyone else on the channel. I also changed the way in which I typed, dropping capitalizations and punctuation. I even practiced sending private messages to other females online.

The most fun I had as a male online was pretending to be a 17-year-old student. I went into CompuServe's teen channel and gave it my best shot. Much to my surprise, many of the girls on the

> **Private Message:** One-on-one communication between two users. Nobody else can see the message except you and the person who sent it. You'll see some examples of private messages in this chapter, and you'll learn more about them in detail in Chapter 13.

145

Part 3 ➤ *What's Going On Out There?*

channel struck up ongoing conversations with me. After experiencing my friendly banter and quick wit, they even started to fight over me. Take a look at the following figures to see how I did.

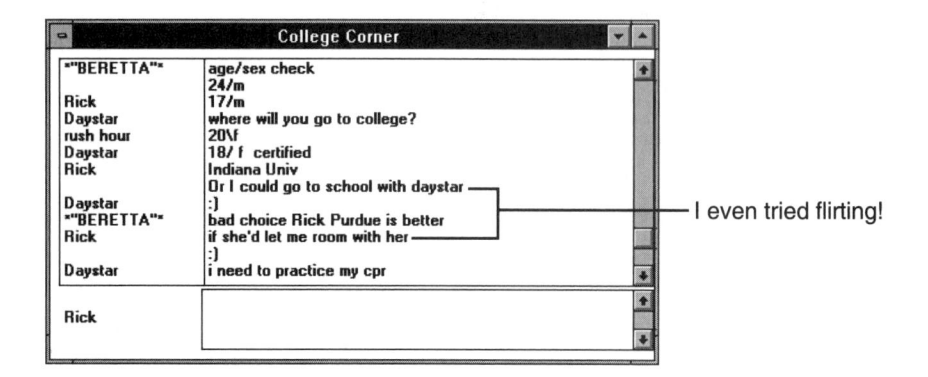

```
College Corner
*"BERETTA"*   age/sex check
              24/m
Rick          17/m
Daystar       where will you go to college?
rush hour     20\f
Daystar       18/ f  certified
Rick          Indiana Univ
              Or I could go to school with daystar ─┐
Daystar       :)                                    │── I even tried flirting!
*"BERETTA"*   bad choice Rick Purdue is better      │
Rick          if she'd let me room with her ────────┘
              :)
Daystar       i need to practice my cpr

Rick
```

Here I am pretending to be 17-year-old Rick.

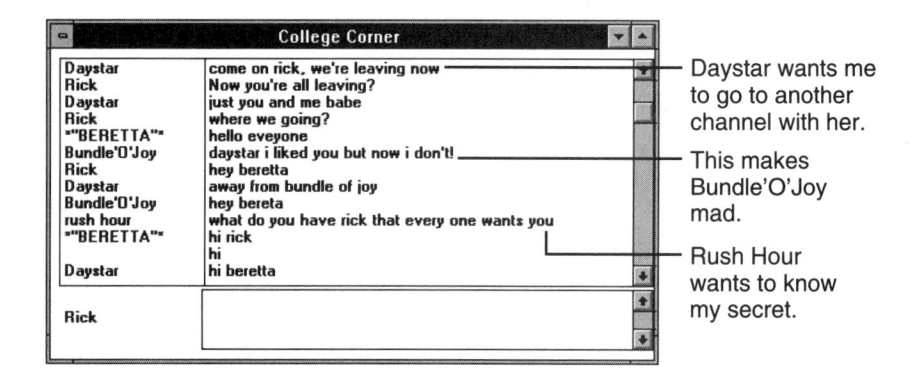

```
College Corner
Daystar       come on rick, we're leaving now ────── Daystar wants me
Rick          Now you're all leaving?                to go to another
Daystar       just you and me babe                   channel with her.
Rick          where we going?
*"BERETTA"*   hello eveyone
Bundle'O'Joy  daystar i liked you but now i don't! ── This makes
Rick          hey beretta                             Bundle'O'Joy
Daystar       away from bundle of joy                 mad.
Bundle'O'Joy  hey bereta
rush hour     what do you have rick that every one wants you
*"BERETTA"*   hi rick                              ── Rush Hour
              hi                                      wants to know
Daystar       hi beretta                              my secret.

Rick
```

I became the envy of all the males.

All in all, my online time as a guy was pretty enjoyable. True, I didn't get as much attention as I did when using a female handle (although I was besieged by a slew of private messages from some psycho gal who got mad when I wouldn't pursue cybersex with her), but it was still a lot of fun. A funny thing would happen to me after I logged off, though. I'd find myself acting a little more aggressively, and I had to reset my speech pattern to my customary "hello" instead of "hey." It's not easy pretending to be someone you're not. It really does take some effort to keep up your charade and figure out where you're going with it.

The one thing that did stand out for me as a "male" user (compared to a female or genderless user) is that I didn't get nearly the same amount of instant messages. There were some females who sent messages *after* we got acquainted in the group chat area. I think this has something to do with the fact that women like to get to know people before going on to more intimate conversations.

I asked my online male friends about their treatment on the chat channels. Most said that they didn't receive as many private messages as they sent. Not all guys, they explained, are looking for cybersex online. Many male users are simply shootin' the cyberbreeze and making friends. Some said they log on just to kill boredom. Maybe this is better than just sitting on the couch watching TV. And when you get bored with online chat, you can always switch channels, right? Welcome to a new age of chat potatoes.

Logging On as a Female

Remember just a few paragraphs ago when I said that the majority of the online population is male? Well, this explains why logging on with a female handle will make you exceedingly more popular than with a male name. During peak online times, there are quite a few guys trolling for love and lust among all the channels. They jump at a female handle like fish to a lure.

To give you some idea of what I'm talking about, here's a collection of private messages that got sent to me merely minutes upon my online arrival.

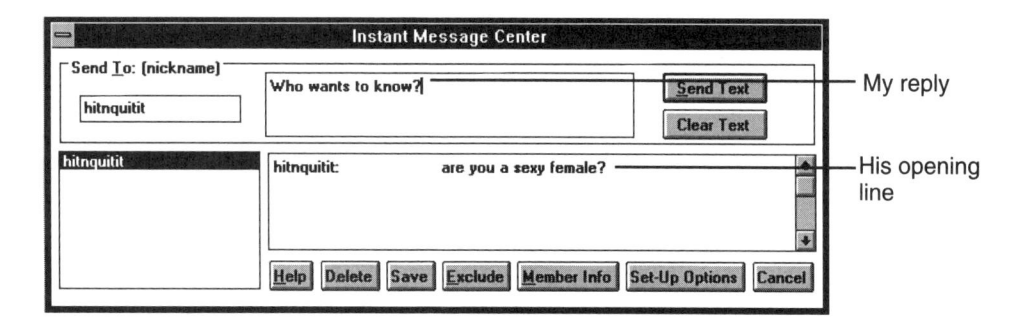

An instant message on PRODIGY.

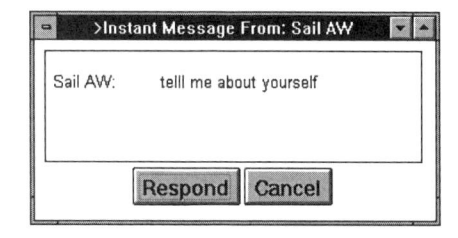

A message on AOL.

Part 3 ➤ *What's Going On Out There?*

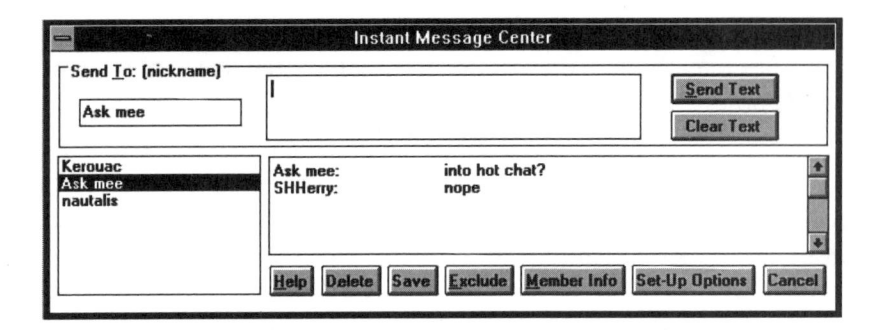

Another PRODIGY message.

Are you beginning to see what it's like as a female online? It seems like everybody wants to talk to you. Just so you know what happens to you when you pursue some of these invitations, here's a sequence of figures showing my private conversation with a guy named Prfct10. He claimed to be a one-time Armani model while in college. I hadn't heard that one before ;).

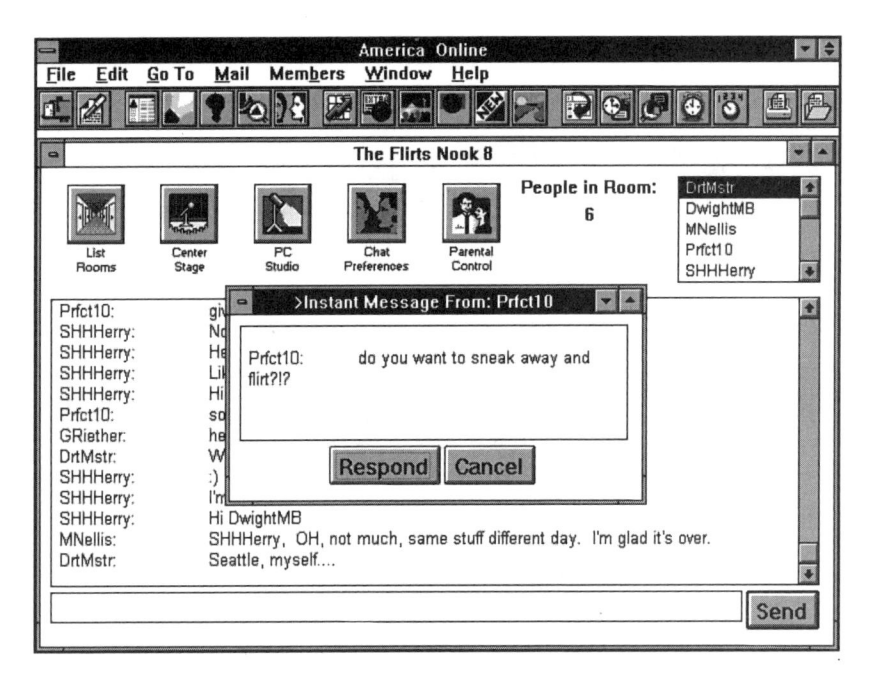

The setup.

148

Chapter 12 ➤ Pick a Sex, Any Sex

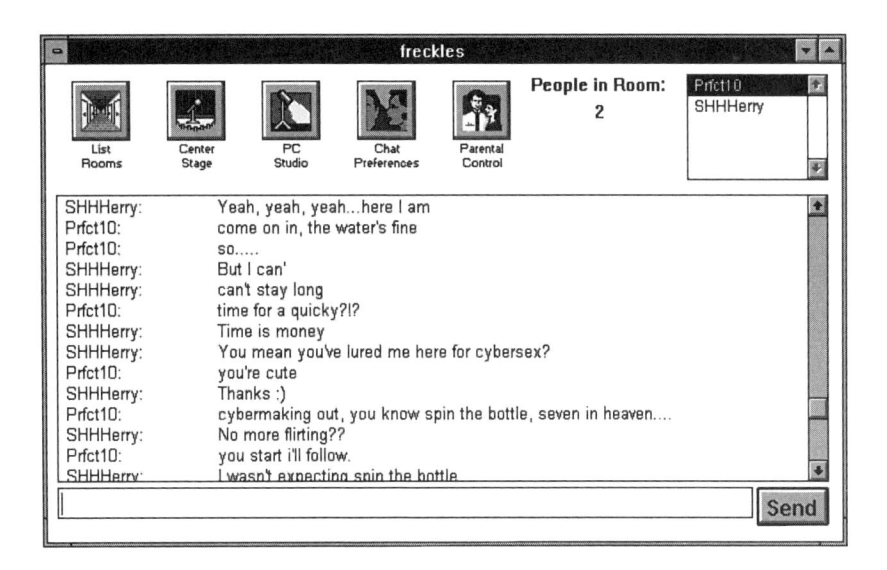

SHHHerry:	Yeah, yeah, yeah...here I am
Prfct10:	come on in, the water's fine
Prfct10:	so.....
SHHHerry:	But I can'
SHHHerry:	can't stay long
Prfct10:	time for a quicky?!?
SHHHerry:	Time is money
SHHHerry:	You mean you've lured me here for cybersex?
Prfct10:	you're cute
SHHHerry:	Thanks :)
Prfct10:	cybermaking out, you know spin the bottle, seven in heaven....
SHHHerry:	No more flirting??
Prfct10:	you start i'll follow.
SHHHerry:	I wasn't expecting spin the bottle

And so the seduction starts.

SHHHerry:	I wasn't expecting spin the bottle
SHHHerry:	when were you an Armani model?
Prfct10:	you mean I'm not going to get first base off of you :)
Prfct10:	six years ago. as a student at oxford
SHHHerry:	Where are you from originally?
Prfct10:	south carolina
SHHHerry:	A southern gentleman?
Prfct10:	tell me about that tan line (is that too fresh)
SHHHerry:	You're a persistent one, aren't you
Prfct10:	girls with freckles better be careful about the sun, can I put some lotion on you?!?
SHHHerry:	Only if it smells nice
Prfct10:	like coconut
SHHHerry:	What happened to that modeling career?

I'm a most uncooperative victim.

SHHHerry:	What happened to that modeling career?
Prfct10:	nice n creamy
SHHHerry:	But not greasy, right?
Prfct10:	spreads on smoooooothly
Prfct10:	where should I start?
SHHHerry:	What did you study at Oxford?
Prfct10:	15th century italian art and architecture. your changing the subject
SHHHerry:	Besides good tailoring?
SHHHerry:	Of course I'm changing the subject
Prfct10:	now.... back to the lotion, yes?
SHHHerry:	Wait...is it greasy? Does it have SPF15 or higher?
Prfct10:	the perfect amount. now shhhhlll I will start with your shoulders, rubbing gently...
Prfct10:	feel goood?
Prfct10:	am I out of line? do you mind?

Notice how I keep trying to change the subject?

149

Part 3 ➤ *What's Going On Out There?*

SHHHerry:	Hmm
Prfct10:	relax
Prfct10:	do you want me to stop? I will
SHHHerry:	You know what?
Prfct10:	what
SHHHerry:	I think I'm allergic to this lotion
Prfct10:	baby powder?
Prfct10:	rub it on me
SHHHerry:	No. Don't like baby powder
Prfct10:	i do!!!
SHHHerry:	You're not a baby, silly
Prfct10:	pretty please
SHHHerry:	Oh....

I think he's starting to get mad at me now.

Prfct10:	you should feel flattered
SHHHerry:	I suppose. You're an odd one, Prfct. Hey, I hate to powder and go....
SHHHerry:	but I must
SHHHerry:	Say goodbye...nicely
Prfct10:	so long
SHHHerry:	lottsa luck with the next one :)

Everything went nowhere fast.

As you can see, inevitably these private messages lead to one thing: cybersex. Failure to cooperate results in a sudden goodbye. But not all chat for females is like this. I met lots of nice guys (and gals) who were wonderful conversationalists. There were some online sessions that I laughed so hard, I cried! So what I'm trying to say is that chat doesn't always have to be about cybersex.

I asked my female friends online what their views were of female treatment. Most were fed up with the online advances. Yes, it was flattering at first, but it got old fast. Some of them had some great one-liners for responding to the flirtations and cybersex invitations. Many changed their online names to get rid of some of the unwanted attention. All in all, that's probably the best advice they gave me—to change my name to something less obvious. Still, despite the cybersex element of online life (when it was annoying), most female users found online chat to be an enjoyable experience. True, the battle

> **Private Messages Annoying You?**
> One of the biggest problems I ran into early on was trying to answer every private message that came my way, even the icky ones. I was raised to be polite, you know. But after awhile, I felt freer to hit the Cancel button when a message popped up, and I didn't feel any remorse for rejecting them.

between the sexes is still present even in electronic form, but the battle manifests itself in words and typing abilities. At least you've got control over these elements—you can always pull the plug, start over as somebody else, or take a course in speed keyboarding.

Try the Genderless Approach

If you'd rather bypass all the wacky gender stuff, give yourself a genderless handle. You won't get nearly the attention a female user gets, but you can expect a lot of questions asking you to identify your sex. A genderless name is the best way to avoid some of the bizarre people.

Like male names, a genderless person has to be brave enough to jump into the conversations and have at it. You won't meet people unless you start talking. The genderless approach is the least-threatening way to communicate with others. After all, who wouldn't want to chat with someone named Sunshine, or RushHour? To give you an example, here's what happened to me when I went online as Jello (a good genderless name if I ever saw one) in the Hospitality Suite on CompuServe.

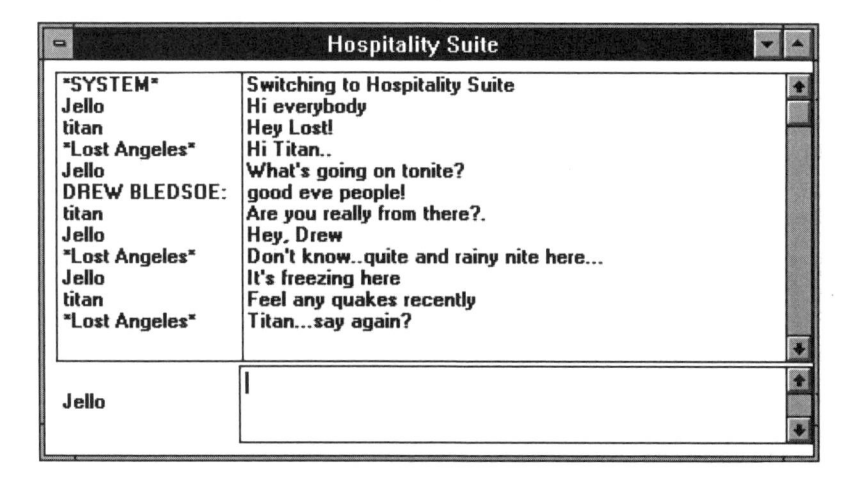

```
Hospitality Suite
*SYSTEM*         Switching to Hospitality Suite
Jello            Hi everybody
titan            Hey Lost!
*Lost Angeles*   Hi Titan..
Jello            What's going on tonite?
DREW BLEDSOE:    good eve people!
titan            Are you really from there?.
Jello            Hey, Drew
*Lost Angeles*   Don't know..quite and rainy nite here...
Jello            It's freezing here
titan            Feel any quakes recently
*Lost Angeles*   Titan...say again?

Jello            |
```

They weren't too receptive at first.

Part 3 ➤ *What's Going On Out There?*

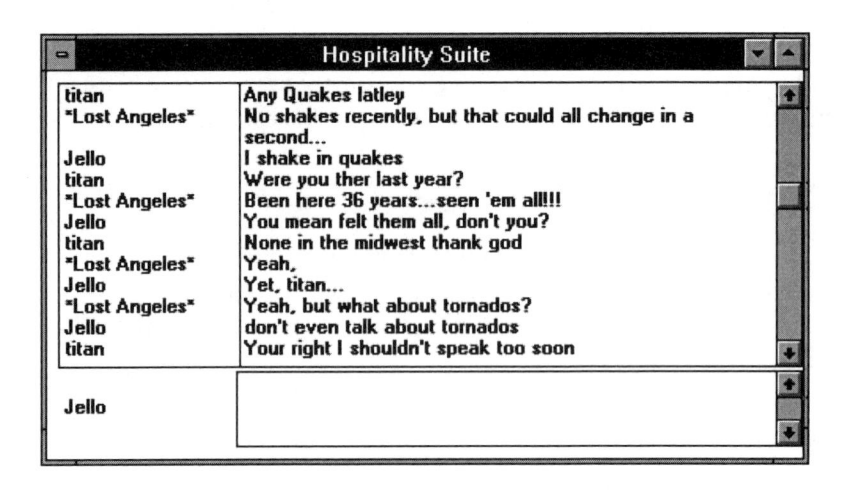

```
┌─────────────────── Hospitality Suite ───────────────────┐
│ titan          │ Any Quakes latley                      │
│ "Lost Angeles" │ No shakes recently, but that could all change in a
│                │ second...                              │
│ Jello          │ I shake in quakes                      │
│ titan          │ Were you ther last year?               │
│ "Lost Angeles" │ Been here 36 years...seen 'em all!!!   │
│ Jello          │ You mean felt them all, don't you?     │
│ titan          │ None in the midwest thank god          │
│ "Lost Angeles" │ Yeah,                                  │
│ Jello          │ Yet, titan...                          │
│ "Lost Angeles" │ Yeah, but what about tornados?         │
│ Jello          │ don't even talk about tornados         │
│ titan          │ Your right I shouldn't speak too soon  │
├────────────────┼────────────────────────────────────────┤
│ Jello          │                                        │
└─────────────────────────────────────────────────────────┘
```

They began to warm up to me after awhile.

You just have to be persistent with your online personality, whatever that may be. If at first you don't succeed, try, try again. Where have I heard that before?

Because of who you are, you won't be able to slip completely out of your gender role. For example, even when I had a genderless handle, some people could still tell I was female. How? By the way in which I phrased my sentences, or the words I used. Unless you're a skilled wordsmith, you'll probably run into the same thing.

In Conclusion

With all three scenarios I told you about in this chapter, male handles, female handles, and genderless handles, you'll find exceptions to the norms. Since online chat is so dynamic, you never really know how things are going to turn out or who you're going to meet. But, hey—if it were predictable, then we all probably wouldn't be online doing this.

The Least You Need to Know

It's a crazy online world, isn't it? Well, at least now you know the various things that you can expect with online roles. Try the gender-switching yourself and see what happens.

- ➤ Online males are more aggressive and send more private messages.
- ➤ Female handles bring lots of attention in most channels. The only exceptions to this were male-dominated channels focusing on subjects like *Star Trek*.
- ➤ A genderless handle is the least-threatening name to use online.

Chapter 13

The World of Intimate Conversations

In This Chapter

➤ Learn what an instant message is
➤ Find out how to talk privately with other online members
➤ Try your hand at electronic mail messaging

After you've been online for awhile (like five minutes on some commercial services!), you may begin to receive private messages sent by other users. These are meant to engage you in private conversations apart from the communal area or channel you're in. These messages are a little confusing (at first) to newbies, but it doesn't take long to get the

Part 3 ➤ *What's Going On Out There?*

hang of them. The first time I was on America Online, some guy sent me an instant message (that's what they call them on AOL). I was completely baffled by where it came from. I just assumed I had hit the wrong button. I must have spent ten minutes trying to figure out what I had done wrong.

In this chapter, I'll show you what private messaging is all about, including how to do it yourself. And speaking about private communication, I'll also tell you about e-mail and how to send it.

Is There Somewhere We Can Be Alone Together?

So far I've told you how to deal with the common conversational areas of BBSs, commercial services, and the Internet. Everything you type into a common conversation area, such as an AOL Lobby room, a CompuServe channel, or an Internet channel, can be seen by everyone else logged onto that area. But what if you want to talk to just one user on the channel without letting anyone else see what you type? You can do that with private messaging.

Private messages go by many names. You may see them referred to as *instant messages*, *IMs*, *sends*, or any other number of names—it all depends on what BBS, commercial service, or Internet connection you use. Regardless of the name, the idea behind them is the same. They're used to send a message to another user and keep it separate from the conversations going on in the channel or room. Private messages are for going one-on-one with another online member. For example, let's say you run into someone in the open conversation channel from the same hometown as you. Rather than engage in an intimate chat of "do you know so-and-so" or "have you ever been to the bookstore on the corner of 5th and Main" in front of everyone else, you can send that person a private or instant message and continue talking amongst yourselves.

An instant message on a GUI program opens up a separate conversation window or box. You can type text into the box, and also see what the other person says. For an example of how this looks on your screen, an instant message from America Online is shown on the next page.

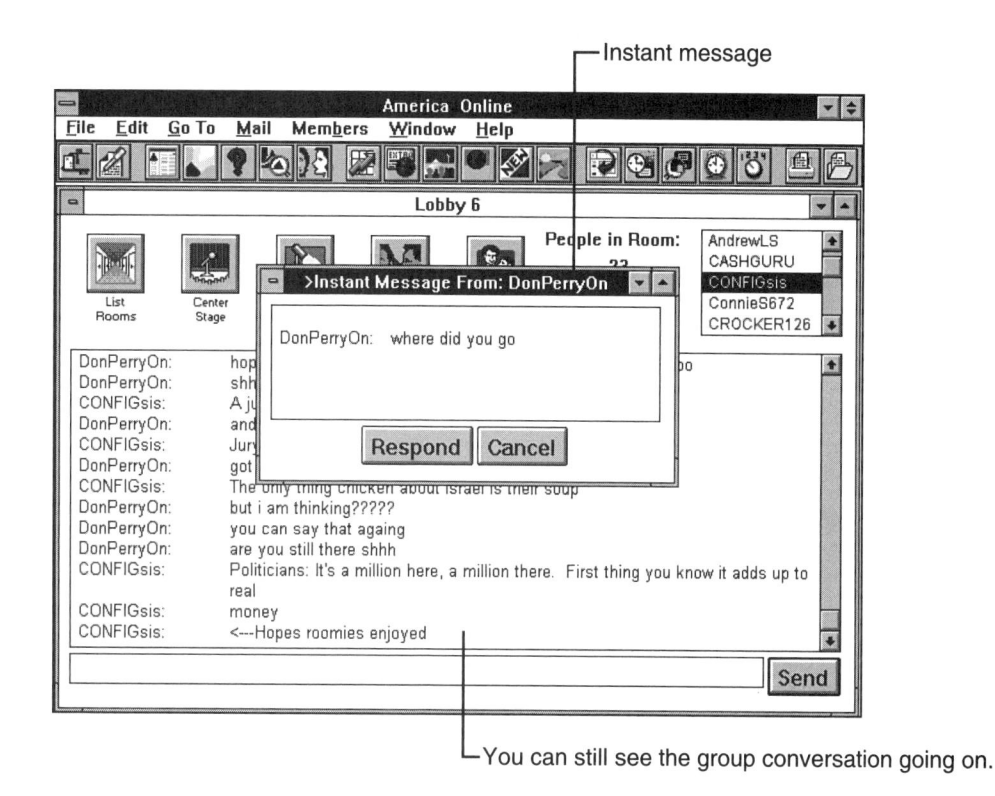

Chapter 13 ➤ *The World of Intimate Conversations*

An example of an instant message on America Online.

If you're not using a GUI program, your private message may appear set off or marked in the midst of the scrolling group conversation. Let me give you another example. This time, I've got a story to go along with it. I was using GEnie's chat feature, which works a little differently from the GUI setup I was accustomed to with CompuServe and PRODIGY. I was in the middle of a discussion and noticed that someone named LA Guy was saying hello. I thought he was on the same channel as the rest of us, so I said hello back. Everyone else on the channel wondered who the heck I was talking to. It turns out that LA Guy had sent me a private message and when I typed hello, everyone else on the channel saw it, but LA Guy didn't. Thankfully, I received a quick lesson in how to respond to a GEnie private message, and I finally got to talk to LA Guy, privately.

Part 3 ➤ *What's Going On Out There?*

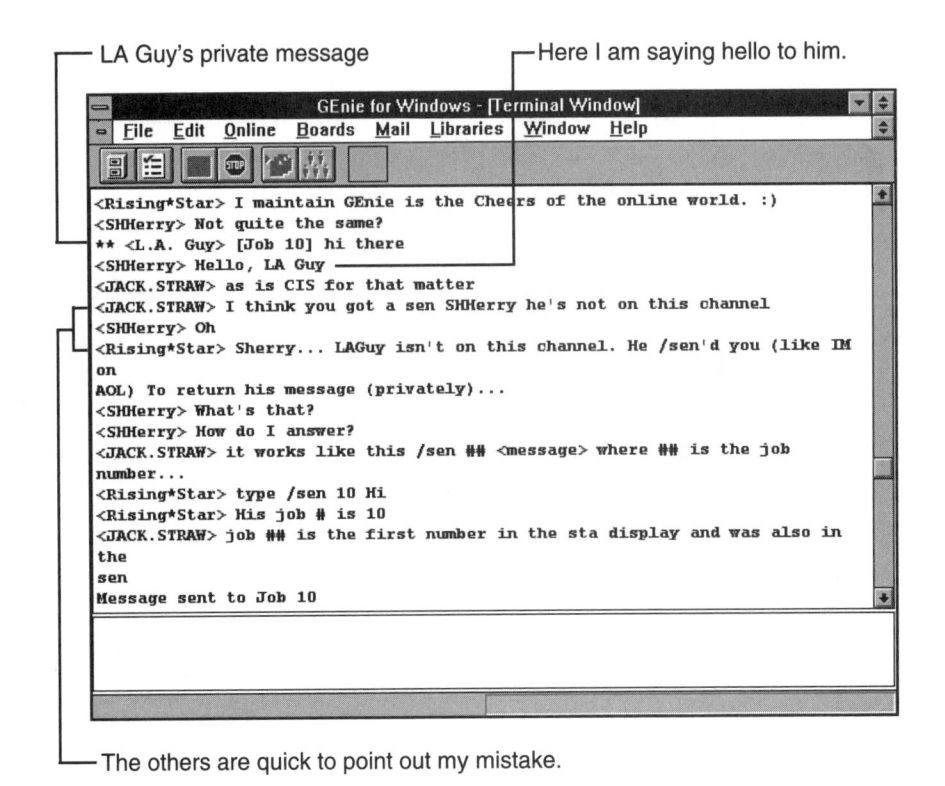

[Screenshot of GEnie for Windows Terminal Window with annotations:

- "LA Guy's private message" points to: `** <L.A. Guy> [Job 10] hi there`
- "Here I am saying hello to him." points to: `<SHHerry> Hello, LA Guy`
- "The others are quick to point out my mistake." points to the subsequent messages.

Terminal contents:
```
<Rising*Star> I maintain GEnie is the Cheers of the online world. :)
<SHHerry> Not quite the same?
** <L.A. Guy> [Job 10] hi there
<SHHerry> Hello, LA Guy
<JACK.STRAW> as is CIS for that matter
<JACK.STRAW> I think you got a sen SHHerry he's not on this channel
<SHHerry> Oh
<Rising*Star> Sherry... LAGuy isn't on this channel. He /sen'd you (like IM on
AOL) To return his message (privately)...
<SHHerry> What's that?
<SHHerry> How do I answer?
<JACK.STRAW> it works like this /sen ## <message> where ## is the job number...
<Rising*Star> type /sen 10 Hi
<Rising*Star> His job # is 10
<JACK.STRAW> job ## is the first number in the sta display and was also in the
sen
Message sent to Job 10
```
]

A private message on GEnie works a little differently than the instant message windows found on GUI programs.

If I had been paying closer attention, I would have noticed that LA Guy's greeting was preceded by two asterisks. On GEnie, these indicate a private message, along with the user's job number. If I had been more experienced, I would have recognized the private message format and responded accordingly. On the other hand, every newbie has to have a first-time experience sometime.

My point in telling you all this is that you'll have to learn to recognize a private message on the service or system you're using. Instant messaging may differ depending on your circumstances and setup.

What Do People Put in Private Messages?

Private conversations can be about practically anything. A lot of flirting takes place in private messages on the major commercial services. In fact, during peak hours, the majority of private messages received on commercial services are pick-up lines. If this becomes too annoying, most of the services have a feature you can activate that will turn off the message-sending and you won't have to see them at all.

You'll also find that lots of people use private messages to engage in cybersex dialog. Others use private messages to simply talk privately, away from the groups of chatterers. You may even run across flaming carried out in private messages. As I said, private conversations can be about anything.

When I first joined several of the large commercial services, I found myself answering every instant message that came my way, regardless of whether the message was flaky or polite. If you're an overly polite person too, you might have to deal with this same dilemma. The problem with doing this, however, is that it gets increasingly difficult to juggle the private messages (especially if there are more than one) and keep up with the group dialog scrolling across your screen at the same time. You also have to remember what's been said in each private message. The more private messages you juggle, the more confusing it gets.

Female users—particularly those identified as such by their handles—tend to receive more instant messages than they send. It's not uncommon during peak hours (evenings) to be absolutely inundated with private messages by hormonally charged or desperately lonely males. In fact, I found that I typically received more messages as a member with a feminine name when I was already engaged in the group conversation going on. Why is that? I think people see that you're willing to talk in the group setting and assume you are willing to talk in a one-on-one setting.

I had to learn to ignore some private messages, like the obnoxious ones and the outright obscene ones, and be more selective about who I talked to one-on-one. At first, it was easier to respond to instant messages than ever dare to send one to another person myself. I'm a little shy, you see. I thought others might consider uninvited messages too intrusive. It didn't take me long to get over this, especially as I was warming up to someone I was already talking to in the group conversation.

On the downside, private messaging can set you up for a lot of rejection. Not everybody likes to respond to such spontaneous invitations. This is especially true for male users trolling for online conquests. Anytime you're dealing with uninvited messages, there's a possibility that the recipient will not be receptive to your intrusion. There's also a possibility that the other user has turned off the message-sending feature. If any of you are planning on becoming professional online Romeos or Juliets, it might be wise to remember that rejection comes with the territory.

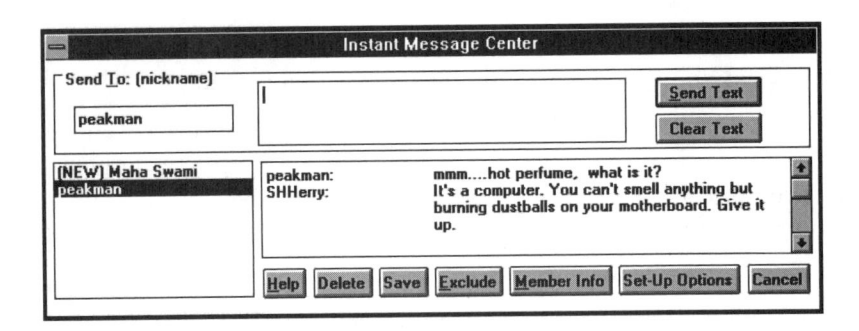

Pow! Another one shot down in flames—ever so gently, of course.

I'd encourage you to try the private messaging feature of the BBS or commercial service you're using, or on the Internet. You really can meet some fascinating people that way. So what if they reject your message. That only means that they weren't worth talking to anyway.

Using the Private Message Feature

Okay. So, I've told you how private messaging works and what it's used for; now I'll show you how to do it on the Internet and the major commercial services.

Private Messaging on IRC

If you want to send a private message to someone else currently logged onto IRC, you'll need to use the /msg command. If you're using UNIX commands to chat, you can type **/who #*channel*** and press **Enter** to find out who's logged onto the channel with you. (Be sure to substitute the name of the actual channel you're logged onto, for example, **/who #australia**.) Once you've found the name of the person you want to chat with, you can use the /msg command to contact them.

To send a private message on IRC, type **/msg *username*** and press **Enter**. (Substitute the person's nickname for *username*, for example, **/msg bobcat**.) To find out details about the person or locate them in IRC (if you don't know where they are), type **/whois *username*** and press **Enter**.

If the user has changed nicknames, you may get a message saying **Username: No Such Nickname**. If that happens, try typing **/whowas *username***, which will tell you who was the last person using that nickname.

> **Private Chat**
> I mentioned this before, but I thought I ought to remind you. Many areas of online chat, such as CompuServe's forums or CB Simulator, let you set up private chat areas for two or more people. So if someone invites you to a group chat, go ahead and participate.

Chapter 13 ➤ *The World of Intimate Conversations*

If you're using WIRC, the Windows version of IRC, you won't have to mess with typing commands unless you really want to. These commands will still work for you, but most WIRC interfaces offer you buttons and dialog boxes to do the same thing anyway.

When someone contacts you with a private message on the Internet, your screen may look like this (if you're using a Windows version):

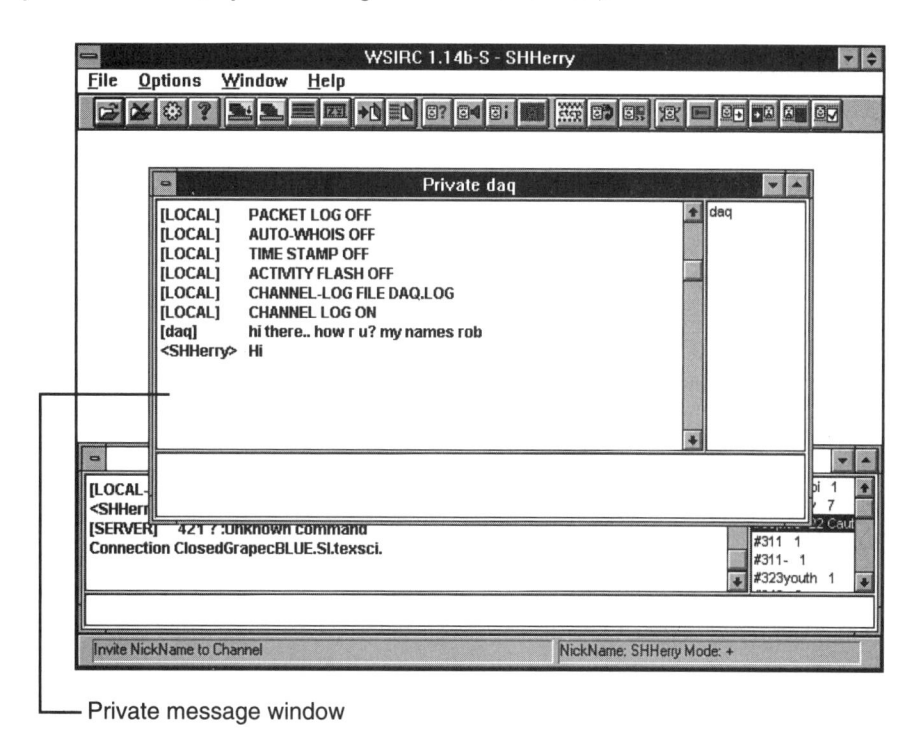

— Private message window

A private message on IRC for Windows.

I have another first-time story for you. The very first time someone sent me a private message while I was logged onto IRC, my screen started beeping like an alarm had gone off. Once again, I thought I had touched the wrong button or set off some kind of Internet security breach or something. Once the beeping stopped, I noticed an icon on-screen. I double-clicked on it, and it turned out to be a private message. At least it got my attention. Depending on what kind of scenario you're in, your private messaging on IRC may work similarly.

> **IRC Chat**
> To see a list of IRC commands, type **/help** and press **Enter**. This will display a complete list of IRC chat commands.

If someone is annoying you with private messages on IRC, you can turn them off. Type **/ignore *username* all** (substitute the offending sender's name for "username") and press **Enter**. To turn them back on again, type **/ignore *username* none** and press **Enter**. If you're using WIRC, you can click on the ignore button.

Instant Messages on the Commercial Services

All of the big online services offer you snazzy ways to send instant messages to fellow members. On America Online, open the **Members** pull-down menu and select **Send Instant Message**. You'll have to fill in the handle of the person you want to contact, but there's not much to this. If someone's messages are bothering you, pull down the Members menu and select **Member Preferences**, then turn off **Instant Message Notice**.

On CompuServe, you'll find private messaging commands located under the **Conferences** menu if you're in a forum. To turn off messages, select **Ignore Invitations** or **Ignore Talks** from the **Conferences** pull-down menu. If you're in CB Simulator, you can use the **People** menu to send messages with the **Invite** or **Talk** command. You can use the **Squelch** command to turn off messages from certain members.

You can use CompuServe's Squelch command to turn off messages from annoying individuals.

On PRODIGY, if you're on a chat channel, you can click on the **Instant Message** button to send a private message to someone. Use the **Exclude** button to shut out unwanted messages.

On GEnie, you can initiate a private message with the /sen command (sen for send). Type **/sen *#jobnumber*** and then your message, then press **Enter**. Each person who logs onto GEnie's chat channels is assigned a job number. You use that job number to send private messages.

BBS Private Message Sending

Private messages on BBSs vary. They mostly resemble Internet chat messages and GEnie chat. You'll have to use slash commands to initiate the message sending. To find out what commands are used on your BBS, you can usually type **/help** and press **Enter**. If you get too confused, locate the sysop for help.

You Can Always Send E-Mail

Although *e-mail* (which stands for *electronic mail*) isn't the same as private messaging, it's still a form of one-on-one communication online. I mean, it's still chatting, it's just not live chat. E-mail is available on just about every BBS, commercial service, and of course, the Internet. E-mail is also available through such services as MCI and Sprint. With e-mail, you can send private correspondence to another user. E-mail can be brief notes, long letters, memos, or any other correspondence you can make using your computer.

Unlike real-time chat, e-mail can take awhile to deliver and to respond to. Sure, e-mail delivery is faster than regular old *snail-mail* (U.S. Post Office), but it may be a day or so before the recipient logs onto the system to check his or her e-mail and respond.

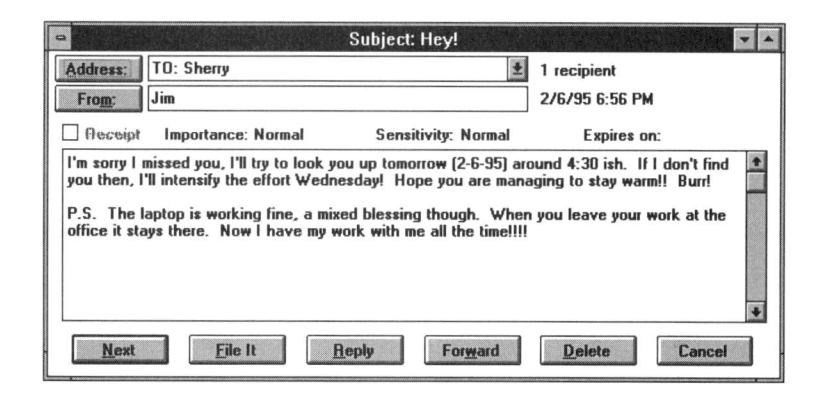

An example of e-mail from CompuServe.

When you sign up for an account with an online service, a BBS, or the Internet, you get your own electronic mailbox. It has its own address, which is usually your name or user ID number. Whenever you log onto the service, it lets you know if you have an e-mail message waiting for you.

Along with an electronic mailbox, most services have an *editor* for composing e-mail—a very simple word processing feature. In an e-mail editor, you can address a message, type the message, and send it on its merry little way. That's about all there is to it.

E-mail is a great way to communicate privately. Keep in mind, however, that with networked computers, electronic privacy is not always what it's cracked up to be. Most of us trust that no one else is going to be reading our e-mail, just the way we trust the Post Office not to open our regular paper mail. With some online services (like BBSs), it's possible for sysops to read the e-mail. Most promise not to let this happen, but it is possible.

If you're not careful addressing your e-mail, it could go to the wrong person, which means it's not too private either. Always double-check the address of the person you're sending online mail to. It only takes one slip of a key to send your confidential message hurtling through cyberspace and into a complete stranger's mailbox.

Although exceedingly slower than real-time chat, e-mail is still a very popular way to communicate and meet people. It's also good for maintaining online friendships started in the chat areas.

The Least You Need to Know

Let's sum up our chapter on private communications:

- ➤ Private messages have many names, depending on which service you're using. They are sometimes called instant messages, sends, or just plain "private messages."

- ➤ Private messages are live messages that are useful for chatting privately with another online user.

- ➤ On the whole, nicknames that seem feminine generally receive more instant messages—and often more unwanted attention—than other kinds of nicknames.

- ➤ Sometimes private messages can become annoying and distracting. You need to learn the steps for turning them off on the service you're using.

- ➤ E-mail is another form of private message, except it's not live. All online options today, from BBSs to the Internet, offer e-mail features for sending electronic correspondence.

Chapter 14

Chatting and Kids: Do They Go Together?

In This Chapter

- See what goes in the chat channels for kids
- Tips for identifying the age of your online conversants
- Things parents should know about online chat

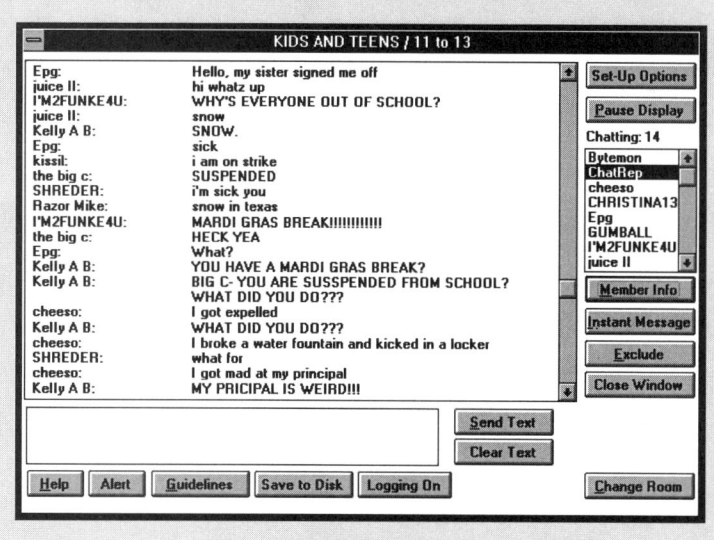

KIDS AND TEENS / 11 to 13	
Epg:	Hello, my sister signed me off
juice II:	hi whatz up
I'M2FUNKE4U:	WHY'S EVERYONE OUT OF SCHOOL?
juice II:	snow
Kelly A B:	SNOW.
Epg:	sick
kissil:	i am on strike
the big c:	SUSPENDED
SHREDER:	i'm sick you
Razor Mike:	snow in texas
I'M2FUNKE4U:	MARDI GRAS BREAK!!!!!!!!!!!
the big c:	HECK YEA
Epg:	What?
Kelly A B:	YOU HAVE A MARDI GRAS BREAK?
Kelly A B:	BIG C- YOU ARE SUSSPENDED FROM SCHOOL? WHAT DID YOU DO???
cheeso:	I got expelled
Kelly A B:	WHAT DID YOU DO???
cheeso:	I broke a water fountain and kicked in a locker
SHREDER:	what for
cheeso:	I got mad at my principal
Kelly A B:	MY PRICIPAL IS WEIRD!!!

It's 10:00—do you know where your kids are online? Computers are fascinating to kids of all ages. There's nothing that sparks their creativity more than a new computer game or program to explore. This is especially true of cyberspace. Most kids are pretty savvy when it comes to knowing about new developments in computer electronics, and that certainly includes the online world. Many schools today have access to the various commercial services and the Internet. We're raising a whole new generation that's technologically hip. It should come as no surprise to you that lots of kids are out there exploring the information superhighway right along with adults.

The question is, however, is it safe for kids to be driving along the information highway without a license? What are the dangers that await them on the open road? In this chapter, I'll tell you about some ways to help kids participate in online chat, and things to avoid on their journey. I'll also show you ways you can set up your computer to keep kids safe.

Should Kids Chat?

Sure they should. They have just as much a desire to talk to other people online as you do. Chatting and kids seem to go hand-in-hand. Granted, there are some online areas that aren't at all suitable for children, even teens, but there's no reason why kids can't chat among the many communal areas of BBSs, commercial services, and the Internet. However, some adult supervision and guidelines should be in place before kids log on and start talking.

Most of the major commercial services, like PRODIGY and America Online, offer kids special channels to chat on. For example, CompuServe and America Online have channels specifically labeled for teens. PRODIGY takes this a step further, and has set up channels for kids of certain ages. For example, they have a kids' channel for ages 10 and under, one for ages 11–13, another for ages 14–16, and yet another for ages 17–19. That's just a few of the kid- and teen-oriented channels. There are more to be found.

Kids also like chatting on channels focused on a hobby (computers or pets, for example). PRODIGY, again, has a great forum for that. You'll also find specific hobby chat areas on CompuServe, America Online, and some of the BBSs out there. Hobby chat on the IRC isn't as common, but it's available too.

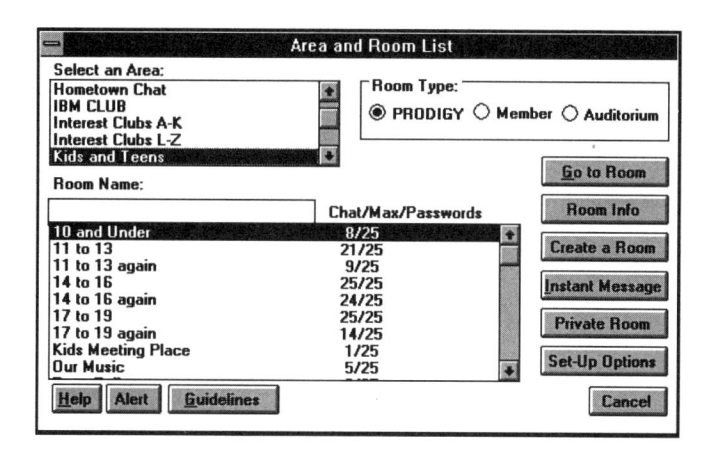

Chapter 14 ➤ Chatting and Kids: Do They Go Together?

PRODIGY offers kids several channels to choose from, based on ages and interests.

Sorting the Kids from the Adults

It's not always easy to figure out whether the person you're talking to online is a kid or an adult. Some of the most comprehensible people I've chatted with online have turned out to be kids or teenagers. However, there are some details that give them away. For starters, when you're chatting with younger children, their response time (the time it takes to reply) is much slower than that of most adults. Why is that? Probably because they don't know how to type very quickly. Most kids haven't had a course in typing yet, and generally employ the old hunt-and-peck technique. (Unless it's a kid who's played millions of computer games and knows his or her way around the keyboard.)

Another giveaway is misspelling, especially more adult-like words. Granted, everyone makes an occasional spelling error, but when you encounter a conversation with a lot of misspellings, then the chances are fairly good that it's a kid you're dealing with. Also look for lingo that kids might use, if you're up on that kind of thing. For example, if the person you're talking to uses the word "cool" a lot, then it's possibly a kid you're chatting with.

One way to find out if the person you're conversing with is a kid or an adult is to do the obligatory age/sex check. Whenever someone types **age/sex** on-screen, the other members type in things like 12/m or 20/f. Of course, we're assuming everyone's telling the truth during an age/sex check, but hopefully this will help determine who your online conversants are. Usually, everyone in the chat channel or room participates in an age/sex check. If too many of these checks happen in a row, people tend to get a little aggravated and don't respond as readily.

165

Part 3 ➤ *What's Going On Out There?*

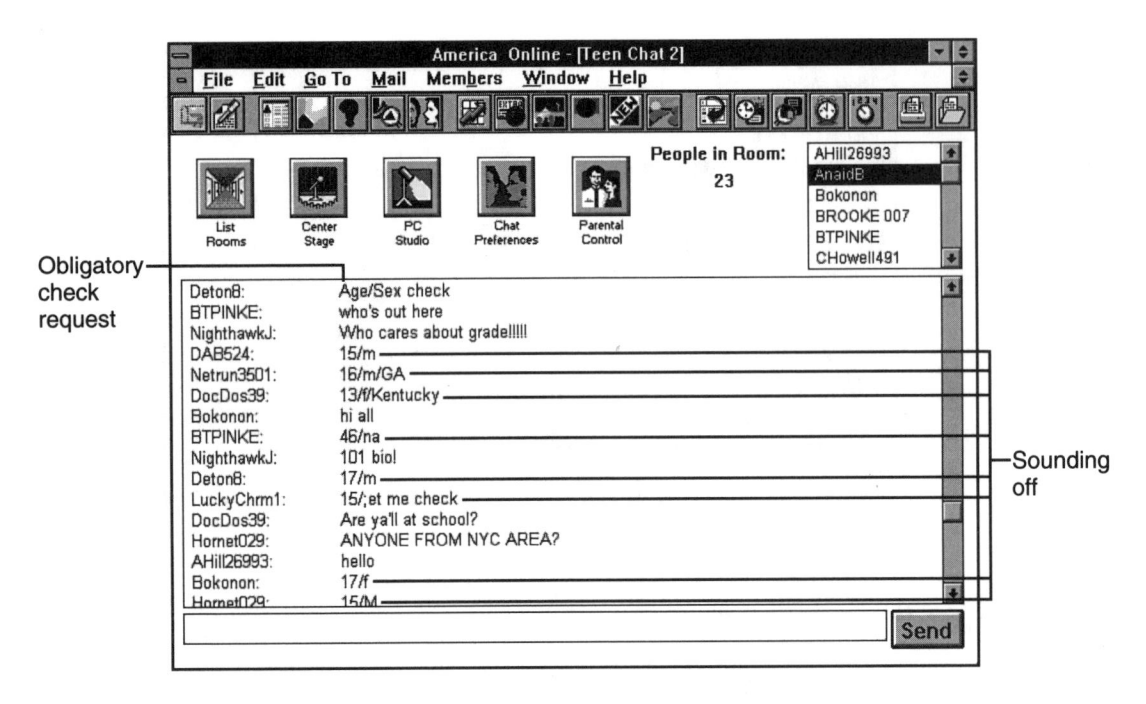

Here's what an age/sex check looks like in AOL's Teen Chat room.

Much of the kid activity online occurs right after school, when everyone gets home from school, fires up the computer, and logs on. Your chances of meeting up with kids increase during the after-school hours.

What's It Like Talking to Kids?

Kids are a lot of fun to talk to online, if you can be patient with their slow typing and misspellings. One of my most enjoyable visits to CompuServe was a 30-minute chat session with a 14-year-old girl from Michigan. I was reading the messages posted on the Pets Forum, when Linda invited me to a live group discussion. We talked about our pets, our love of horses (I was quite an enthusiast in my youth), and summer camp. Linda was very polite (her parents would be proud) and chatted easily. I was happy to talk to her, even though I had other things I needed to do. (I'm a nurturing person at heart.)

Another time, I was in PRODIGY's Computer Interests area and had an extremely pleasant talk about computers with Jason, a 12-year-old from Connecticut, who just got a new PC (IBM-compatible) for his birthday. He even gave me some good game tips to try. I was really enjoying his expertise until his mother made him log off for dinner. Aw, well.

Chapter 14 ➤ *Chatting and Kids: Do They Go Together?*

As an adult, be sure to be on the lookout for children in all the online chat areas. They like to chat as much as adults, and can even help you out with computer problems from time to time.

But not all chat experiences for children are pleasant encounters. Chatting has an ugly side that you may not want your child to be exposed to. To fully understand what goes on among the various kid-oriented chat channels, I secretly disguised myself as a kid and logged on. Sometimes I was a 12- or 13-year-old male, other times I was a 16- or 17-year-old female. What was it like? It was pretty scary at times. As far as subject matter, anything seems to go. The language is exceedingly graphic, more so than most adult channels. It bears repeating: parents really need to get involved and check this out.

Kid Chat: What Is It?

Kids often have their own language. When you enter a kids' chat channel or room, you may not always understand what they're talking about. Don't forget what it was like at their age—lots of wacky band names, goofy slang words, and the typical "attitude" displays. Online chat room discussions aren't much different than the banter that goes on in class or in the hallways at school. Kids are kids, you know. That also means you'll run into the occasional bully or two. But when it comes to online chat and bullies, words are your only true weapons.

What Goes On on a Kids' Channel?

Well, there's *not* a lot of talk about quantum physics going on or anything like that. There's plenty of idle chitchat amidst all the typos, and lots of silliness too. School, sports, dating, and music are big topics. A lot of chatting among the younger kids involves "How old are you?," "What's your favorite video game?," or "I wish school was over."

The following page shows examples of the kind of chat you might find on PRODIGY's Kids and Teens area. The first figure shows a good moment online. The second is another look at the same channel when I logged back on later.

Part 3 ➤ *What's Going On Out There?*

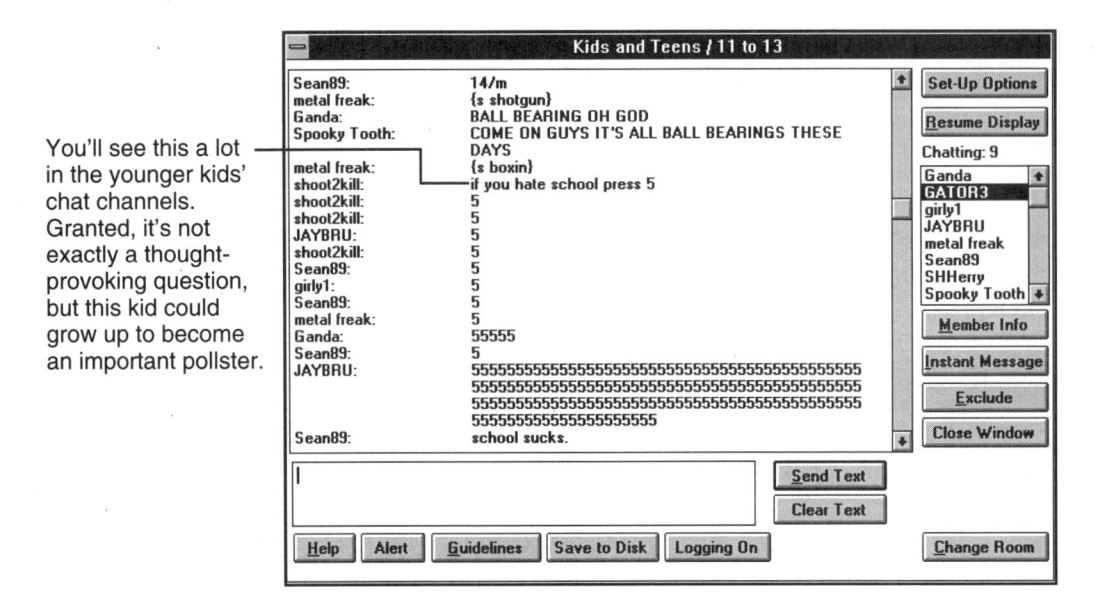

You'll see this a lot in the younger kids' chat channels. Granted, it's not exactly a thought-provoking question, but this kid could grow up to become an important pollster.

```
┌─────────────────────── Kids and Teens / 11 to 13 ───────────────────────┐
│ Sean89:        14/m                                      │ Set-Up Options │
│ metal freak:   {s shotgun}                               ├────────────────┤
│ Ganda:         BALL BEARING OH GOD                       │ Resume Display │
│ Spooky Tooth:  COME ON GUYS IT'S ALL BALL BEARINGS THESE ├────────────────┤
│                DAYS                                      │ Chatting: 9    │
│ metal freak:   {s boxin}                                 │ Ganda          │
│ shoot2kill:    if you hate school press 5                │ GATOR3         │
│ shoot2kill:    5                                         │ girly1         │
│ shoot2kill:    5                                         │ JAYBRU         │
│ JAYBRU:        5                                         │ metal freak    │
│ shoot2kill:    5                                         │ Sean89         │
│ Sean89:        5                                         │ SHHerry        │
│ girly1:        5                                         │ Spooky Tooth   │
│ Sean89:        5                                         ├────────────────┤
│ metal freak:   5                                         │  Member Info   │
│ Ganda:         55555                                     ├────────────────┤
│ Sean89:        5                                         │ Instant Message│
│ JAYBRU:        5555555555555555555555555555555555555     ├────────────────┤
│                5555555555555555555555555555555555555     │    Exclude     │
│                5555555555555555555555555555555555555     ├────────────────┤
│                555555555555555555                        │  Close Window  │
│ Sean89:        school sucks.                             │                │
│                                          ┌─────────────┐ │                │
│ │                                        │  Send Text  │ │                │
│                                          ├─────────────┤ │                │
│                                          │  Clear Text │ │                │
│ ┌──────┬───────┬──────────┬─────────────┬─────────────┐ ┌────────────────┐│
│ │ Help │ Alert │Guidelines│ Save to Disk│ Logging On  │ │  Change Room   ││
└─────────────────────────────────────────────────────────────────────────────┘
```

As you can see in the ongoing conversation, there was some earlier discussion about skateboard ball bearings, but then the dialog quickly moved on to more important matters.

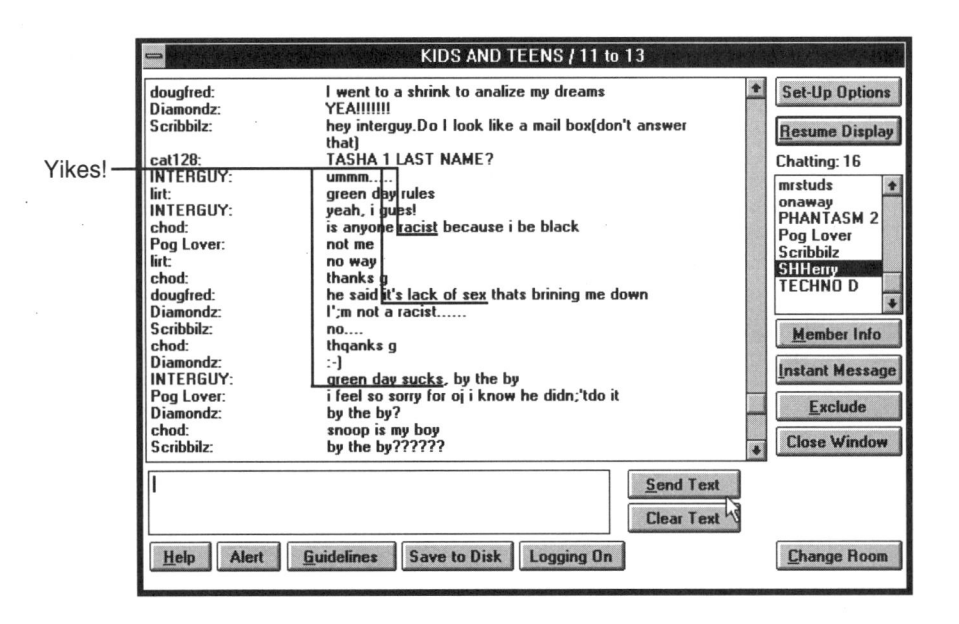

Yikes!

```
┌─────────────────────── KIDS AND TEENS / 11 to 13 ───────────────────────┐
│ dougfred:     I went to a shrink to analize my dreams   │ Set-Up Options │
│ Diamondz:     YEA!!!!!!!                                ├────────────────┤
│ Scribbilz:    hey interguy.Do I look like a mail box(don't answer│Resume Display│
│               that)                                     ├────────────────┤
│ cat128:       TASHA 1 LAST NAME?                        │ Chatting: 16   │
│ INTERGUY:     ummm.....                                 │ mrstuds        │
│ lirt:         green day rules                           │ onaway         │
│ INTERGUY:     yeah, i gues!                             │ PHANTASM 2     │
│ chod:         is anyone racist because i be black       │ Pog Lover      │
│ Pog Lover:    not me                                    │ Scribbilz      │
│ lirt:         no way                                    │ SHHerry        │
│ chod:         thanks g                                  │ TECHNO D       │
│ dougfred:     he said it's lack of sex thats brining me down ├──────────┤
│ Diamondz:     I';m not a racist......                   │ Member Info    │
│ Scribbilz:    no....                                    ├────────────────┤
│ chod:         thqanks g                                 │ Instant Message│
│ Diamondz:     :-)                                       ├────────────────┤
│ INTERGUY:     green day sucks, by the by                │    Exclude     │
│ Pog Lover:    i feel so sorry for oj i know he didn;'tdo it ├────────────┤
│ Diamondz:     by the by?                                │  Close Window  │
│ chod:         snoop is my boy                           │                │
│ Scribbilz:    by the by??????                           │                │
│                                          ┌─────────────┐│                │
│ │                                        │  Send Text  ││                │
│                                          ├─────────────┤│                │
│                                          │  Clear Text ││                │
│ ┌──────┬───────┬──────────┬─────────────┬─────────────┐┌────────────────┐│
│ │ Help │ Alert │Guidelines│ Save to Disk│ Logging On  ││  Change Room   ││
└─────────────────────────────────────────────────────────────────────────┘
```

Yes, there is some questionable language and subject matter in this conversation, but this is relatively mild compared to some of the stuff I saw.

Chapter 14 ➤ *Chatting and Kids: Do They Go Together?*

(I had some more examples to show you, but I can't, because this is a nice, decent, morally upstanding book.) If you expect your child to log on and meet only polite young people with excellent manners and language skills, you can forget it. Yes, there *are* some polite young people with great manners and language skills, but there's also a lot of bad language, sexual innuendo, and flaming going on. Nobody ever said it was a perfect world.

Apparently, a lot of parents let their children wander wherever they want online without any restrictions. Some children behave themselves and follow netiquette, others behave like spoiled brats. Sometimes you'll find the latter interrupting adult conversations among the communal chat areas with silly typing, scrolling, and other attention-getting acts. It can be a very frustrating experience for all.

If you stick around a kid's channel long enough, you'll see the typical scrambles for attention, pleas for instant messages, discussions about the day's events, and so on. Along with that is a lot of flaming, although in kid-terms flaming usually just involves insults. In the figure below, someone named FLIFFY M18 was getting yelled at for being in the wrong kids' channel. His ID, M18, signified he was a male, 18 years old. He's kindly asked to leave the channel, in a kid-like way.

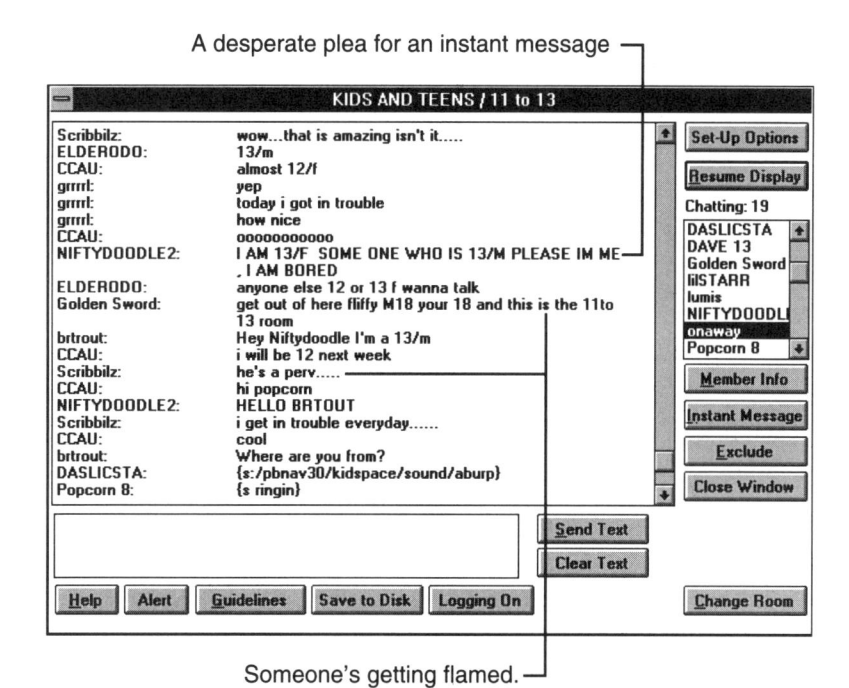

Another average day in PRODIGY's Kids and Teens area.

What Are the Teens Up To?

I was a little surprised about the content of subject matter discussed in the teen rooms. Some of it is pretty graphic. Perhaps this reflects today's society. A lot of the teen chat revolves around relationships and music. And when it comes to relationships online, things can get really mushy.

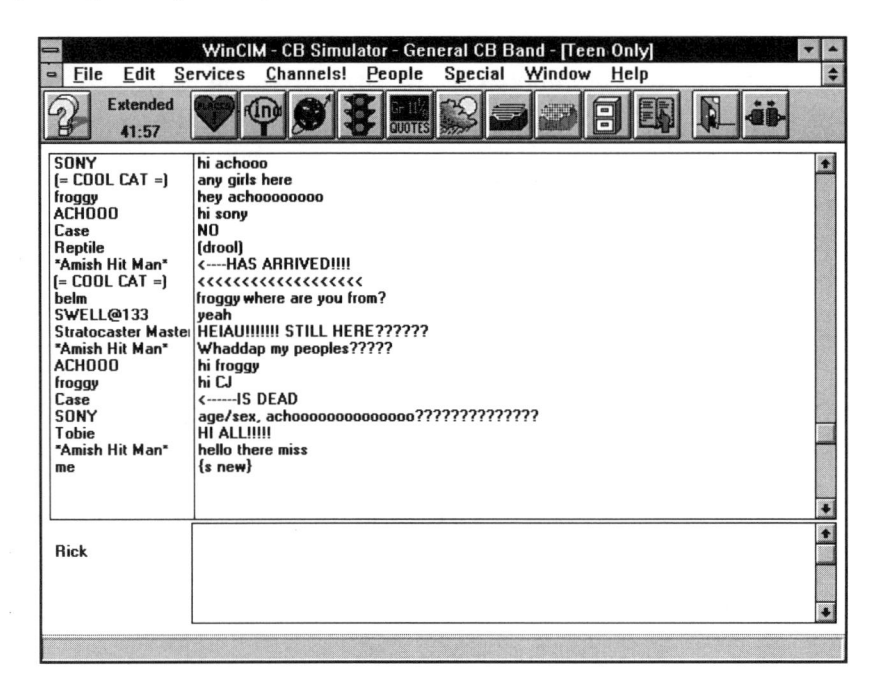

A conversation from CompuServe's teen room.

I'd have to say, out of all my online experimentation, my encounters in the teen chat channels during peak hours (after school) were the most bizarre. I couldn't believe some of the things they were talking about. And there was so much male posturing (like peacocks during a mating dance) going on. It's amazing how online anonymity makes many male users so brave in what they say. Sure, it was entertaining, but sometimes it was downright disgusting. There was also a lot of computer romance going on. I witnessed at least one online wedding (that's where two online chatterers pretend to get married) and a lot of online dating (some pretend to go steady).

Being the somewhat cynical person I am, I found myself doubting that many of the "teens" talking in the teen channels were actually teenagers. Something didn't quite seem right about some of the participants. I suspect that adults often sneak into the teen channels, trying on their youthful personas for fun or cheap thrills (or other, more

Chapter 14 ➤ *Chatting and Kids: Do They Go Together?*

licentious reasons). A phenomenal thing to witness, however, is when a crowd of teenagers expose an adult pretending to be a teen. Whew, do those flames fly! It's like watching the Frankenstein monster get tarred and feathered by a mob of angry torch-bearing villagers. I guess there is safety in numbers sometimes.

Safegard Your Kids

In the next few paragraphs, I'll tell you how to make online chat safe for your kids. It takes some effort, but it's well worth it in the long run.

Is Kid Chat Safe?

The reality is that a lot of parents aren't monitoring the chat channels their kids use, and have no idea what's going on. Another problem to contend with is the fact that some of the users logged onto kid channels may *not* necessarily be kids or teenagers themselves. (This is a drawback no matter what the focus of the channel, whether it's for adults or children.) Some users just pretend to be kids (hey—I had to for research!), and some have other motivations (read Chapter 16 where I warn you about online pedophiles).

What I'm trying to tell you is that online chat isn't always safe for kids. It really requires some adult supervision, guidelines, and assistance. Not all of the kid-chat is bad, but as a parent or concerned adult, you need to be aware of it and prepare your own children for what they'll encounter online. I certainly wouldn't let my kids online without supervision or guidelines intact, and I hope you wouldn't, either. The real world's dangerous enough—why let the electronic world become dangerous as well?

How to Make Your Kids Safe Online

You can do several things to help keep kids safe online. The first thing you can do is sit down with your kids and tell them what they can expect from the various online chat areas. Explain to them how real-time chat and messaging works. Set up some guidelines about how to use the chat feature of your service, including how to handle the offensive stuff, aggressive members, and other online elements. Warn them about getting personal with strangers. Make sure they understand they're not to give out any personal information, such as your home phone number or your account password. That goes for e-mail correspondence too.

Teach your kids all about online netiquette and what happens when it isn't followed. I've heard stories of accounts that were kicked off the service because children abused the chat feature, annoying other users and causing trouble. You as a parent need to learn about the service or BBS your kid is using.

Part 3 ➤ *What's Going On Out There?*

Also warn your kids to never, *ever* make arrangements to meet with someone they've met online unless you're involved with the meeting too. If you really want to keep your kids safe, participate in their online chat.

With many of the BBSs, commercial services, and Internet providers, you can set up controls that regulate who uses your account and what they are allowed to do with it. For example, America Online offers a Parental Control feature that lets you close off certain areas of online chat or all of it, and block off the instant message option. Be sure to check your own service for similar options.

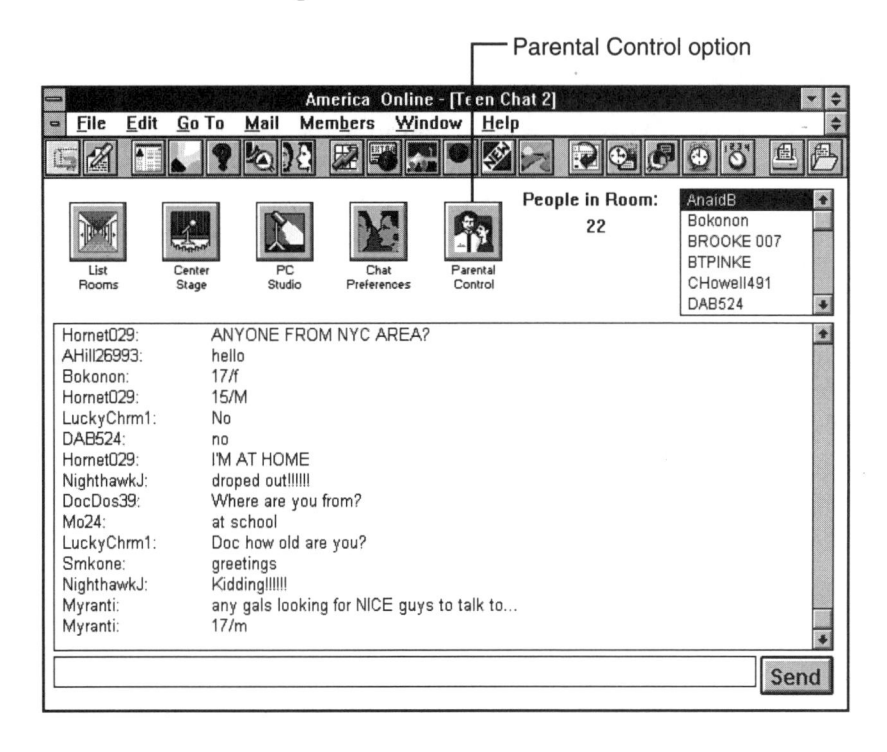

You can control which chat rooms your kids enter with AOL's Parental Control option.

It's a good idea to turn online time into a family activity, and to participate with your child as he or she chats on a service or BBS. It's also a good idea to keep your computer in a neutral area, like the family room. That way you can easily monitor their online activities, and keep control of the service.

172

Chapter 14 ➤ *Chatting and Kids: Do They Go Together?*

The Least You Need to Know

I hope I haven't scared you parents away from online chat. Remember, it's not all bad—you and your kids just need to be careful.

➤ Kids like chatting just as much as adults.

➤ The larger commercial services offer chat areas focused completely on kids and teens.

➤ To find out the age of the people you're chatting with, do an age/sex check.

➤ Some of the chatting that goes on in the kid channels isn't very pleasant. Be sure to set up guidelines for your own kids to follow.

➤ Teach your kids how to handle questionable subject matter and online harassment.

➤ Be sure to monitor your children's time online; use the parental control options available on the service you've subscribed to.

> **More info!**
> There's a brochure put out by the U.S. National Center for Missing & Exploited Children along with the Interactive Services Association that has some great guidelines for kids and cyberspace usage. You'll find this brochure on CompuServe: type **GO MISSING** and look for the **CHISAF.TXT** file.

Chapter 15

Chatting for Fun or Profit

In This Chapter

➤ The lowdown on newsgroups and boards

➤ Tips for advertising in cyberspace

➤ Find out where to network among professionals and peers

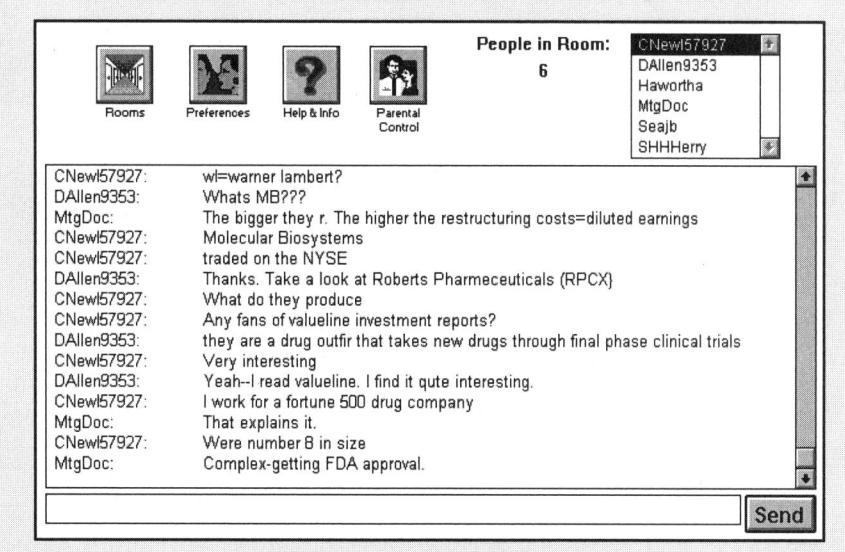

	People in Room:	
Rooms Preferences Help & Info Parental Control	6	CNewl57927 DAllen9353 Hawortha MtgDoc Seajb SHHHerry

CNewl57927:	wl=warner lambert?
DAllen9353:	Whats MB???
MtgDoc:	The bigger they r. The higher the restructuring costs=diluted earnings
CNewl57927:	Molecular Biosystems
CNewl57927:	traded on the NYSE
DAllen9353:	Thanks. Take a look at Roberts Pharmeceuticals (RPCX}
CNewl57927:	What do they produce
CNewl57927:	Any fans of valueline investment reports?
DAllen9353:	they are a drug outfir that takes new drugs through final phase clinical trials
CNewl57927:	Very interesting
DAllen9353:	Yeah--I read valueline. I find it qute interesting.
CNewl57927:	I work for a fortune 500 drug company
MtgDoc:	That explains it.
CNewl57927:	Were number 8 in size
MtgDoc:	Complex-getting FDA approval.

[Send]

Online chat doesn't have to be all fun and games, although most of us like it that way. There's plenty of online chat focused on serious discussions, business topics, and networking with your peers. In this chapter, I'll show you how to work the online ropes to conduct business, surveys, and serious learning.

Business on the Net and Beyond

The Internet was not invented for financial gain. It was originally intended for nonprofit communications. However, things have changed since the Internet's early days of "peace on earth and goodwill toward men." The same could also be said for BBSs and commercial services. These days, the Net is a booming business. When I say Net, I'm referring to all of cyberspace, including commercial services and BBSs, not just the big Internet network. Today, all these online areas are connected in one way or another.

Because of such vast connections and such a humongous audience of online users, lots of people are jumping online and wondering how to go about selling something or meeting other professionals. Before you jump anywhere, you need to find out what's acceptable and what's not when it comes to business practices, advertising, and communicating with your peers. Can you conduct business through chatting, or should you stick to a more static form of communication—the posted message? Good question. Keep reading.

Newsgroups and Boards

Let's start by examining the concept of newsgroups and boards. The Internet's message posting areas are called *newsgroups*. Newsgroups are discussion groups that meet via public messages to discuss everything from horticulture to auto mechanics. Basically, the Internet's newsgroups are the equivalent of CompuServe's forums, PRODIGY's bulletin boards, and AOL's message boards, or any of the boards found on BBSs. Regardless of the name, the purpose is still the same—newsgroups or boards focus on specific topics.

> **OOPS!** Check your spelling! Always proofread your message before posting. Spelling errors can make you look hurried, disorganized, and unprofessional.

Chapter 15 ➤ *Chatting for Fun or Profit*

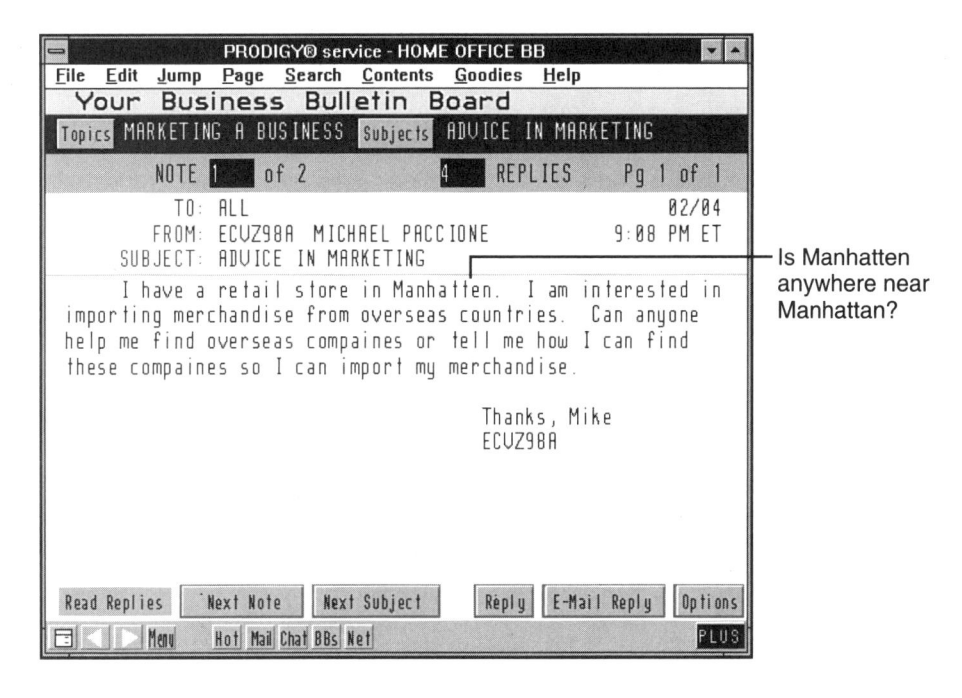

An example of a business bulletin board on PRODIGY. This figure shows a business-related message posted on the board.

(Callout: Is Manhatten anywhere near Manhattan?)

In each newsgroup or board are posted articles. These articles are notes left in the newsgroup or board to communicate with the other people who stop by and read them. Those notes can range from simple comments, to mind-numbing discussions, to out-and-out flaming. Each reader has an opportunity to respond to another's posted message or post a new message of his own.

Probably the best analogy to explain the concept of newsgroups and boards is the image of an electronic cork board. Somewhere in cyberspace, there's a room or hallway dedicated to a specific topic, such as scuba diving, for example. If you're interested in scuba diving, you can log on and find your way to the scuba-diving room or hall, then stand there and look at all the notes posted about the subject on the electronic cork board. If you come across a note you'd like to add to, or disagree with, you can type up your own comments and reply to the note. If you have something new to add to the scuba-diving cork board, you can type up your thoughts and tack them onto the board, too.

Not everybody's standing in front of the scuba-diving board at the same time. The note you're responding to, for example, may have been posted by someone yesterday, or just a few minutes before your arrival. Unlike real-time chat, boards and newsgroups don't require all the members to be logged on at the same time to communicate.

So, as you can see, newsgroups and boards are where ideas and information are exchanged. It's ongoing communication. Because it's so dynamic, it offers users a chance to meet new people and see new ideas. This is especially true when it comes to business. There's such a variety of topics scattered among the thousands and thousands of newsgroups and boards out there, it's a little mind-boggling to know where to start. Most BBSs and commercial services have access to the Internet's many newsgroups. You'll also find plenty of message-posting boards on the BBS or commercial service you're using.

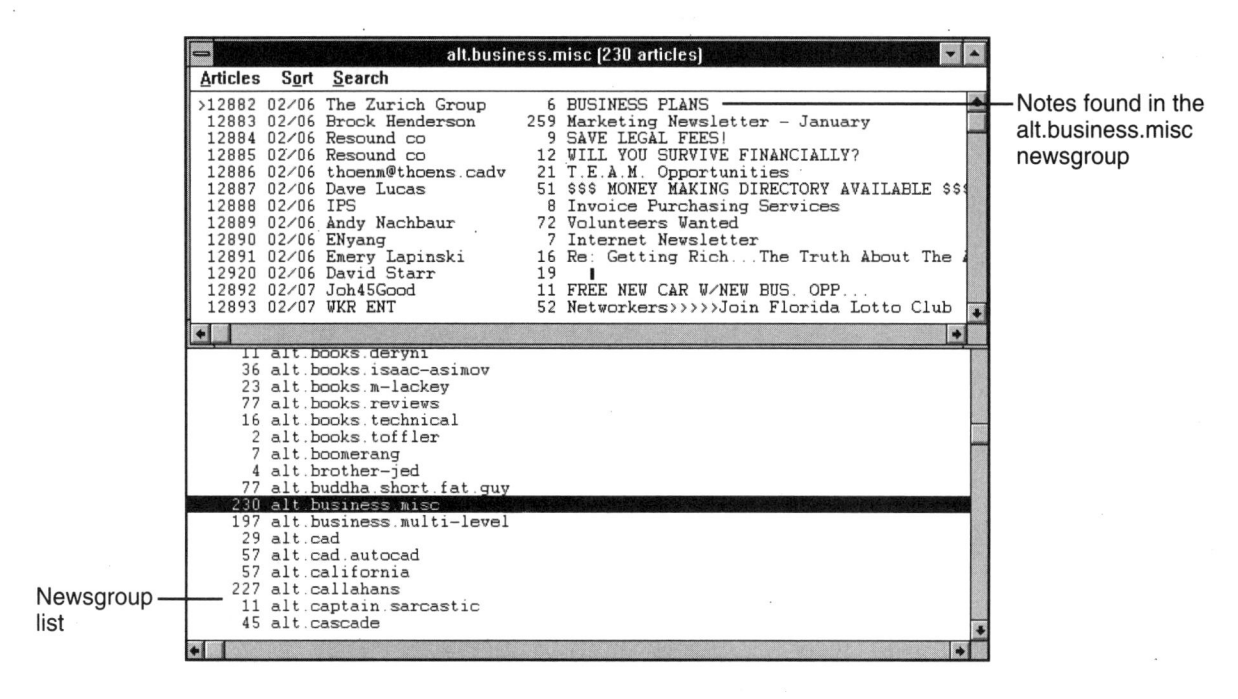

```
                alt.business.misc [230 articles]
 Articles  Sort  Search
>12882 02/06 The Zurich Group       6 BUSINESS PLANS
 12883 02/06 Brock Henderson      259 Marketing Newsletter - January
 12884 02/06 Resound co             9 SAVE LEGAL FEES!
 12885 02/06 Resound co            12 WILL YOU SURVIVE FINANCIALLY?
 12886 02/06 thoenm@thoens.cadv   21 T.E.A.M. Opportunities
 12887 02/06 Dave Lucas            51 $$$ MONEY MAKING DIRECTORY AVAILABLE $$$
 12888 02/06 IPS                    8 Invoice Purchasing Services
 12889 02/06 Andy Nachbaur         72 Volunteers Wanted
 12890 02/06 ENyang                 7 Internet Newsletter
 12891 02/06 Emery Lapinski        16 Re: Getting Rich...The Truth About The
 12920 02/06 David Starr           19
 12892 02/07 Joh45Good             11 FREE NEW CAR W/NEW BUS. OPP...
 12893 02/07 WKR ENT               52 Networkers>>>>>Join Florida Lotto Club

  11 alt.books.deryni
  36 alt.books.isaac-asimov
  23 alt.books.m-lackey
  77 alt.books.reviews
  16 alt.books.technical
   2 alt.books.toffler
   7 alt.boomerang
   4 alt.brother-jed
  77 alt.buddha.short.fat.guy
 230 alt.business.misc
 197 alt.business.multi-level
  29 alt.cad
  57 alt.cad.autocad
  57 alt.california
 227 alt.callahans
  11 alt.captain.sarcastic
  45 alt.cascade
```

— Notes found in the alt.business.misc newsgroup

Newsgroup list

Here's an example of an Internet newsgroup list.

Who Runs the Boards?

Good question. Who oversees these boards and newsgroups and keeps them organized? Usually, one or two people are responsible for the upkeep of a board. They make sure current notes are posted, and they handle the archiving of old notes. When necessary, they also censor the messages that get posted. (Watch your cybermanners!)

FAQs

Many of the newsgroups and boards you'll run across have a special area containing frequently asked questions, or *FAQs* for short. FAQs can give new users information about a particular board, how business is conducted, how the system works, policies, and more. Be sure to read any FAQs you come across before attempting to post a note of your own. Failure to read the FAQs can cause you serious trouble later.

What kind of trouble? Well, if you post a message asking a question already covered in the board's FAQs, you'll be royally flamed by all the other board users. This means plenty of nasty comments about your intelligence or even some negative e-mail. Play it cool—read the FAQs before diving into any newsgroup or board.

Advertising on the Net

The most common way to sell something on the Net is by posting advertisements. Just a warning: Advertising isn't always acceptable on every board you come across. In fact, the Internet service provider you signed up with may not even allow it (nor the BBS or commercial service, for that matter). Always make sure it's okay before trying it.

If you think you've found a board that represents the audience you want to sell something to, be sure to read the board's FAQs before attempting to post your advertisement. Read the other messages to see if anyone else is advertising and if the other users find this acceptable.

If it looks safe to post, then here are a few suggestions. Keep it simple and short. Cyberspace isn't exactly a visual medium, so the success of your message depends on your use of words. Don't post anything longer than one screen in length. Include a name or an Internet address (or other address) where readers can contact you for more information. Make sure you're not relying on hype and style to convey your message. Since you're dealing with words, content and quality are the keys to making it work online. Message boards are two-way streets. Anything you post can be responded to, either in a positive or negative manner.

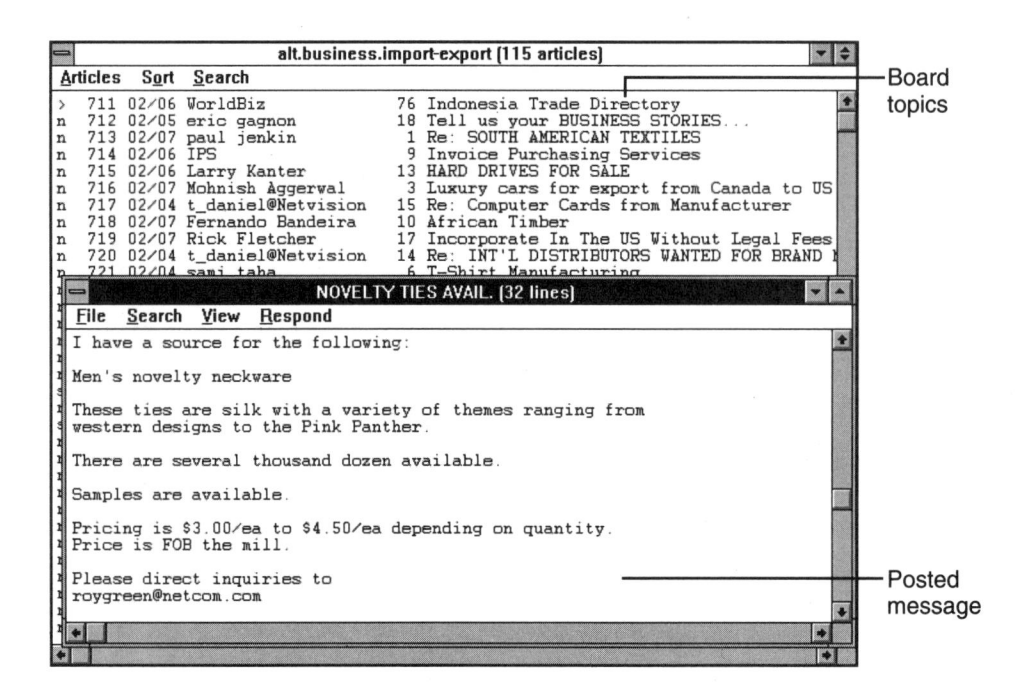

Here's an ad found on the alt.business.import-export newsgroup.

By far the best advice I can give you is to do your research. Scope out what's going on and how people are responding. Read the FAQs, the posted messages, and the replies. Study what other businesses are doing online. Start small, then aim higher later. Don't even think about plunging in and advertising your latest product or service *without* knowing what the netiquette is or who's in your newsgroup audience. If you're not too sure of what you're doing, then everybody's going to pick up on it. Be prepared to handle the response to your business endeavors. That includes the positive as well as the negative.

Never *ever* send mass postings to all the newsgroups or boards available (this is known as *spamming* in Internet lingo). You'll get in big trouble if you do. A husband and wife law firm, Canter and Siegel, tried spamming the Internet's newsgroups by advertising their legal services for obtaining green cards... for a price. Boy, was that a big mistake. For one thing, green cards are free. For another, they posted the advertisement everywhere— never once targeting the proper board that represented their audience. They also didn't respond very nicely to users who pointed out their misuse of the system. Thousands and thousands of angry users e-mailed them, thus forcing Canter and Siegel off the Net.

Let this be a lesson to you. Stick to the board that best represents your audience. If you can't find such a board (hard to imagine), then you can make your own board or newsgroup.

Can I E-Mail Everyone Instead?

Whoa! *Don't do that.* Nobody likes junk mail in real life, and they certainly don't like junk e-mail in cyberlife. You really need to know who you're e-mailing to; don't go about it blindly. It's okay to send advertising through e-mail, if the recipients are receptive to it. If they're not, you can really take some heat. E-mail's great for business correspondence and networking, but it's not always a good source for advertising.

Networking Among Newsgroups and Boards

If you're interested in networking with your peers, then boards and newsgroups will offer you a more formal medium. Depending on your area of expertise (or the area you *want* to be an expert in), you'll find plenty of peers to exchange thoughts with. Find your way to the newsgroup or board that you're interested in and start reading the messages posted there. That's how you begin networking on the Net.

It's up to you to find out who's who among the messages, but with time and energy, you can seek them out and begin your own correspondence, whether it's just in the form of posted messages or private e-mail. Relationship-building is a tough task, especially when you can't see or hear the person you're communicating with. On the other hand, online text really gives you an opportunity to express your intelligence and your writing (both admirable traits in the business world).

Survey Says

Online surveys are becoming quite common throughout the Internet. Basically, they're like the surveys you would find in magazines, trade journals, or at the mall. You simply fill out a questionnaire and your response is recorded electronically.

Surveys are becoming quite popular among the Internet's WWW pages. WWW, which stands for World Wide Web, is a special hypertext system for looking around on the Internet. With hypertext, certain key words are linked to open other pages or places on the Internet. The information is related, and can jump you around from topic to topic. For more information about WWW, pick up a copy of *The Complete Idiot's Guide to World Wide Web* by Peter Kent.

Online surveys are a good marketing tool for collecting data about a particular target group. Some companies even disguise their surveys as contests, or entry blanks. Travel and vacation companies are notorious for these kinds of gimmicks. I filled out a survey on CompuServe for a Florida agency in the hopes of winning a grand prize vacation. I got an actual phone call later that month wanting me to buy a vacation package, even though I hadn't won the prize. Those darn telemarketing people!

Job-Seeking Tips

Networking on the Net is also a good way to get your name out for potential jobs that arise among your peers or in your area of interest. There are specific areas on large BBSs, some commercial services, and the Internet's newsgroups where you can post your résumé. If you have trouble finding them, ask around.

Be careful about the amount of information displayed in an online résumé, and be discreet about where you post it. Always make sure you're in the right place. In the case of sending a résumé by e-mail, double-check to make sure you've got the correct address.

There are also specific areas where jobs openings are posted. If you're looking for a job, check these areas frequently. It also pays to ask your peers and ferret out information about upcoming openings.

Finding Business Chat on the Chat Lines

When you're ready to talk business, find your way to a live business-oriented conference. Some of the more business-related services, like CompuServe or Delphi, have such places to exchange business ideas and discussions.

For example, CompuServe's business forums are full of conference rooms for discussing business topics. Some of these chats are scheduled in advance by the operators in charge of the forums; others are impromptu when several people meet spontaneously. The scheduled conferences, however, are more heavily attended by members.

CompuServe's forums use conference rooms for live chat.

You can also do your professional networking through the Internet's many IRC channels. Granted, you have to pick and choose the one that's best for you, but you can meet many of your peers on IRC. It's a great way to exchange thoughts or tips, and get help with problems. Aren't friends wonderful? Especially the ones who are trusted experts in their fields.

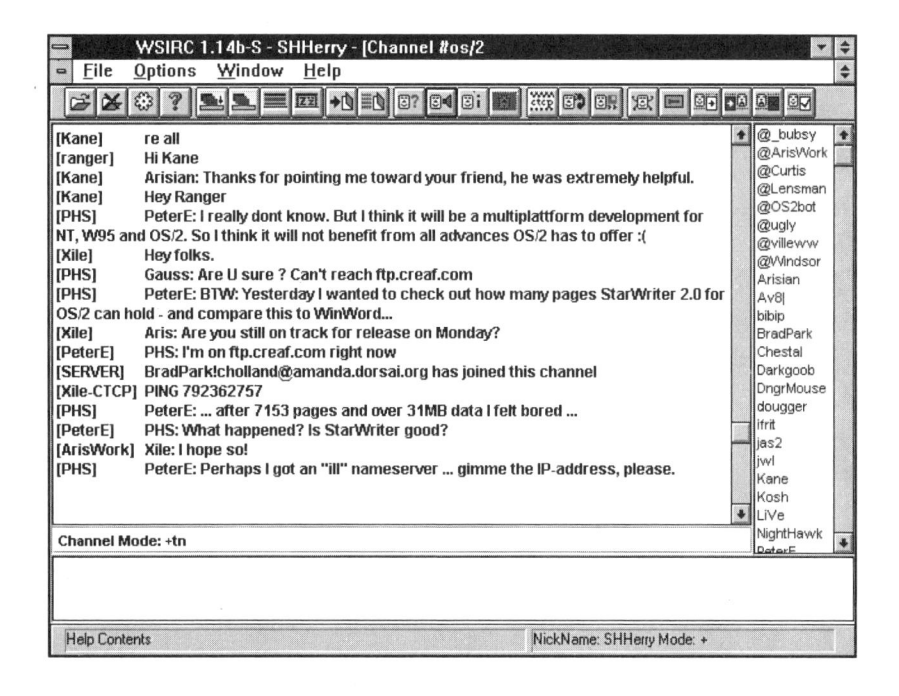

Business and technical chat on IRC's OS/2 channel.

Enroll in Online School

Many of the commercial services and BBSs offer educational sessions that teach about software and a variety of other topics. Some of the business-oriented services even offer career development classes and sessions focusing on entrepreneurial tips. For example, AOL has a learning and reference area and an interactive education center. Classes are taught by professional instructors. (Type the keyword **education** to locate AOL's classroom areas.)

Perhaps you haven't thought about using the online medium for education, but that's another development to keep your eye on. Many of the services are participating in online education. The ImagiNation Network, for example, has educational classes for children and adults. All you have to do is sign up and log on at the appropriate meeting time. Look for educational sessions on your favorite service or BBS. You never know what you could learn on your computer.

The Least You Need to Know

Chat and other online communications aren't all fun and games. You can conduct serious business in cyberspace, and sometimes it's even more efficient than in real life.

- ➤ Newsgroups and boards are used to post messages about specific topics.
- ➤ A board's FAQs are a collection of frequently asked questions. New users can read the FAQs to find out how to communicate on a board, the etiquette of message-posting, and any other rules to follow.
- ➤ Advertising on the Net works a little differently from the advertising you're accustomed to on TV, in newspapers, and in magazines. Net advertising is more direct, relying on the power of words, not images.
- ➤ You can connect to peers through message boards and online chat areas. You can even look for jobs online.
- ➤ Business chat is usually conducted in channels and forums that are apart from the regular chat areas. For example, CompuServe offers business chat in forum conference rooms.
- ➤ You can take a class online to learn about the latest software, or any other number of topics. Check your own BBS or commercial service for online educational opportunities.

Chapter 16

Online Dangers

In This Chapter

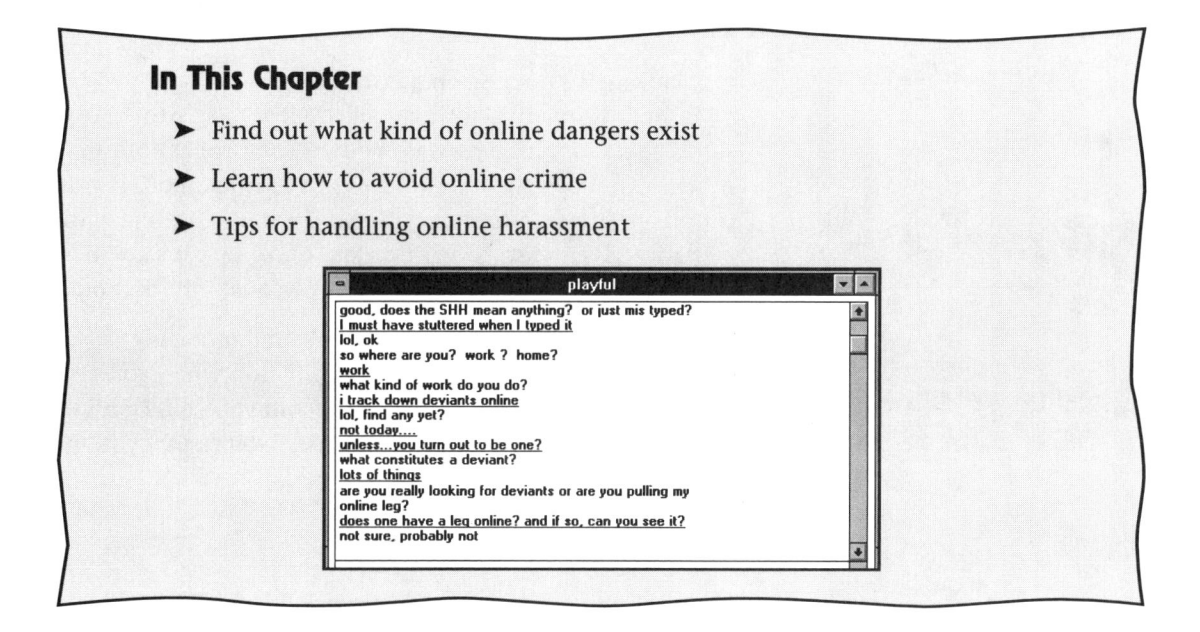

➤ Find out what kind of online dangers exist
➤ Learn how to avoid online crime
➤ Tips for handling online harassment

```
playful
good, does the SHH mean anything?  or just mis typed?
I must have stuttered when I typed it
lol, ok
so where are you?  work ?  home?
work
what kind of work do you do?
i track down deviants online
lol, find any yet?
not today....
unless...you turn out to be one?
what constitutes a deviant?
lots of things
are you really looking for deviants or are you pulling my
online leg?
does one have a leg online? and if so, can you see it?
not sure, probably not
```

Computer crimes. They're out there lurking in the most unsuspected places. Be careful, or you could be the next victim. The electronic community is susceptible to crime just like every other part of your life. Bummer, huh? Hundreds of online users fall victim to electronic scams and robberies each day. It can be scary, especially because you can't "see" it happen.

Those seemingly innocent masses you're conversing with in the online chat areas may not be so innocent after all. In this chapter, I'll tell you all about the online dangers that exist for users, plus ways you can make yourself and your computer safe.

It's a Jungle Out There

What kind of online crimes am I talking about? Theft is a major one. Online criminals are looking to steal your credit card numbers, telephone numbers, and even your account passwords. Why? Because they can then sell the info to someone else, or use your account when you're not and run up your bills. Scary? You bet, so you'd better be careful out there.

In the following paragraphs, I'll describe some things to watch out for, and ways you can protect yourself.

Guard Personal Information

One of the first rules of thumb is to never give out personal information with your modem or network connection. Granted, you may be using your modem to talk to your stockbroker or bank, but watch out. Some people pose as officials and legitimate businesses just to rip you off. If you ever have any doubts about the service you're dealing with electronically, get some verification. Make sure it's all on the up-and-up before divulging any personal information.

> **OOPS!** If you do need to give out some personal information, don't do it in a chatting area or in a services message-posting feature. Do it through e-mail. It's a little more private.

I'm not talking about your name and modem number—you have to give that information when you sign up with an online service. But guard yourself. Don't give out your credit card number unless you're sure you know who you're dealing with.

Keep Your Passwords Safe

A second rule of thumb is to never give out your password to anyone, especially to someone online. Online service employees and sysops (systems operators or administrators) would never ask you for your password, so don't fall for that. If someone keeps trying to obtain your password, note their user ID and report them to the service officials (sysop, service provider, whatever). It's a good idea to keep your password and any special user ID in a safe place in your home or office. It's also smart to change your password occasionally.

Watch Out for Free Offers

Don't fall for anyone offering you free things that would normally cost money. One popular online scam is an offer for free long distance calling. (Free long distance? Ha, ha, ha. We've seen enough long distance commercials to know it's never free.) There is no such thing, and it's probably someone using a stolen account number. Stay away from this scenario. The same goes for telling an online friend your personal telephone number. Make sure you know who your "friend" really is first.

> **Sysop:** Short for systems operator, someone who oversees a BBS or an online area. Sysops make sure everything is in order, especially uploaded files. They also monitor online activities and make sure everything is more or less civilized.

Don't Get Involved with Illegal Software Distribution

Also be careful about what software you upload or download with your modem. It's illegal to upload or download commercial software. It's a violation of copyright laws to do so. If it's *shareware*, *freeware*, or *public domain* (all three of which will say so), it's okay to upload or download those. Look for the words "shareware" or "Registration Fee" on the screen to tell you what type of software it is.

I'm not trying to frighten you, but copyright infringements are pretty serious. You can be prosecuted if you're caught doing illegal things with commercial software programs. I just read a story about a BBS operator who's being held responsible for illegal software files available from his BBS. The guy's going to court and possibly to jail.

> **Commercial Software:** A program that you purchase through a store or catalog that usually comes on disks that you use to install the program onto your computer. Commercial software includes programs such as Microsoft Word, Lotus 1-2-3, or Aldus PageMaker.

> **Thanks for Sharing**
>
> You'll run across the terms *shareware* and *freeware* quite often while exploring online. You can test shareware programs before you buy. You can download one onto your computer, try it out, and if you decide you want to use it, pay a registration fee to the person who wrote the program. Freeware programs are those you can download and use for free. You can't sell them to others because of their copyrights. There are many great shareware and freeware products out there, so dig around. Be careful, though. Always check for viruses before installing the programs onto your computer.

Get Virus Protection

You'll also want to use a virus-protection program anytime you download files onto your computer. A *virus* is a program designed to wreak havoc on unsuspecting computers. It vandalizes your system and can cause a lot of damage. A virus can destroy your system files, reformat your hard disk, erase data files, and more. A virus-protection program will help prevent viruses from invading your system.

More Heinous Dangers

Who knows what evil lurks in the hearts of men? (Well, *besides* the Shadow, that is.) Online scams and thievery aren't the only criminal activities to watch out for online. As in the real world, there are seriously disturbed people online, ranging from psychos to deviants. Perhaps you've heard stories or watched television news reports of innocent online users being stalked electronically? It's creepy, but it's true.

I don't know how many stories I've run across in the past year about pedophiles who are caught trolling the online areas for young children and carrying it through to real-life meetings with the children. Typically, the pedophile slowly begins courting children through online chat or message-posting areas (bulletin boards), striking up friendships. More often than not, the adult poses as a child to establish these friendships. Over time, the friendships become more intimate, and the pedophile eventually attempts to meet with the child in person.

Thankfully, there are online police out there looking for such individuals. But as an online user, you need to be aware of what's happening—and if you have children, take steps to protect them. The information superhighway has its share of pornography, even child pornography. Even though fewer than 5% of the Internet's bulletin boards specialize in X-rated stuff, they're still easy to find, even for children.

Hackers are another type of criminal altogether. Unlike the mentally disturbed deviants, hackers are simply technological wizards walking on the bad side of the cybertracks. Hackers are people who specialize in breaking into other computer systems, whether to explore, trespass, wreak havoc, or steal. (Those who do so strictly for criminal gains are called *crackers*—criminal hackers.)

Most hackers do it for the thrill, but there are plenty who make money stealing corporate secrets, breaking codes, and plundering computer systems (ranging from banks to telephone companies). Believe it or not, there are professional cybercrooks roaming the information highway's roads looking for all kinds of ill-gotten financial gains. Those gains can involve innocent citizens like you.

> **Virus:** Yes, computers can catch diseases too. A virus is a program designed to vandalize other computers. A virus usually gets to your computer via a floppy disk or a file copied from another computer with a modem. Once on your system, a virus can do a lot of damage. To avoid a virus, use a virus-protection program to watch out for these deadly infections.

Strangely enough, though, these hackers are pointing out areas of weaknesses in our computer networks, as well as sloppy administration. We should be aware that all is not safe on the vast Internet, and we should never take any of it for granted.

Handling Online Harassment

For those times when you meet up with online bad guys who deliberately and frequently harass you, there are some actions that you can take. The first thing to try (though it's usually futile if you're dealing with a disturbed person) is to tell the person that you don't appreciate their behavior, and if it doesn't stop, you're going to report them. Remember, a lot of online services have specific buttons or commands for turning off private message-sending features or unwanted e-mail.

If the person continues to bother you after such a warning, it's time to check your online service or sysop for steps to follow. You may even have to file a report. If someone harasses you repeatedly, definitely report the person (and his/her ID) to the online service administrators. Those in charge of the service can kick harassers off the system and revoke their accounts.

The PRODIGY service has a special button on the chat window for summoning an online authority. It's important to report harassment and violations right away so the online representative can come to the chat area on-the-double and witness what's going on. Other services encourage users to record the conversation using a log mode to document the violation.

Part 3 ➤ *What's Going On Out There?*

The Least You Need to Know

I hope you've learned a few things to keep yourself safe online. Here's a summary of what to do and not do:

➤ Never give out personal information, like addresses or phone numbers, to people you chat with. You never know who it is you're dealing with.

➤ Never give out your password.

➤ Don't fall victim to online scams like free long distance calling.

➤ Don't stay involved with a BBS you suspect of letting users download commercial software.

➤ Be sure to use a virus-protection program on files you download from cyberspace.

➤ If someone's harassing you online, contact a service representative or a sysop for help.

Chapter 17

Online Troubleshooting

In This Chapter

➤ What to do when your screen gets stuck

➤ What to do when you're kicked off the network

➤ A handy table of online troubles and their solutions

➤ Tips for finding online help

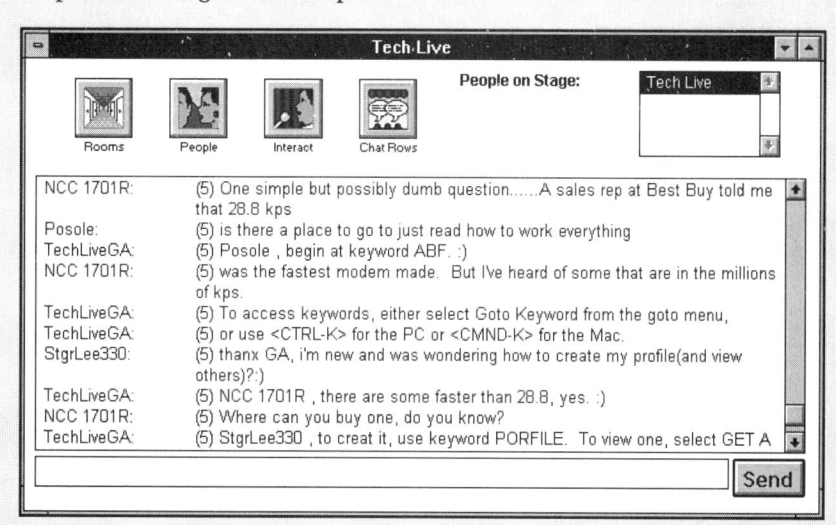

Tech·Live

People on Stage: Tech Live

Rooms   People   Interact   Chat Rows

NCC 1701R:	(5) One simple but possibly dumb question......A sales rep at Best Buy told me that 28.8 kps
Posole:	(5) is there a place to go to just read how to work everything
TechLiveGA:	(5) Posole , begin at keyword ABF. :)
NCC 1701R:	(5) was the fastest modem made. But I've heard of some that are in the millions of kps.
TechLiveGA:	(5) To access keywords, either select Goto Keyword from the goto menu,
TechLiveGA:	(5) or use <CTRL-K> for the PC or <CMND-K> for the Mac.
StgrLee330:	(5) thanx GA, i'm new and was wondering how to create my profile(and view others)?:)
TechLiveGA:	(5) NCC 1701R , there are some faster than 28.8, yes. :)
NCC 1701R:	(5) Where can you buy one, do you know?
TechLiveGA:	(5) StgrLee330 , to creat it, use keyword PORFILE. To view one, select GET A

[Send]

Part 3 ➤ *What's Going On Out There?*

Any time you start dealing with computers, you're going to experience technical difficulties... eventually. This is doubly true when you increase the number of computers you're dealing with. When it comes to the online world, you not only have to worry about your own computer functioning properly, but you also have to wonder about the computers or network servers you're contacting. This includes the computers at your Internet service provider, the computers at the big commercial online services, and the computer in the basement of your favorite BBS operator.

In this chapter, I'll show you how to handle online turmoil when it comes to technical difficulties.

Hey—Something's Wrong!

You're in the middle of a brilliant online discussion on the politics of international scientific research when your screen suddenly freezes. *What do you do?* You've just navigated your way into your favorite chat channel where all your online friends are waiting for you, and there's an ominous click on your modem line. *What do you do?* You haven't been online in over a week and you're suffering from withdrawal symptoms. You instruct your computer to call up your favorite BBS, but your modem doesn't even blink. *What do you do*, what *do* you *do*? (Ever see that movie *Speed* with Keanu Reeves? I was just wondering.)

It's times like these when computers can be a real pain in the [*insert your own word of choice here*]. Because there's such a variety of hardware and software that people use—and a variety of online connections—there's usually a variety of technical troubles you can suffer from. Sometimes your problems are common, and there are common solutions for them. Other times, your problems will be unique to your situation. Is this what your auto mechanic tells you when you take your car in to be fixed?

Well, when it comes to computer technology, it's a lot like car engines. Depending on how you "drive" your computer, who manufactured your computer, its make and model, and what kind of "gas" you've been using, your troubles could mean a lot of different things. I'm going to address some common problems you'll encounter online (and off)—and how you can handle them.

My Screen's Stuck

Has this ever happened to you? You're in the middle of something on the computer and suddenly your screen freezes? No, I'm not talking about a sudden drop in temperature, I'm talking about a loss of mouse movement or the ability to select items on-screen. (This happens to me while I'm using software programs.) Basically, all action comes to a standstill, like a stalled vehicle.

Unfortunately, when this happens you aren't left with many options to pursue—except to restart your vehicle. Try pressing your **Esc** key to see if that clears anything. If not, you'll probably need to exit the program or disconnect from the service. How are you supposed to do that when everything on-screen is jammed? Try your keyboard. If it's operable, you can use shortcut keys to open menus and select the **Exit** command. On many Windows programs, for example, you can hold down the **Alt** key and press **F** to open the **File** menu, and then press **X** to exit the program.

If that doesn't work and your PC is running DOS, you'll have to follow emergency evacuation procedures. Walk, do not run, to the keyboard and press the old **Ctrl+Alt+Del** keys (simultaneously) to reboot your computer—or turn your computer off and on.

If your modem does not disconnect from the service you were calling, you can also shut off the modem to hang up the call. Be warned, however, that this method of disconnecting does not always tell the computer you were in touch with that you've hung up. This means that your connect-time meter is still running until the service computer figures out that you've disappeared from the line. If possible, always try to follow the proper logoff steps to disconnect from the service you're calling.

I Just Got Thrown Off!

What's the deal? There you were, innocently minding your own online business when suddenly a message pops up on your screen telling you you've been kicked off the system. What's this all about? Don't panic. When this happens, it's the host computer that's having a problem.

There's not much you can do when you've been thrown off the host computer; just get back up in that saddle and ride again. Simply contact the service or network and log on again. If they're having technical difficulties, you may not be able to log on right away, but try anyway.

I've been thrown off AOL's computers several times in the past six months. This may have something to do with the ongoing changes they are making to their system. Don't get mad at them—it's just a fact of computer life. Some systems do automatic maintenance late at night, so if that's when you're calling, you could easily get dumped.

Another reason you may have been thrown off is that you've gone over your time limit. Some BBSs only allow you to call for a certain amount of time. Once you go over your limit, you're kicked off. Also, if you haven't made any recent selections on-screen (perhaps you've fallen asleep at the keyboard), the host computer might think you've abandoned ship and automatically hang up. Or you might also get kicked off if someone else in your home picks up the phone while your modem is using the line.

> **Someone Logged Me Off!**
>
> Did you notice that menu selections were suddenly happening and you didn't select them yourself? Did it look like a ghost was using your computer? The system's sysop can log you off automatically this way. Why would they do such a thing? They can dump people who violate the rules at any time, so you'd better behave yourself.

Speed Needs

If you're connecting to the online world through a modem, you really need to be aware of the different modem speeds you can use. For example, did you know that you *can't* call up some commercial services if your modem's speed is 14.4 kilobits per second? As modem technology has blossomed, they've come out with faster and faster modems. But just because you bought a super-fast modem doesn't mean the places you call will be able to communicate at that speed. Another bummer, huh?

Most likely they'll increase their speed parameters and such eventually, but it just takes awhile to catch up to the technological developments. For example, today you can get a pretty good deal on a 28.8 modem (28,800 bits per second), but you won't find many services that can talk back to you at that speed. Your modem will have to slow down to the speed of the service you're calling.

Speaking of speeds, you ought to know that some services charge you more for using higher-speed modems than they do for slower modems. Be sure to check out the service or provider for details about pricing the usage of various modem speeds.

> **What's the Deal with Modem Speed?**
>
> Modem speed is based on how many bits of data can be sent through the phone line per second. This measurement is called *bits per second*, or *bps*. The more bits a modem can send, the faster its speed. Today's modems transmit anywhere from 9600 to 28,800 bps and higher. Ideally, the faster your modem, the quicker you can exchange data with the computer that you connect to. Speed really starts to pay off when you're downloading files from the host computer onto your computer. If you have a fast modem, the transfer goes quickly, and you don't spend as much time or money tying up the phone line.

Something's Wrong with My Phone Line

Continuing with modem problems, here's another one for you. If your modem is sharing a telephone line with your regular phone, you'll run into some difficulties if you have a call-waiting feature on your phone. You need to disable call-waiting by setting up a special code.

When you set up your *phone list* (the list of online services, BBSs, service providers, or friend's modems that your software dials automatically for you) on your communications software, precede each number with ***70**. (If you don't have Touch-Tone service, precede each number with **1170**.) This code will disable the call-waiting feature while your modem is in use.

Other Problems

Some of the other problems you may encounter when using your modem to go online are various differences in your communications settings. If you're using a commercial service like AOL or PRODIGY, the installed service-specific software makes sure that your computer and their computer can talk to each other. But if you're using your own communications software program to call up a local BBS, *you'll* have to worry about the details instead.

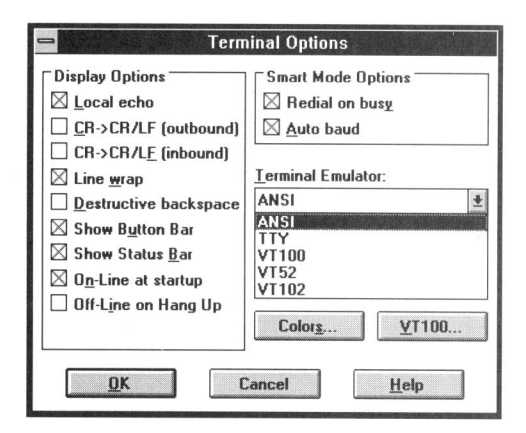

You may have to make adjustments to your software settings, such as echo and terminal emulation, to improve your connection.

Chapter 7 explained a little about BBS connections. The parameters, such as Echo and Duplex, or settings such as Terminal mode (also called *terminal emulation*), are important options that have to be fiddled with in order to get a good connection. If you're experiencing difficulties when calling up other computers, you'll need to adjust the settings on your own modem and communications software. Be sure to consult your manual for tips, and don't hesitate to contact the software or hardware manufacturer's technical support line for additional assistance. The people who run the technical support lines are trained to know how to help you with your computer problem.

Since you never know what kind of problems you're going to run into, how about if I make a list that you can check when the occasion arises? (Am I thoughtful, or what?)

My modem's lights don't come on (external).

Make sure it's plugged in and turned on. Double-check your cables and see if they're plugged in too. Also check your power outlet to see whether it's working properly. If the modem lights never come on, it's time to return your modem. I hope you kept the sales receipt.

The screen says "Device not present" or "CTS signal not detected."

Is your modem turned on? If so, your cable could be bad, or your software doesn't know which COM port the cable's plugged into. Double-check these things.

Nothing happens after my modem dials.

Is your phone cord plugged in? If nothing happens after your modem dials, then you've probably got a phone line problem. Make the necessary checks (plug in a regular phone to see if it works) before summoning the phone company.

My modem won't call at its fastest speed.

Sounds like your software isn't set at its fastest speed. Check your dialing directory and set a higher speed.

When I connect to a BBS, I get gobbledygook on my screen.

Check your communications parameters. 8-N-1 is most common, unless you're dialing up CompuServe (without CIS). Also, try calling back at a slower modem speed.

I see strange characters instead of the BBS menu when I call.

Switch your terminal emulation mode. Try **ANSI**.

Chapter 17 ➤ *Online Troubleshooting*

My online text is missing letters.

Turn on the **RTS/CTS** hardware-handshaking setting (9600 modem) or turn on your **Xon/Xoff** software flow-control setting (2400 or slower modem).

I'm seeing two of everything I type.

Change your **Duplex** setting to **full** or your **Echo** setting to **off**.

I can't see anything I'm typing.

Switch your **Duplex** setting to **half** or your **Echo** setting to **on**.

How to Holler for Help

If you run into online trouble, and your screen isn't frozen, you can always look for a live online person to talk to for help. Where do you look? Most of the commercial services and BBSs have special Help menus or areas where you can go for assistance. If you're using an Internet service provider, they may also offer you a Help menu or live assistance.

Let me give you an example of an excellent help service. AOL's Member Services area features something called Tech Support Live. It's a special chat lobby that you can enter to ask a technical question when you haven't been able to find the answer amid all the files and message boards.

AOL's Member Services feature a variety of ways you can seek help, including a live support lobby and phone support.

Part 3 ➤ *What's Going On Out There?*

AOL's special tech support channel is set up like an auditorium. Depending on what row you "sit" in, you can ask different kinds of questions. The rows are staffed by technical support people who stand by waiting for your questions. This is, by far, the most sophisticated and user-friendly online help I've seen yet. There's something rather comforting about knowing that there's a live person you can talk to about your technical problem.

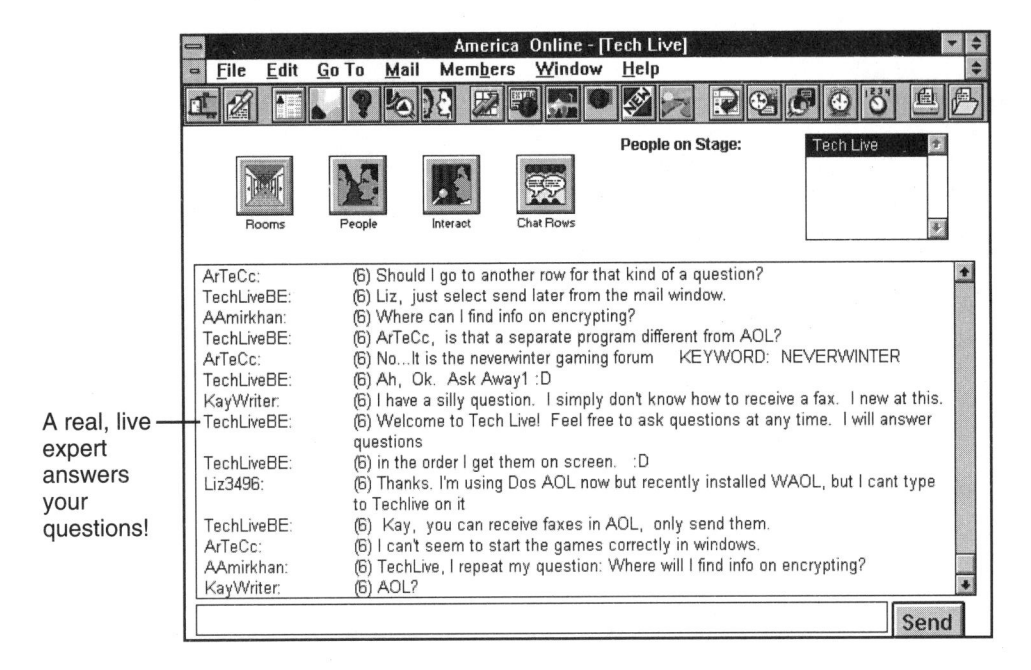

A real, live expert answers your questions!

At any given moment, dozens of people are in the Tech Live lobby asking questions about problems with AOL, their modems, their computers, and more.

AOL's Tech Live lobby is open during normal business hours and some evenings. It's truly a life-saver when you're having trouble.

The other commercial services and BBSs have support areas also, but they work a little differently. Most involve message posting to a sysop or administrator. You enter the help area, post your problem in the form of a message and wait. A day later, they answer your message.

Chapter 17 ➤ *Online Troubleshooting*

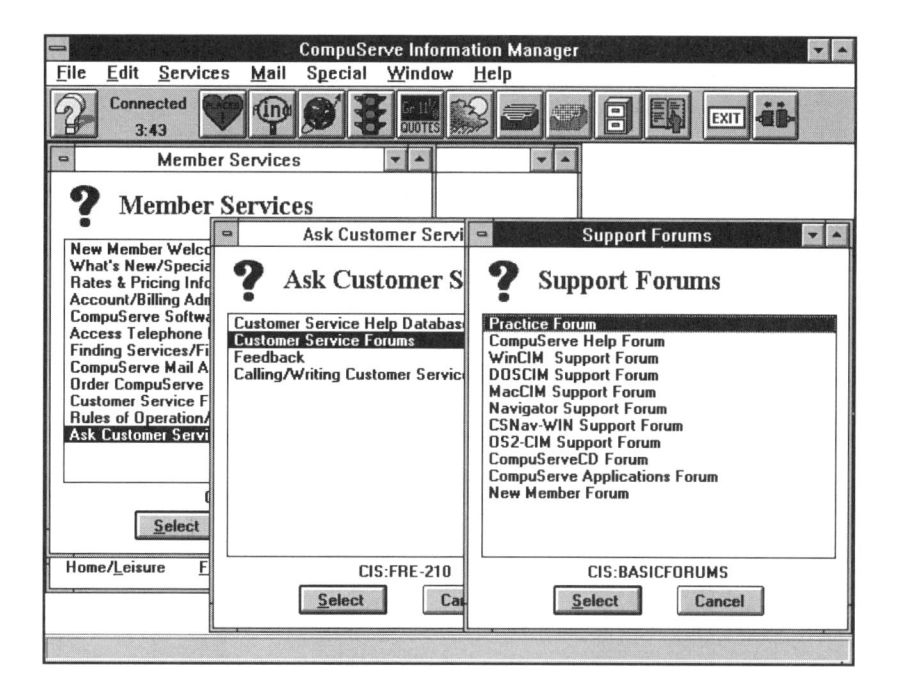

CompuServe's support forums let you post your problems as notes.

Make sure you know where your service's tech support area is. It may be listed under a different name, such as *member support*, *member services*, *customer services*, or simply as a *help* selection. You can also turn to other live users for advice and input when the going gets tough. There are quite a few IRC channels where people hang out to discuss problems with operating systems, hardware, software, and games.

The Least You Need to Know

Feel a little better knowing what steps you can take when things go wrong? Be sure to consult your manual for additional help.

➤ When your screen freezes, try pressing the **Esc** key. If that doesn't work, you'll have to reboot your system.

➤ If you've been thrown off the system, it may not have been your fault. Log back on and try again.

➤ Your modem's speed and communications parameters play an important part in your online success. Make sure you know how to change your settings and when to do so.

➤ If your modem connection is sharing a line with your regular phone, you'll need to watch out for call-waiting and for other family members who pick up the receiver.

➤ Don't be afraid to contact online help sources for assistance. Most BBSs, online services, and Internet service providers can offer you some help when you're in trouble.

Part 4
Confessions of an Online Junkie

Once you get involved in online chat, chances are pretty high you'll become addicted. Why? Because, it's fun, it's exciting, and it's all happening through the miracle that is your computer! Besides, if you don't go online and chat, you'll miss out on everything. Anyway, in this final portion of the book, I'll give you advice for getting the most out of your own online chat sessions. You'll find out who's first in the big commercial service race, and all the best chat channels to hang out on. I'll also give you some money-saving tips and lists to help make your online ride a smooth one. Hopefully, this will help you avoid costly therapy for your own chat addiction down the road (it will happen, I know it will).

Chapter 18

How to Become an Online Addict

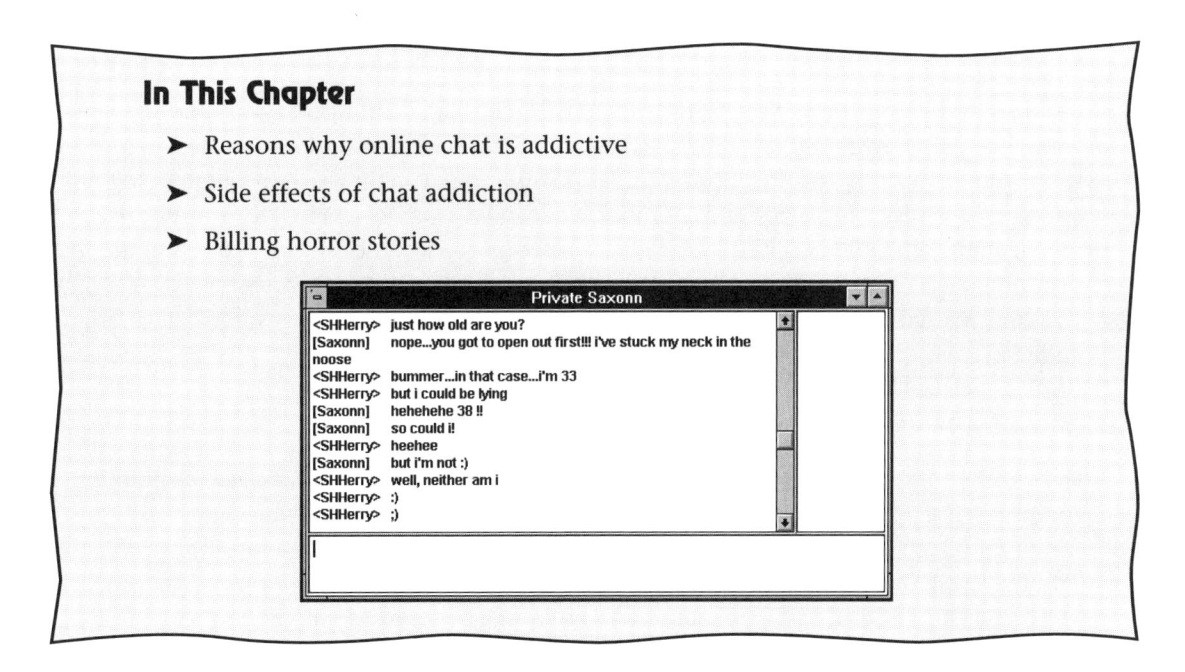

Jimmy, you've got a monkey on your back.

Very funny.

In This Chapter

➤ Reasons why online chat is addictive

➤ Side effects of chat addiction

➤ Billing horror stories

```
                         Private Saxonn
<SHHerry>  just how old are you?
[Saxonn]   nope...you got to open out first!!! i've stuck my neck in the
noose
<SHHerry>  bummer...in that case...i'm 33
<SHHerry>  but i could be lying
[Saxonn]   hehehehe 38 !!
[Saxonn]   so could i!
<SHHerry>  heehee
[Saxonn]   but i'm not :)
<SHHerry>  well, neither am i
<SHHerry>  :)
<SHHerry>  ;)
```

If you've made it to this chapter, you've survived the first three sections of this book. Either that, or you're cheating and reading ahead. In any case, you're here. In this chapter, I'm going to tell you about the addictive side of online chat. Yes, it's hard to believe, but online chat is not always a bed of roses. It can be addictive, expensive, and you could end up in therapy.

Confessions of an Online Addict

It happened slowly. I didn't just wake up one day and decide to become a cyberchat junkie. It took awhile. I would log on once or twice a week, check my e-mail, download some files. But it was never anything serious. Then I started exploring, playing the online games, joining forums and message boards. It wasn't long before I had my first craving to actually meet other people online. One day, I tried the chat channels. It was scary, but fun. I lurked in the background, running away if anyone attempted to talk to me. I wanted to make sure I understood how this worked before committing myself to an actual conversation. Once I felt comfortable, I started adding my own thoughts to the scrolling dialogue, humbly typing in comments here and there, then engaging in longer discussions.

At first, I thought this online chat stuff was a silly thing to do, a mindless activity for killing time. I just couldn't imagine logging on solely for the purpose of talking to people in cyberspace. Unlike some people who are introduced to chat by their friends, I found my own way into this fascinating online world. I got braver and braver in my conversations, jumping in here and there, trying to monopolize the dialogue. Then I started flirting and flaming with the rest of them. It was then that I knew—I was hooked.

When I wasn't logged on, I always had this nagging feeling that I was missing something, that everyone was talking without me. I'd be in the middle of drawing up sales figures on my spreadsheet program, and would be overcome with an urge to log on and see who was in my favorite AOL room. I began writing down PRODIGY announcements about scheduled celebrity chat guests. I set up regular meetings with online friends on CompuServe. I asked for a subscription to *Boardwatch Magazine* for my birthday. I secretly started keeping a list of my favorite Internet newsgroups. I was hopelessly addicted.

I'm Exaggerating... Sort Of

Okay, okay, maybe I don't *really* have a subscription to *Boardwatch Magazine* (although that would be a good gift idea), but I do need to warn you—online chat *is* addictive. In fact, a lot of users say so. Why's it so addictive? Like any new phenomenon, it attracts a lot of interest, but because of its dynamic interaction between users, it appeals mainly to our social side. With live chat or static chat (message boards and e-mail), you can get the attention you crave, share thoughts and quips, or simply meet people who are trying to make heads or tails out of this ever-changing technology—just like you.

Chapter 18 ➤ *How to Become an Online Addict*

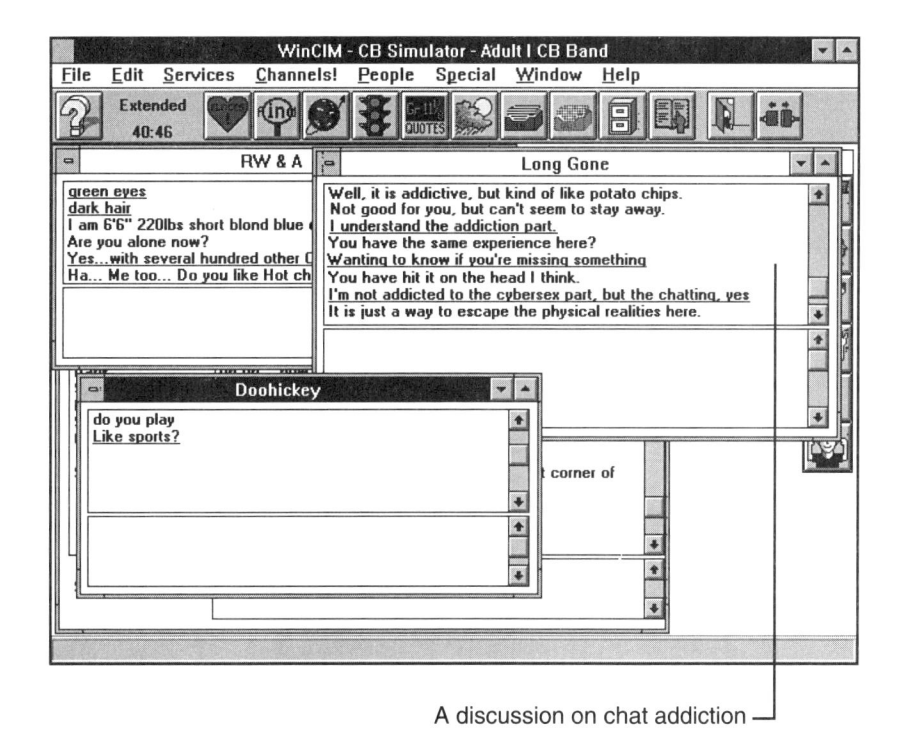

A discussion on chat addiction

Lots of people talk about the addictive side of online chat.

Some people compare online addiction to the pull that electronic games have, like computer games, Nintendo, and such. There's always something new you can get out of the experience. No, it's not like you can chat your way to a new level and beat the bad guys or anything. But, each time you log on to try live chat, something new can happen, whether it's meeting new people, trading new lines, or new insults. Live chat really is unpredictable. (I've said that a hundred times already, haven't I?)

Live chat is also very challenging at times. Long-time users admit that online chat has really forced them to improve their typing skills. There's nothing more exhilarating than being able to respond to a question or comment with lightning speed to beat the other conversants to the punch. Typing is the key to your online communication. That's not to say slow typists aren't going to enjoy themselves—as long as you've got a keyboard, you can talk with everyone else.

Just How Addictive Is It?

It's pretty powerful. The vast majority of users log on after they get home from work; some can't even wait till after dinner. Some chat for hours on end, others just for small increments of time. People who are hooked up to a service through their work computer often conduct online chat when they need a break from the pressures of the day. (This can be a little dangerous though, you slacker, you. Don't get caught by the boss.)

Newbies will find that live chat is most addictive during the honeymoon phase. That is to say, the newness of the technology has greater appeal when you're first trying it out. It's the same thing you run into with anything new. For example, computer games are most addictive when they're new and unexplored. After the newness wears off, the usage goes down. Remember the first time you played a video game or a pinball machine? Once is never enough, you've got to try it again and again until you've mastered it. Live chat has a similar appeal.

I found that after I went through the honeymoon phase, I would only chat periodically, maybe several times a month. But when I was really bored and there was absolutely nothing on TV, live chat filled that entertainment void. I'm not saying I have to be constantly entertained, but the reality is, that's what our culture has been conditioned to. Unlike passive entertainment, however, live chat is engaging, fresh, and full of surprises. It takes more mental effort than sitting in front of the television. You have to think, type, ask, and answer.

Seek Treatment

Some people do go overboard with live chat. During the online research I conducted in the writing of this book, I ran across quite a few individuals who frequented the online chat areas on a daily basis. I began to notice that some people seemed to "live" on the channels, never leaving, not even to go Net-surfing or channel-surfing. They just stayed on the same channel for hours on end. Among the various big commercial services, I ran across at least five users who were online on the same channel for most of the day or evening. No matter what time of day I logged on, they were there.

Is that too much? Were they obsessed? Possibly. Perhaps that's all they had to look forward to each day; maybe it was their only contact with the outside world. Or perhaps they have unlimited bank accounts and can afford all those hours of service. Who knows? My only advice, unless you have very deep financial pockets, is not to let online chat rule your life. Sure it's addictive and fun, but don't ever lose sight of the fact that there's more to life than the box of electronic components that is your computer. You won't find everything under the sun inside your computer, no matter how far across cyberspace you can reach with it. For crying out loud, try to get away from your monitor screen occasionally; take a walk, listen to the birds sing... do something! (You can always log back on later.)

What to Do When They Close Your Account

Online chat doesn't come without a price tag. That's important to remember, especially when you find yourself suffering from online addiction. I explained the various billing scenarios you'll encounter back in Part 1 of this book. Unless you've got some kind of free hookup (such as a free Internet connection), you have to shell out some bucks to keep yourself online.

Those guys running the various services are pretty smart cookies. Most of them have placed live chat under the umbrella of online "extras," which means that chat costs above and beyond your basic services. For example, to engage in live chat on CompuServe, you have to pay an additional usage charge every time you go into CB Simulator. Sneaky? You bet, but it's all part of the savage laws of capitalism.

What I'm trying to tell you is that you need to be careful of how much time you spend chatting. It adds up fast. Granted, it still beats the cost of a long-distance phone call, but there's still a bill to be paid. If you've become a real online junkie, you may be juggling some startling credit card bills.

Online Billing Horror Stories

I can't count how many times I've heard users talk about receiving their first online bill and practically fainting because of its staggering cost. Most people don't realize how much time they spend online, especially in the chat areas. It's quite common to run across people online who have spent $200–$600 dollars a month. That's a lot of chatting, if you ask me.

How many hours of chat does it take to create such a bill? It takes a lot of hours. One guy told me he logged 60 hours on one online service to the tune of $200.00. That doesn't seem too surprising for someone who's online for three hours a day, five days a week. Can you imagine how much those users who are logged on *eight* hours a day are spending?

Yes, chatting is tons of fun, but don't get carried away with it—or it will carry you away financially! I also heard stories about people who overdid it on the chat feature and their spouses disconnected the service, or about teens who charged up enormous bills before their parents closed the account. How do these large bills happen? Easy—time just slips away from you when you're chatting on the computer—it's easy to forget that it rings up charges just like a long distance call. I advise you to keep a clock nearby so you know how long you're on.

So What if You're Addicted and They Close Your Account?

Find another hobby. Take up reading, or basket-weaving, or something like that. Maybe your computer friend next door will let you use his account. Don't worry—each year brings more online services and BBSs you can try, plus the Internet's only going to get easier and easier to use. If you lose your account, you can always pay off your debts, save your money, and try it again.

No doubt about it, online chat is a hot new phenomenon on the online front today. You're going to continue to hear about it as more and more users log on and discover the thrills of communicating with people they've never seen before. Who knows—maybe years from now you'll tell your grandchildren about the first day you logged on. By then, the online world will have corrected its visual weaknesses and you'll be able to actually *see* the people you're chatting with. On the other hand, this might very well be the downfall of online chat. Much of its romance today lies in the fact that you can't see who you're talking to. There's a certain amount of wonder and mystery about who you're really dealing with and what they're really like. If that goes away, the unconscious pull of live chat might go away too.

The Least You Need to Know

If you've got a personality type that's easily addicted to new technology—and an insatiable desire to communicate—then you may find yourself glued to the online chat channels. To gauge whether or not you're a true online addict, answer the following questions:

- Is the computer the first thing you turn on when you get home at night?
- When you log on to your favorite BBS, are you up and chatting within 10 minutes or less?
- Is IRC your favorite place on the Internet?
- Do you know all the regulars who hang out in AOL's Best Little ChatHouse room?
- Can you send a private message blindfolded?
- Have you lost sleep at night trying to think up new and creative handles or nicknames?
- Have your modem's external lights burned out from overuse?

Chapter 18 ➤ *How to Become an Online Addict*

- ➤ Do you consider the screeching sound your modem makes when connecting to be music to your ears? (And have you started to hum along?)
- ➤ Have you memorized the e-mail addresses of all your online friends?
- ➤ Does everyone on GEnie know your name?
- ➤ Are the characters on your keyboard keys wearing off?
- ➤ Have you been tempted to play hooky just to find out who chats on CompuServe's Breakfast Club channel during the day?
- ➤ Is your skin pale from never leaving the house?
- ➤ Do you get more e-mail than regular mail?
- ➤ Are you missing your nightly soak in the tub just to stay online longer?
- ➤ Have you begun typing smileys into your regular correspondence?
- ➤ Would you rather chat online than talk to your own family?
- ➤ Have you had to declare bankruptcy and foreclose on the house just to cover your chatting bills?
- ➤ Has your bottom side become permanently attached to the chair in front of your computer?

If you answered yes to eight or more questions, you're suffering from online addiction. Face it, pal, you're hooked.

Chapter 19

The Good, the Bad, and the Ugly

THE GOOD   THE BAD   THE UGLY

In This Chapter

- Techniques for making friends and losing enemies
- Find out the best times and places to log on
- Learn how to deal with the ugly side of online chat

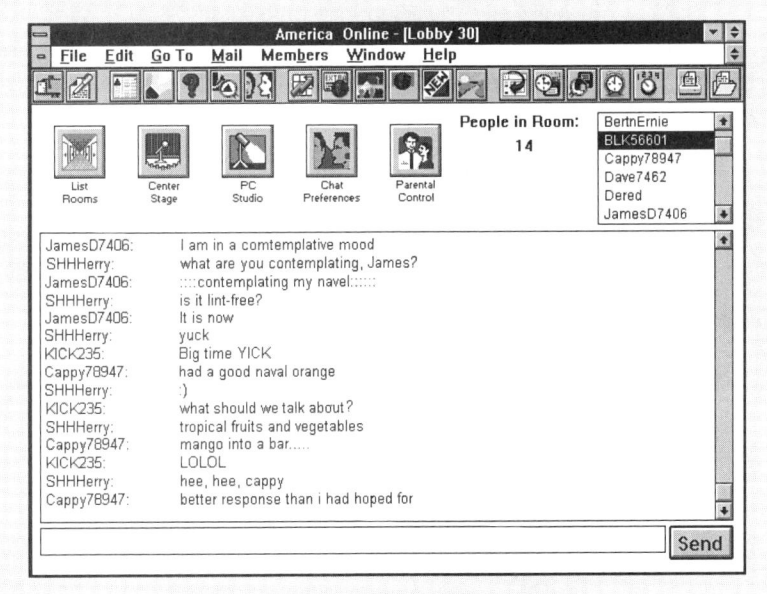

```
JamesD7406:    I am in a comtemplative mood
SHHHerry:      what are you contemplating, James?
JamesD7406:    ::::contemplating my navel::::::
SHHHerry:      is it lint-free?
JamesD7406:    It is now
SHHHerry:      yuck
KICK235:       Big time YICK
Cappy78947:    had a good naval orange
SHHHerry:      :)
KICK235:       what should we talk about?
SHHHerry:      tropical fruits and vegetables
Cappy78947:    mango into a bar.....
KICK235:       LOLOL
SHHHerry:      hee, hee, cappy
Cappy78947:    better response than i had hoped for
```

In this chapter, I'm going to give you my best advice for navigating the chat channels. In the previous chapters, I told you what you can expect online (such as private messages) and the various activities going on (such as flirting and flaming). Now it's time to tell you how you can get the most out of the chat channels yourself.

My Best Chatting Advice

I've logged some considerable hours online myself. I've tried all the services, sampled plenty of BBSs, and jumped around the IRC channels on the Internet. Being an experienced veteran of online chat, I can give you some good advice about what to do, where to go, what time to go, and what will happen when you get there. Of course you don't have to listen to any of this—you can just log on and waste your own sweet time figuring everything out. But, if you want to cut to the chase, here's what I would do…

Lurk First

If you're a newbie to chat, it's always best to lurk first and see how the other members are behaving and what they're saying. (Same thing goes for message boards and newsgroups.) Spend some time acclimating yourself to the environment, but don't feel pressured to join the conversation unless you're up to it. However, if someone says hello to you when you enter a room, go ahead and respond. It's bad cybermanners not to return a greeting. I like to check out what's being talked about before even saying hello myself. That way, if I don't like what they're discussing, I can quickly move on to another channel.

The best places to lurk are the crowded channels, such as AOL's lobbies, PRODIGY's Meeting Place channel, and Channel 1 on CompuServe's CB Simulator, to name a few. If you're on the Internet, try hanging out in channels named #20plus, #30plus, #australia, and #chatzone. If the channels are crowded, you won't be noticed—you can lurk and observe all you want.

Try Different Channels

Speaking of moving on, don't feel obligated to stay and chat in just one channel. There are lots of channels to choose from. I warned you about flitting around from channel to channel in Chapter 11, but you also have to explore a little bit to see what else is out there. Some chat channels have a specific topic or theme for discussion, but I've found that most of the time, the people on that particular channel aren't necessarily talking about the topic. So, just because a chat channel is labeled "News Room" doesn't mean they're talking about news.

AOL's got a great list of generalized channels to pick and choose from—including The Flirts Nook, Thirtysomething, and Best Little ChatHouse, among others. If you're using PRODIGY, try the General area and channels like Meeting Place.

Try the Less-Populated Channels

Traffic flow can often affect your enjoyment of a chat channel. The more people on a channel, the harder it is to communicate. Why's that? It's more difficult to follow the conversational threads in the more heavily populated channels than in others. Conversational threads are when certain people are talking about a particular topic, but their lines of dialog are interspersed with other threads of conversation conducted by others on the channel. The lines of text related to the topics weave in and out of your scrolling screen. It's hard to follow threads when different clumps of people are taking about different things. It's also harder to get a word in edgewise. For that reason, I like starting out on a channel that doesn't have many people on it.

> **Want to See Who's Chatting?**
> Most chat channels have a command or option you can use to view how many people are on the channel. Some options even list the names of everyone on the channel and where they're calling from.

For example, on AOL, each chat room can hold 23 people. That makes for a crowded room. I look for rooms that have fewer than 10 people in them. It's easier to start up a conversation with fewer people than it is to jump in the middle of a large group. This may not work for you, but it certainly works for me! You also have more control of the conversation when there are fewer people. It gives you more opportunity to make friendships and to find out information about the other members. The bottom line is this—you'll find it easier to participate yourself if you chat on less-populated channels.

There's More Chat During Peak Times

You'll run into more people chatting during peak times, which are typically in the evening or on weekends. It's been my experience that the heaviest traffic among the chat channels occurs after 6:00 p.m. during weekdays. The peak hours run from after work to around 10:00 or 11:00 p.m. More adults are logged on during that time. There are also lots of chatterers logged on during the weekend; you run across more kids then, too.

> **BBS Tip!**
> If you're a member of a relatively small BBS, you may have trouble getting online during peak periods. Some BBSs have only a few lines for members to call into.

Part 4 ➤ *Confessions of an Online Junkie*

> **Who's Online?** Be sure to check the weekly schedule of speakers and guests on your favorite service or BBS. You never know who you'll run into online. Events may be posted in an area you'll see when logging on, or among the many message board areas.

Evening chat has a more relaxed feel to it than any other time of day. Weekday evenings are also when most of the big online services sponsor special guest chats. You can log on at a set time and place and ask questions of your favorite celebrity. Celebrities range from actors and authors to people famous in the computer industry. Just to give you an example, during the month that I was writing this chapter, I could log on and talk to Christian Slater, Ed MacMahon, Sally Fields, and Alex Trebek. Online chat is so hip these days, all the major Hollywood players are rushing online to promote movies and television shows.

Find Things You Have in Common with Other Users

When chatting with people, it's best to look for something you have in common with them. Start with location. Ask where everyone's from. I like finding people online who are from the same general area I am, or who have passed through the vicinity. PRODIGY has a special area called Hometown Chat, which has a chat channel for each state in the U.S. Another common topic is weather. Weather discussions are plentiful in the chat channels because there's always weather going on somewhere, right? Other common topics to chat about are children, jobs, pets, music, television, movies, and the hottest news stories.

Use Humor

There's nothing wrong with telling a good joke or swapping stories online. Just be careful that it fits the channel you're on (remember: lurk before you leap). I *wouldn't* try using an off-color joke in a channel that has both kids and adults. Try to use some good taste, okay? It's lots of fun to swap stories revolving around your online experiences. Those range from the various kooks you run into to silly pick-up lines.

Humor online is a must, in my opinion. You're online to have some fun, so lighten up. Of course, this doesn't apply to serious conferences or forums. I'm just talking about humor in the general meeting areas, the common conversational grounds like AOL's lobbies or PRODIGY's General area. Written text gives you some wonderful opportunities for play-on-words and clever repartee, as well as quotes and such. Online chat without humor is... incredibly boring. But online humor is also a little tricky at times. The people you're conversing with can't always tell whether you're kidding or not, so be sure to use emoticons to help get the point across.

You will run into people with absolutely no humor or patience for humor. They may not get your jokes or cleverness at all. Don't worry if they do not understand your humor; if they bore you, move on to the next channel (or maybe they'll move on instead).

Keep Up Relationships Through E-Mail

One of the best parts of online chat is the friendships you cultivate. It takes time and energy, but the bonds you establish with your fellow online travelers can last a long time. However, these relationships are fragile. They are based solely on communication, so if you fail to keep open the lines of communication, the friendship fades. That's why I highly recommend that you take advantage of e-mail to keep in contact with friends during those periods when you're not online with them.

Take Time to Help Other Newbies

Another good side of online chat is passing along what you know to others. I get a kick out of helping newbies figure out what's going on. I encourage you to watch out for newbies when they enter the chat channels, and be sure to pass along the tips and tricks you learned about chatting to help them out. They're usually very grateful, and you can be content in your good deed for the day.

In this day and age, when chivalry is dead or dying (and even good manners are getting scarce), it's nice to see a helping attitude survive online. For the most part, online users are very helpful and offer advice freely, much more so than in real life. Why? It's easy to be helpful under the cover of anonymity.

Weeding Out the Bad Stuff

Okay, you've read all my good advice—now you're ready for my bad advice. Just kidding—I won't give you any of that. But I will go over the not-so-good elements of online life. That's what the next few paragraphs will cover.

Learn to Handle Online Rejection

Rejection is a bummer. The online world is full of rejection. Some of the chat channels are monopolized by cliquish groups; "intruders" rarely get any attention from them. I've seen some who don't even acknowledge your greeting or presence. If you stumble across such a channel, don't feel rejected, just move on to another channel.

If you're planning on becoming an online Romeo or Juliet, you're going to face lots of rejection. Not everyone's logged on for a fling at cybersex or romance, you know. Just accept it and move on. If you make a habit of flaming people, or picking on them for no reason, you'll experience rejection too.

For those of you aspiring to online love or lust, try hanging out in AOL's Romance Connection room, or look among AOL's many member rooms (special rooms created by AOL users). You can also check out the love/lust action in PRODIGY's Pseudo area and its many channels.

Online Rudeness Is a Fact of Life

You'll also encounter people who just can't carry on a discussion, or are far too sensitive to what's being said. It doesn't pay to be too sensitive online, so toughen up a little. To give you an example, some guy named Spiderman contacted me with a private message on AOL. I responded and started joking around about his name and occupation—after all, he's the one who chose the name of a well-known comic-book superhero. I got the feeling that he didn't seem too impressed by my clever banter about superheroes. After awhile, our conversation turned to jobs. I told him I was working even as I was talking to him. He asked what I did for a living. I told him I write computer books. He didn't believe me. In fact, when I said I was doing research for a book, I think he began feeling very apprehensive. He kept saying he didn't believe me, then he rudely left in the middle of our conversation.

I have no idea what he was looking for in our conversation. Maybe he was just trolling for a cybersex relationship. The lesson here is that you should expect to encounter some rude behavior in your own online adventures, and you'll run into some incredibly sensitive people, so watch out. You'll also find people who are online solely to pick a fight with someone and carry out their frustration or anger. Learn to avoid these types, but above all, *don't take it personally* when you become of victim of flaming, rudeness, or disbelief.

Learn to Deal with Cyberviolators

There's a lot of ugliness on the chat channels. No, I'm not talking about appearances, I'm talking about attitudes and behavioral conduct. I really dislike the belligerent people who insist on typing questionable language in the common conversational areas for the sheer thrill of offending everyone else. I don't care if you normally swear like a sailor (so to speak)—it's not necessary in group conversations. And I'm not talking about the typical swear slang, but the hard-core stuff. I'd love to be a chat-channel policeman and nab those users who insist on violating cybermanners. I think it would be very satisfying to bounce them right off the system. Despite the good intentions of cybermanners and the people in charge of the system or service, you will encounter this ugly element of online chat, so be prepared.

There's not a whole lot you can do about ugliness when it occurs. You can certainly speak up and tell the person it's not appropriate on that channel. If it persists, you can even warn them that you're summoning the online administrators or sysops. Other than that, if you're unhappy with the language, you may just have to switch to another channel or log off.

Expect to Encounter Some Private Messages

The online sexual advances get a little old after awhile, too. There's only so many private invitations to cybersex you can stand while in the middle of a group conversation in the general chat channels. The instant messages become distracting and annoying, like flies buzzing around your head. It seems there isn't a single channel out there that's safe from these advances.

The worst private messages are the ones that are out-and-out distasteful; the ones that are so vulgar they leave you shocked that someone dared to type them. It makes you want to flame each one you encounter, but you hate to give them any more attention than they're already getting. If you're not too keen about these messages, find the command or option for turning them off. Otherwise, be prepared to deal with them.

There are other annoying aspects of online chat, just as there are annoying aspects of all communications, written or verbal. You'll inevitably have to deal with the bad and ugly side of chat at one time or another. Just try not to let it get the best of you, or you'll find yourself wasting precious time flaming the many kooks, jerks, and morons in cyberspace.

> ### You Need a Sound Card to Hear Sound Waves
>
> I find sound waves on chat channels annoying. A lot of people have sound cards on their computers. I don't (do you feel sorry for me?). People with sound capabilities like to send sound waves in the various chat rooms. If you don't have a sound card, you can't hear them. However, they're usually characterized in the on-screen text by a funny symbol and a brief description of the sound, such as {welcome (creates the sound of a voice saying "welcome")}. Since I don't have a sound card, I find the whole thing kind of annoying and I feel left out. Pooey on me, right?

The Least You Need to Know

So, that's my advice for getting the most of the chat channels. Now for a recap for those of you who left the room to get a snack:

- Lurk first to see what's going on.
- Try the various channels to see which one suits you best.
- Look for less-populated channels for better communication.
- Online chat is at its peak during evening weekday hours.
- Look for things you have in common with other users.
- Feel free to use lots of humor in your online conversations.
- Keep your online relationships going through e-mail contact.
- When you run into a newbie, help out.
- Get used to online rejection—it happens.
- Watch out for the rude people and the ones who violate cybermanners.
- Learn to deal with private messages.

Chapter 20

Rating Online Chat

In This Chapter

- Find out which commercial service ranks first in chat
- Learn how to use the very best in pick up lines
- Tips for saving money online

```
Doing It
did we talk
Of course not
do you want to
I am talking...that's what you call this
ok, then what about
what's with the name?
what do you think?
It could mean you're vacuuming for all i know
```

This is it, the end of the book. Our journey together is over, if you don't count the obligatory glossary and index. This is our final chapter together. Sniff, sniff.

Did you learn all you wanted to know about online chat? Are you going to become an online junkie yourself? Good—we can always use another newbie online. In this final chapter, I've compiled a bunch of lists I think you'll find helpful in evaluating the various services, money-saving tips, suggestions for conversation starters, and much more.

Part 4 ➤ *Confessions of an Online Junkie*

Rank and File

Do you want to know which commercial service is the best? Do you want to find out where the best or worst chat channels are? You've come to the right place. I'm going to give you my evaluations of the online world. It's up to you to try them out for yourself. Most of the evaluations focus on the larger commercial services and the Internet. I didn't purposefully leave out BBSs; it's just that there are far too many BBSs out there to try, and it would take me a year to call them all up. But, hey—if you've got the time and money, give them all a try!

The Best and Worst of the Commercial Services

All of the major commercial services are undergoing changes. By this, I mean there's heavy competition for your online dollar. This has forced the big players to shape up their GUIs and features, and the race is on to offer the most and best stuff online—including tons of Internet access. AOL introduced an improved interface in 1994, and CompuServe has unveiled a new one in 1995. PRODIGY has continually worked on its interface. GEnie and the rest of the pack have got to hustle to keep up with the big three. The coming years will also bring additional commercial services into the fray, so watch out for the up-and-comers, like Apple's eWorld and the Microsoft Network.

Who's got the best commercial online service when it comes to chatting? It's a tough call, but I'd have to say AOL beats the others by a nose or two. Let me tell you why. AOL is the easiest service to use in terms of visual appeal. AOL's screens really look nice; they're very intuitive, and it's incredibly easy to get to the chat rooms. Ease of use and visual appeal are what really counts when chatting online. AOL more than fulfills those requirements.

AOL's chat rooms are also very friendly. I like the fact that there are guides assigned to some of the lobbies to help out newcomers. If I could change a few things about AOL chat, I would extend the view of the list of other available rooms and I'd set up the instant messages so that you could press **Enter** to send a reply instead of having to click on the **Send** button. Other than that, AOL's chat rooms are pretty top-notch.

The race for second place was a tight one between CompuServe and PRODIGY. I'll rate CompuServe the second-place position. CompuServe edges out PRODIGY because it's a little easier to use, though CompuServe's chat area is also harder to find. They've made some improvements to get you to CB-Simulator, but it's not as easy as AOL. I don't like the fact that they've set up the CB-1 band and the CB-2 band as two separate areas. You have to assign yourself a new handle each time you enter a band. I also wish they had more topically named channels to choose from.

PRODIGY comes in at third place because (1) it's not as visually appealing, and (2) it's incredibly slow-going to find your way to the chat area. They also need to improve the flexibility of the chat windows themselves. It would be nice to be able to enlarge the windows as needed. Bonus points to PRODIGY for continuing to improve its chat topics; they've added quite a few more areas and channels that focus on particular subjects or themes.

GEnie comes in at fourth place, mainly for only one reason—it's not too appealing in the visual sense. I hope they're going to continue to work on their front-end GUI programs. As it is now, live chat looks the same (basically) whether you're using the GEnie GUI or not. In its favor, however, the people who use GEnie chat are some of the friendliest people I've ever encountered online.

It might help to know that some of the online services are geared to certain users. For example, AOL has focused more on the home user. If that's your niche, you'll probably enjoy everything AOL has to offer. If business is your game (and you have the money), CompuServe is the logical choice. CompuServe has built a reputation of being very business-oriented. GEnie and DELPHI are also heavily focused on the business user. PRODIGY has targeted the entire family in its scope, offering something for everyone, from children to adults.

The Up-and-Comers

On the online horizon are new and just-starting networks from Apple to Microsoft. Apple's eWorld service was launched the summer of '94, targeting Mac users first, then encompassing Windows users as well. eWorld's appeal is mainly to the Mac world, but keep your eye on them.

Microsoft is starting The Microsoft Network with the release of its Windows 95 product. Naturally, this network is targeting Windows users all around. Some other services to watch for are the Interchange Online Network, and AT&T PersonaLink Services. These are just a few of the new services cropping up. Most of these will take a year or two to get going, but you should definitely check them out when you get a chance.

The Best Places to Chat

The best places for generalized banter are in the common chat areas, like any of AOL's lobbies. AOL's public rooms are full of constant dialog and there's always heavy traffic flow in and out of the rooms. If you're looking for more intimate chatting, then try AOL's member rooms. Scrolling through the list of member-named rooms is like searching through the want ads.

Part 4 ➤ *Confessions of an Online Junkie*

> **Other Chat Areas** Don't forget, a lot of chatting takes place in other areas online. For example, AOL's clubs and CompuServe's forums also offer online chat opportunities. Be sure to look for scheduled conferences too. (Try MTV's chat area on AOL.)

Chatting comes easily on CompuServe's CB-1 band on CB Simulator. It's worth your time to check out the Newcomers channel, or Channel 1. If you prefer more adult chat, switch to CB-2. You can expect more private messaging and more adult language on the CB-2 band.

PRODIGY's got a lot of chatting going on day and night in the General area. There are plenty of broad-topic-based channels to choose from in the General area. If you're looking for a chat about your favorite hobby, try the Interests area, channels focusing on hobbies broken down alphabetically. I highly recommend that you check out PRODIGY's Hometown area and connect to people in your own state. If you prefer more adult-like banter, then go to PRODIGY's Pseudo area, a collection of adult channels with a variety of names.

If you're chatting on GEnie or any of the smaller commercial services, look for the more populated channels to find the best chat. If you're using BBSs to chat, you'll find a variety of channels and topics to choose from.

The best Internet chat can be found on channels like #30plus, or #chatzone. You'll know you've found a hoppin' chat channel if it has 10 or more people on it.

The Worst Places to Chat

Probably the worst places to chat (for grownups, at least) are on the teen channels. Yuck. They do all kinds of annoying things in the teen channels, like scrolling—typing one letter at a time, one line at a time, or the same letters over and over again, filling the conversation window. There's also a lot of teenage slang, offensive language, raging hormones, and all-out silliness going on. Teens tend to shout at each other and flame each other constantly. After researching the teen channels for this book, I vowed never to step onto a teen channel again.

There are lots of other bad channels out there, but you'll find those on your own.

Top-Ten Lists

To get in the spirit of fun online chat, here are some top-ten lists to check out. Some of these lists are serious, some are silly. These lists can help you with your own online communications, and save you money to boot.

Ten Ways to Save Money Online

Everybody wants to save money, right? Here are some tips for saving your online money.

1. Always keep track of how long you're online, especially when you're chatting.
2. If you plan on composing a lot of e-mail, use an *off-line navigation program* to create your messages before ever logging onto the service. (Some service-specific software lets you do this already.) An offline navigation program lets you compose mail without being logged onto the system. That way you don't waste precious time online typing them up; instead, you can just log on and send them all at once.
3. Find a local access number to use in your modem calls. Local numbers cost a lot less than long-distance numbers. It's also cheaper to find a local Internet service provider than use one that's far away from you.
4. Always know exactly how you're going to be billed by your BBS, commercial service, or Internet service provider. Watch out for extra charges based on modem speed and time of call.
5. Make your calls during off hours. It's sometimes cheaper to call on evenings and weekends than during prime daytime hours.
6. If you plan on doing a lot of downloading (copying files onto your computer), use your fastest modem speed.
7. If your service charges a monthly fee that includes a set number of online hours, be sure you're getting your money's worth. If you find you aren't using all of your allotted hours, you may need to find another pricing plan.
8. Look for special deals and offers before you sign up with a commercial service or Internet service provider. Some deals offer you free online time or usage when you sign up, or bonus time if you get a friend to sign up too.
9. If your BBS or service sponsors contests, be sure and try your luck. Sometimes the prizes involve free memberships, bonus online hours, and more.
10. Make sure you know exactly what you want to accomplish in your online session before logging on. That way, you won't waste time figuring out what you want to do or where you want to go.

The Ten Most Popular Opening Lines

For all you online Romeos and Juliets, here are some helpful pickup lines to try in your own private messages to members of the "seemingly" opposite sex. I've listed 10 lines for male users to try out on women, and 10 lines for female users to try out on men. (First make sure your sense of humor is online!) Okay, maybe they're not the best lines to use, but I thought you'd find them amusing... and yes, I've actually seen some of these online myself.

Top Ten Pickup Lines (Male)

1. What's a nice girl like you—you *are* a girl, aren't you—doing in a place like this?
2. Hey, baby, what's your sign? (No, not the one that says "Not Interested.")
3. Haven't I seen you here before? (Or somebody who types just like you?)
4. Hi, I like your handle.
5. Would you like to come over and see my .GIF collection? (I've got virtual champagne, imaginary candlelight...)
6. What are you wearing? (Is it as thin as this line?)
7. Hey, you've got a great smile :)
   (Use this line after someone's typed in an emoticon. If it's a snarl, try, "Hey, you've got a great snarl.")
8. I have a 30-inch screen. (But I hear it's what you *do* with it that counts...)
9. Hello there, are you on this channel often?
10. Does your mother know you're online?

Top Ten Pickup Lines (Female)

1. Is that your mouse, or are you just happy to see me?
2. Excuse me, but what modem speed are you using?
3. Hi, I like your handle.
4. My, you're very dexterous.
5. Oops, I must have pressed a wrong button. Can you help me out?
6. Is that a floppy disk or a hard disk you're using?
7. Can you tell me how to find the hotchat channel?
8. I like the quote in your profile.
9. What's your handle mean?
10. Are your fingers always this slow (or fast)?

Chapter 20 ➤ *Rating Online Chat*

Ten Ways to End an Online Conversation

One of the most difficult chat situations you'll run into is the graceful exit situation. That's when you've run out of time and need to log off, and you really need a way to close your current conversation. Here are ten distinct ways you can end an online discussion fast:

1. I gotta go, my mother's calling.
2. Wait, I think I heard someone on the stairs. There's someone coming into the room. HELP ME… HELP ME… NOOOOOOOOOOOOOooooooo
3. Hey, Melrose Place is on!
4. Schrruzz, screasgruzz, scrizzschroz… We must have a bad connection.
5. I'm originally from Mars, but I've lived on Earth for about 10 years now.
6. I think I left the stove on.
7. Oops, I'm outta online time.
8. I wonder what would happen if I touched this button?
9. Yikes! The cat's on fire!
10. I have to leave now. The men in white jackets just pulled into my driveway.

Ten Ways to Start an Online Fight

Got some aggression you need to work out? Then try your hand at picking an online fight. Here are some lines guaranteed to stir up some trouble:

1. You're spelling iz lousy. Did you flunk grammar?
2. Watch your manners, pal. Were you raised in a barn?
3. Liberals are losers.
4. My 486 can take your 486 any time. (Other variations include "My Motorola chip can take your Pentium chip any day," Mac versus Windows, and numerous other conjectures.)
5. Your mother wears army boots. (Actually, anything derogatory about the other person's mother will work.)
6. Why don't you go chat on the teen channel?
7. You call that typing? I thought a snail was using your keyboard.
8. What a stupid handle.

9. Do you work hard at being a complete moron, or is it just genetics?
10. Are you calling me a liar?

Ten Ways to Respond to Instant Messages

It's kind of a challenge sometimes to reply to the myriad of private messages that get sent to you. How about some snappy one-liners to the most common instant messages you come across?

➤ Message says: What do you look like?
Possible replies: I don't know, let me go check my mirror.
Which one of us?
Before or after the operation?
(Pick a celebrity, any celebrity.)

➤ Message says: How old are you?
Possible replies: Is that in dog years or human years?
I'm only as old as I feel.
Old enough to know better.
(Type in a mathematical equation.)

➤ Message says: What are your measurements?
Possible replies: Let's do yours first, starting with IQ.
From top to bottom, or side to side?
In which dimension?

➤ Message says: What are you wearing?
Possible replies: Sackcloth and ashes.
I don't know, but it's making me scratch like crazy.
Just my blue-ribbon smile.

➤ Message says: Want to have some cyberfun?
Possible replies: Want a cyber-punch-in-the-face?
I don't know—does it involve Ferris wheels?
Not tonight, dear, I have a headache.

The Least You Need to Know

That's all she wrote. I hope this book appeased your curiosity about the online chat phenomenon. You can now log on and chat with the best of them. Lotsa luck to you in your own online adventures. See you in cyberspace… unless they close all my accounts!

The Important Extra Stuff

In This Section

- ➤ A summary of important UNIX commands
- ➤ A list of the big online services' phone numbers you can call to set up an account fast
- ➤ A list of Internet service providers
- ➤ A list of BBSs
- ➤ Crucial information about buying a modem without getting ripped off
- ➤ Helpful hints on what to look for in communications software
- ➤ Tips for caring for your modem so you can chat for the next five years without incident
- ➤ Instructions for modem-to-modem chatting with your closest computer friend

UNIX Command Summary

If you're stuck surfing the Net using only a UNIX environment, you'll appreciate this handy collection of specific commands. Keep this book open when online so you won't have to wrack your brain to remember what to type at the UNIX prompt.

Understanding UNIX Commands

To find out the structure of a UNIX command and all the options and arguments you can use with that command, type the command and -? and press Enter. You'll see a usage statement—something like this:

```
commandname [-option(s)...] [arguments...]
```

The brackets [ ] indicate that something is optional. If you see a | as part of the command structure, you can choose between one or the other option, but not both. Finally, if you see ellipses (...), you can use more than one option or argument.

> **More UNIX?**
> If you find you want more information on UNIX, just pick up a copy of *The Complete Idiot's Guide to UNIX* at your local bookstore.

UNIX Command Table

Use This Command	To
cd[*directory*]	Change to a new directory
cd	Go to the home directory
cp [-i] ...*directory*	Copy a file to a directory
-i	Inquire before replacing an existing file
cp [-i] ...*file copyname*	Copy one file
-i	Inquire before replacing an existing file
grep [-i] *text* [*file*...]	Search files for specified text
-i	Ignore differences between upper- and lowercase letters
ls [-aFl] *directory*...	List contents of a directory
-a	Show all files, including hidden ones
-F	Show file types (/ is a directory, * is a program)
-l	Show long file listing
pwd	Show current directory
man [-s n] *command*...	Get help on a command
-s *section*	Look only in part *n* of online manual

The Important Extra Stuff

Use This Command	To
mkdir *directory*	Make a directory
mv *oldname newname*	Move (or rename) one file
mv *file ...directory*	Move a file to a directory
lp *file ...*	Print a file
rm [-ifr] *file ...*	Remove a file
-i	Inquire before removing a file
-f	Remove files without inquiring (force)
-r	Remove directories and contents
rmdir *directory...*	Remove an empty directory

Some Useful IRC Commands

Use This Command	To
/channel #*channelname*	Select a channel
/help	See a list of IRC commands
/join #*channelname*	Join a channel
/list	Display list of available channels
/msg *handle*	Send a private message to another handle
/quit	Exit IRC
whois *handle*	View information about the handle in question
whowas *handle*	View information about who was on the channel

Phone Numbers to Reach All the Big Online Services Fast

Following is a quick summary of what each of the big online services looks like and phone numbers you can call to reach them.

The Complete Idiot's Guide to Sex, Lies, and Online Chat

CompuServe

800-848-8199 (voice phone)

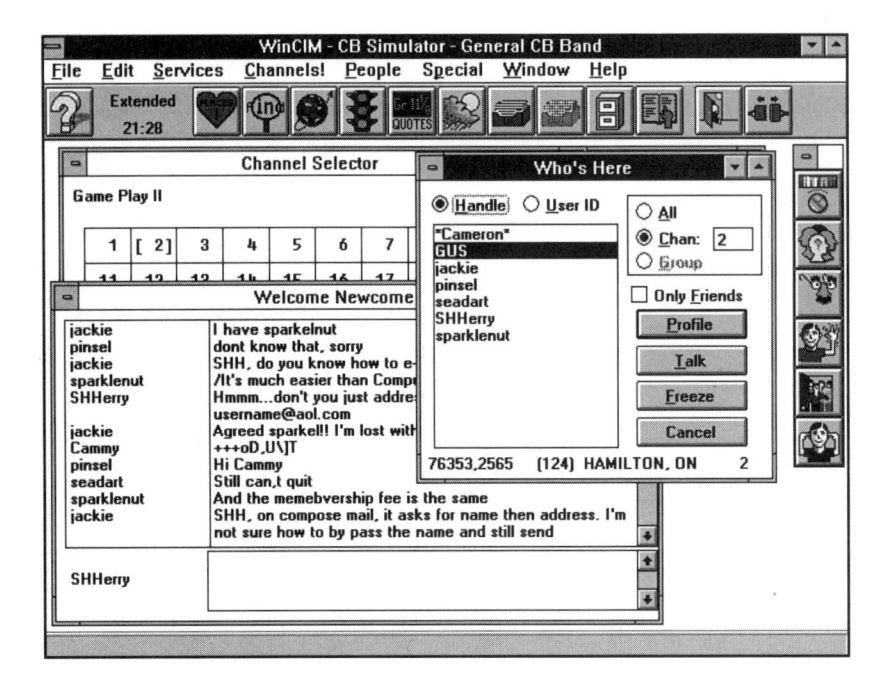

CompuServe's CB Simulator.

America Online

800-827-6364 (voice phone)

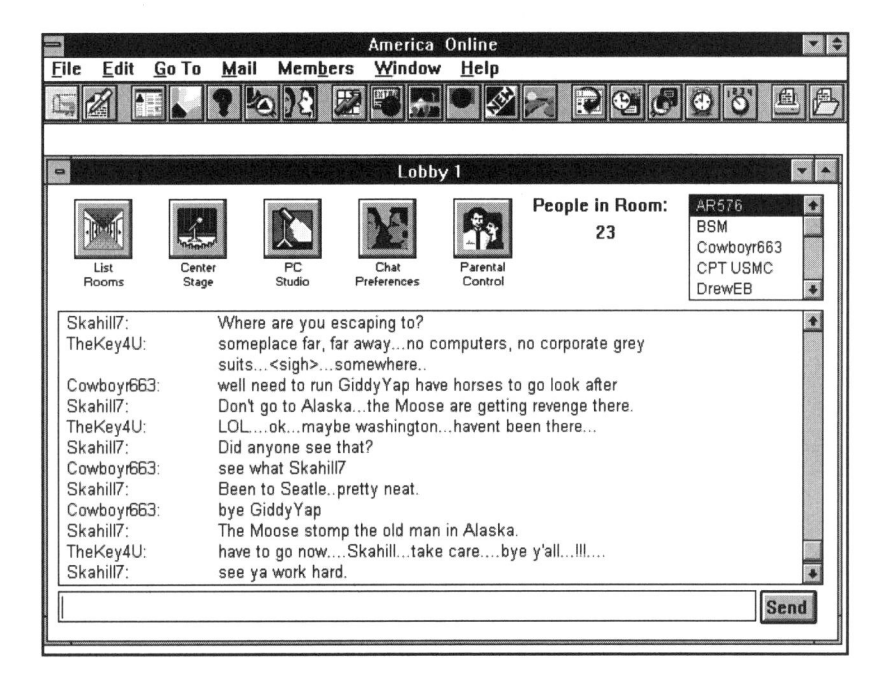

Chatting on America Online.

PRODIGY

800-776-3449 (voice phone)

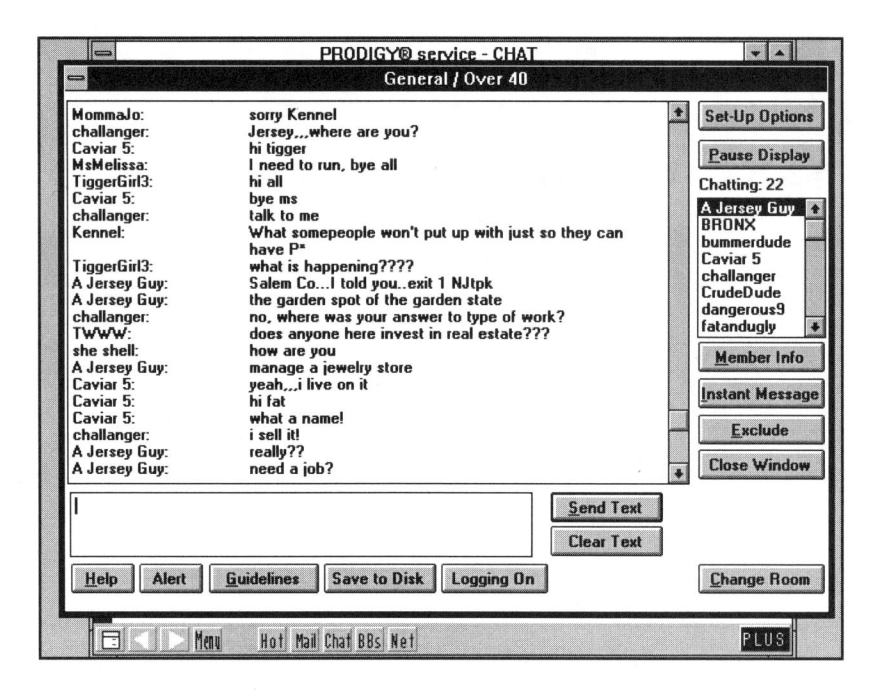

This is what conversations on PRODIGY look like.

GEnie

800-638-9636 (voice phone)

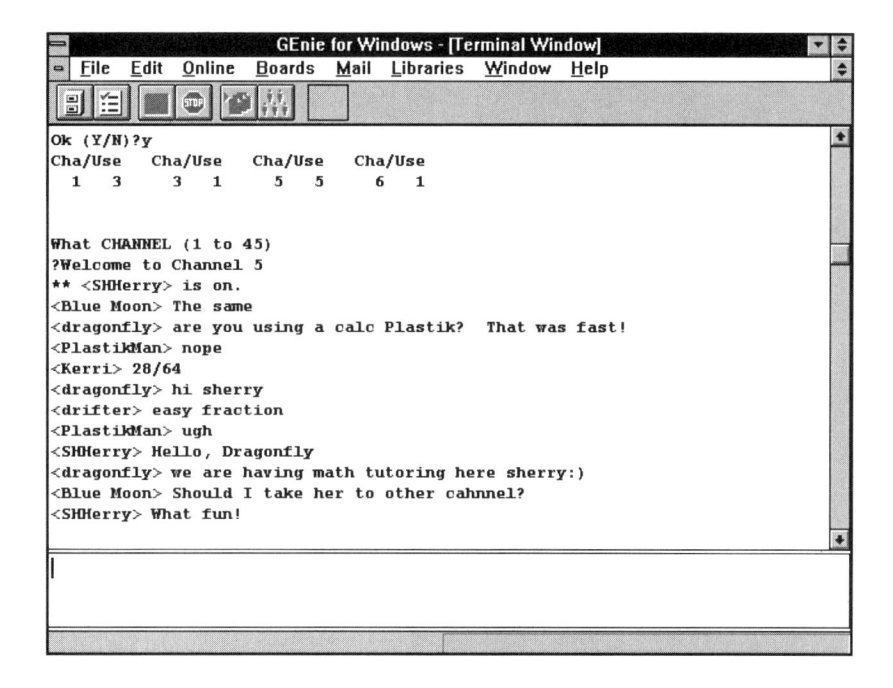

```
GEnie for Windows - [Terminal Window]
 File  Edit  Online  Boards  Mail  Libraries  Window  Help

Ok (Y/N)?y
Cha/Use    Cha/Use    Cha/Use    Cha/Use
  1   3      3   1      5   5      6   1


What CHANNEL (1 to 45)
?Welcome to Channel 5
** <SHHerry> is on.
<Blue Moon> The same
<dragonfly> are you using a calc Plastik?  That was fast!
<PlastikMan> nope
<Kerri> 28/64
<dragonfly> hi sherry
<drifter> easy fraction
<PlastikMan> ugh
<SHHerry> Hello, Dragonfly
<dragonfly> we are having math tutoring here sherry:)
<Blue Moon> Should I take her to other cahnnel?
<SHHerry> What fun!
```

Chatting on GEnie looks a little different.

A List of Internet Service Providers

Service Provider	Phone Number
Colorado Supernet	303-273-3471
PSInet	703-620-6651
a2i Communications	408-293-8078
BAARNet	415-725-1790
Demon Internet Limited (UK)	081-349-0063
MIDnet	402-472-7600
OARnet	614-292-8100
JVNCnet	800-358-4437
MBnet (Manitoba, Canada)	204-474-8230
MichNet	313-764-9430
MSEN, Incorporated	313-998-4562
CSUnet	310-985-9661
BCnet (British Columbia)	604-291-5029
CICNet, Inc.	313-998-6104
CONCERT	919-248-1999
Internet Transit	315-453-2912, ext. 230
The Well	415-332-4335
PSINet	800-827-7482
PREPnet	412-268-7870
NevadaNet	702-895-4580
NetILLINOIS	708-866-1825
WVNET	304-293-5192
UUNET	800-488-6384
World dot Net	206-576-7147
NOVX	800-873-6689

The Important Extra Stuff

Service Provider	Phone Number
NYSERnet	315-453-6147
SESQUINET	713-527-6038
SURAnet	301-982-4600
NETCOM	800-501-8649
Portal	408-973-9111
ICNet/Innovative Concepts	313-998-0090
The World	617-739-0202
MV Communications	603-429-2223
ANSRemote	800-456-8267
CERFnet—General Atomics/CERFnet	800-876-2373
Gateway to the World	305-670-2930
Network Information Services Center	415-859-5318
InterNIC Information Services Referral	619-455-4600

A List of BBSs

BBS Name	Phone Number	Location
Monterey Gaming System	408-655-5555	Monterey, CA
The INDEX System	404-924-8472	Woodstock, GA
The File Bank, Inc.	303-534-4646	Denver, CO
Ultimate BBS	217-792-3663	Mt. Pulaski, IL
The Rock Garden	602-220-0001	Phoenix, AZ
Compass Rose	916-447-0292	Davis, CA
Tampa Connection	813-961-8665	Tampa, FL
Micro Message Service	919-779-6674	Raleigh, NC
Top City	612-225-1003	St. Paul, MN

continues

Continued

BBS Name	Phone Number	Location
Capital City Online	206-956-1123	Olympia, WA
Tech Talk	407-635-8833	Titusville, FL
Point Blank	516-755-3000	Plainview, NY
Possibilities	619-748-5264	Poway, CA
Synergy Online	201-331-1797	Parsippany, NJ
24th Street Exchange	916-448-2483	Sacramento, CA
Infinite Space BBS	407-856-0021	Orlando, FL
PC-Ohio	216-381-3320	Cleveland, OH
Software Creations	508-368-7139	Clinton, MA
EXEC-PC	414-789-4360	New Berlin, WI
Blue Ridge Express	804-790-1675	Monterey, CA
Deep Cove BBS	604-536-885	White Rock, BC
America's Suggestion Box	516-689-5390	East Setauket, NY
Chrysalis	214-690-9295	Dallas, TX
Springfield Public Access	413-536-4365	Springfield, MA
Wizard's Gate BBS	614-224-1635	Columbus, OH
Hello Central	206-641-7218	Bellevue, WA
Crystal Quill	703-241-7100	Arlington, VA
Network East	301-738-0000	Rockville, MD
Starship II BBS	201-935-1485	Lyndhurst, NJ
City Lights	612-633-1366	Arden Hills, MN
ExecNet Information Systems	914-667-4066	Mt. Vernon, NY
The Doctor's Office	703-749-2860	Vienna, VA
MicroFone InfoService	908-205-0189	Metuchen, NJ
Father & Son BBS	610-439-1509	Whitehall, PA

BBS Name	Phone Number	Location
The Nashville Exchange	615-383-0727	Nashville, TN
Aquila BBS	708-820-8344	Aurora, IL
Garbage Dump	505-294-5675	Albuquerque, NM
Channel 1	617-354-8873	Cambridge, MA
Hotlanta BBS	404-992-5345	Atlanta, GA
West Coast Connection	619-449-8333	ElCujhon, CA
Windows Online	510-736-8343	Danville, CA

Tips and Tricks for Buying a Modem

Let's talk about this. What exactly are you looking for in a modem? Speed, intelligence, raw beauty—or just plain old companionship? Whatever you're looking for, there's a modem out there for you. Unless, of course, you already have one sitting on your desk. The following sections offer some serious help for finding a modem that's right for you.

How to Read a Modem Box

Any time you go shopping for electronics—and that includes computer stuff these days—you quickly find there's a lot to choose from and a lot of different prices to pay. If you trot down to Ed's Computer Warehouse for a modem today, you'll find recognizable and unrecognizable brand names, warranties and extended warranties, and an endless parade of model numbers.

You'll also find commission-driven salespeople just waiting for an innocent victim such as yourself. (If you're a salesperson, I mean no offense—I'm just talking about the stereotypical ones, of course.) Try to avoid them when possible, and head straight for the modem boxes like you know what you're looking for. If they do try to bother you, just keep chanting "I can get this wholesale... I can get this wholesale..." and they should leave you alone.

Once you've made it past the salespeople, start looking for the right modem. There are many strange codes on a modem box. For example, I'm staring at my new modem's box, and it says "14,400 V.32bis." It also says "Super high-speed V.32bis protocol; hardware controlled V.42 error detection and control; V.42bis data compression; PM14400FXMT V.32bis." You will find similar cryptic codes on the modem boxes in stores across the globe. You may as well arm yourself with the know-how to read them. If you're ready, we'll commence with a discussion on modem standards.

Ye Olde Standards

Engineers and manufacturers set standards. These standards usually develop over the years into a certain set that is acceptable to everyone. Standards typically involve many numbers and letters that stand for particular specifications and hardware features. Of course, these standards are never in plain English and rarely make any sense unless you're in the know about the technology. However, these numbers and letters stamped onto a modem's box supposedly represent engineering specifications that tell you what the modem supports and complies with.

Some of the standards you'll see on a modem box date back to early modem development. Other standards are recent. Whether old or recent, modem standards have one thing in common—they're confusing. I'll help you translate what these standards mean. Think of this as an archeological adventure, like reading hieroglyphics on a pyramid wall. In no time at all, you'll unlock the mysteries of the vee-dot symbol, V.32.

Bell Standards

Good old Ma Bell established some of the very first modem standards. She managed to get in on this modem stuff before the big breakup and the proliferation of Baby Bells. Knowing this, finding Bell standards listed on a modem box won't surprise you. Until the early 1980s, the standards established by Bell Laboratories were used in most U.S. modems. These early standards were designed for the 300 bps and 1200 bps modems. So if you see a **Bell 103** or a **Bell 212A** on your modem box, that means that the modem can talk to old modems with these standards.

The MNP Standards

Microcom, Inc. developed its own set of standards for error control and data compression and called these standards *Microcom Networking Protocol*, or MNP for short. The MNP standards break down into nine classes; the first four pertain to error correction and the last five cover data compression.

Classes MNP 1–MNP 4 are error correction-related, and classes MNP 5–MNP 9 are for data compression. MNP 1, 2, and 3 work to control errors that may occur when the modem's phone line is "noisy." You see these standards listed under the hardware features on a modem box. MNP 5 and 7 determine a modem's data compression; either standard can compress data at a ratio of 2 to 1. Wow, that's squishy.

According to my new 14,400 modem box, my modem has MNP 2, 3, and 4 when it comes to error control. It has MNP 5 when it comes to data compression. Look under these categories on any modem box to see the MNP standards listed.

CCITT Standards

In Europe, an international committee agreed upon modem standards. They called themselves the Consultive Committee on International Telegraphy and Telephony (CCITT). One of their major recommendations was the V-series, which is a series of recommendations for interfaces and voice-band modems. The standards set up by the CCITT determined those mysterious vee-dot symbols on today's modem box, such as V.32.

You only have to deal with four or five of these vee-dot symbols, and some of them have *bis* added to the end of them. Bis means that it's the second version of the original standard. It's kind of like a "new and improved" label on your favorite laundry detergent. Confused? Let me straighten it all out with a helpful vee-dot table.

The V-series Numbers You Need to Know

Series Number	What It Does
V.22	Communicates at 1200 bps.
V.22bis	Communicates at 2400 bps.
V.32	Communicates at 9600 bps.
V.32bis	Communicates at 14,400 bps.
V.42	Error correction that works with MNP standards.
V.42bis	Data compression that packs data tighter than MNP 5.
V.32terbo	Communicates at up to 19,200 bps.
V.Fast	Communicates at up to 28,800 bps.

When you're looking at the various modem boxes, you'll notice that the listed features may include more than one vee-dot standard. That tells you which standards the modem supports. For example, my new modem is a V.32bis modem, yet it supports V.32, V.22bis, V.22, and V.21. Essentially, this means that although it's a fast modem, it can still talk at slower modem speeds. If the modem box lists V.42bis and V.42, that means it can use those particular error control and data compression standards. Are you beginning to get the hang of this?

Speed Bumps

Of course you're going to examine the modem box to determine it's speed, right? Hopefully, you've already figured out which modem speed you're looking for. Remember, there are several popular speeds to choose from. In most mainstream retail stores, the most popular modem speeds offered are 9600 bps and 14,400 bps. You may have difficulty finding anything slower offered in the major computer hardware outlets.

How about another table to illustrate modem speeds and how they compare? Please, there's no need for applause; I'm just doing my job.

Modem Speed Comparisons

Modem Speed	How It Stacks Up
300 bps	Forget it. This is a modem artifact.
1200 bps	Not so good either. This is also ancient modem history.
2400 bps	S-l-o-w. You may even have trouble finding this in a store.
9600 bps	Today's average modem speed, very common.
14,400 bps	The next average, fast and sleek as a racehorse.
16,800 bps 19,200 bps 28,800 bps	These three speeds are the modems of tomorrow. The technology is still new, and you'll have trouble using these modems except with similar-speed modems.

The bottom line is this: as long as your modem has at least one modulation (speed) standard in common with another modem, communication can occur. And that's what modems are for, anyway.

Summing Up Standards

Now that you know about standards, let's see if we can make some sense out of them when you see them listed on a box. Most modem boxes list technical specifications as well as hardware features. Under technical specifications, you'll find a listing of what the modem is capable of complying with. For example, my new 14,400 modem says it complies with CCITT V.32bis, V.32, V.22bis, V.22, V.21, Bell 212A and 103, V.42, and V.42bis. Simply put, that means it can talk at the lower modem speeds. So, if I call a friend with a 1200 bps modem, I can still communicate with him even though I have a 14,400 bps modem.

The Important Extra Stuff

Under the hardware features on my modem box is list of error control and data compression codes. My 14,400 box says my modem has V.42 LAPM and MNP 2, 3, and 4 error correction capabilities and V.42bis and MNP 5 data compression. This means my modem will detect phone line noise and control errors as well as compress data by a ratio of 2 to 1 or even tighter. The MNP 5 compresses data 2:1, and the V.42bis compresses it 4:1.

Still confused about reading a modem box? Here's another little table to help you.

Common Modem Standards to Look For

Standard	Name	What's It Do?
Speed	Bell 103	Communicates at up to 300 bps.
	Bell 212	Communicates at up to 1200 bps.
	V.21	Communicates at up to 300 bps.
	V.22	Communicates at up to 1200 bps.
	V.22bis	Communicates at up to 2400 bps.
	V.32	Communicates at up to 9600 bps.
	V.32bis	Communicates at up to 14,400 bps.
	V.32terbo	Communicates at up to 19,200 bps.
	V.Fast	Communicates at up to 28,800 bps.
Error Correction	MNP 1, 2, 3	Checks for phone line noise and controls errors.
	MNP 4	Checks for errors and adapts to phone line conditions.
	LAPM	Error protection.
	V.42	Combines MNP 2, 3, and 4 with LAPM.
Data Compression	MNP 5, 7	Compresses data 2:1.
	V.42bis	Compresses data up to 4:1.

Who's Hayes and Why Are All the Other Modems Talking to Him?

Another feature you'll find listed on a modem box is *Hayes compatibility*. This is definitely something you want your modem to have. The Hayes Microcomputer Products Company has been around since 1978, and they've made quite a mark on the modem industry. A Hayes modem is the most popular brand of modem sold today. They've helped establish many standards, including a set of commands that control how modems call and hang up. These commands are the *Hayes AT Command Set*. It's an industry standard, which means everybody uses it. It's kind of like when you say, "Hand me a kleenex." You don't really care if it's a Kleenex-brand or some other brand, you just want a stupid tissue. The word *kleenex* is synonymous with tissues. Hayes is synonymous with modem commands.

The Hayes AT Command Set is a special group of commands for controlling a modem using the keyboard. This group (named for its first command, AT) means "attention." (This command wakes up the slumbering modem and tells it to get ready.) You can type AT commands to make your modem dial a number, hang up, and even control your modem's speaker. Just about every modem-maker out there has adopted this standard. That's not to say that every Hayes-compatible modem truly utilizes all of the AT Command Set, but more than likely they use enough to get you by.

Does It Fax?

Just to throw a monkey wrench into your modem shopping preparation, there are also sets of fax modem standards to be aware of. Most of the modems being sold today also double as faxes. This means that not only can you communicate with other modem users, but you can also call fax machines. Wow.

Mind you, faxing is different from modem communications. When you dial out with your modem to send a file, you're breaking the file down into analog signals. When you fax a document, you're sending a complete visual picture to a receiving fax machine. The fax part of a fax modem handles the sending differently. It even uses a separate set of electronics to handle its job. Fax modems also use different protocols. They're just different!

Miscellaneous Modem Features

Along with all of the other standards and features, there are some others you may want to consider when you make your modem purchase. The first of these is the phone socket. If your modem needs to share the same exact line as your phone, you may want to plug your phone into the modem itself. Some modems have a socket (labeled PHONE) on the back in which you can plug the telephone unit. If the modem you want to buy doesn't have a place to plug in a regular phone, you can always buy a splitter for your wall jack and plug in your phone that way. (Stop at Radio Shack while you're out shopping.)

If you're looking at a modem with a speaker, it's probably a good idea to investigate the speaker volume controls. If there's no speaker knob, make sure the modem supports the Hayes AT Command Set commands that control volume. If you qualify for TDD service (Telephone service for the Deaf and Disabled), make sure the modem you buy supports Bell 103 operations. Your local phone company can assist you with setup instructions for utilizing TDD communication.

Where to Shop

Where does one go to hunt big modem game, you may wonder? Modems run wild over the countryside, and you can easily capture one with a credit card. Computer equipment and accessories are quickly finding their way into all sorts of strange places these days. Don't be too surprised in the near future if you pull into a gas station and they're having a printer paper sale, or they're offering a free mouse pad with a fill-up.

As for buying a modem, there are numerous places to investigate. Start by checking out the Sunday paper and see who's having a sale. Electronics stores and large computer superstores are always advertising computer goods. You should also check out large office supply stores for good deals. All of these places specialize in large quantities and low prices. Don't expect the store personnel to be computer experts, but the prices will be competitive. Plus there's always a carnival atmosphere and lots of demonstrations to entertain anyone you choose to drag along with you on this quest.

> **Eavesdropping**
> If you really want to find out if a superstore is worth its salt, check out its return counter. Eavesdrop if you have to. If the customers are angry and upset or the store employees are belligerent and not the least bit accommodating, then this isn't the place to buy computer stuff. What a great tip, huh?

Smaller stores that specialize in computers and electronics are also good places to research a modem purchase. Despite slightly higher prices, the sales help usually possesses more expertise. Whether it's a chain or just a franchise, these smaller stores can offer you more personal service. The same with business computer stores. Large companies and businesses purchase big quantities of computer equipment from these stores. However, don't rule them out for a simple modem purchase. Such stores offer expertise and savvy advice, even if you do mistake them for office furniture showrooms.

Many stores offer installation, especially if you purchased the modem at their store. If you're wary about installing an internal modem, for instance, the extra cost to get the store's expert to install the modem may be well worth it.

Mail-order shopping is another avenue for buying a modem. There are direct mail catalogs to choose from as well as multipage advertising in the back of every known computer magazine. Generally, mail-order suppliers are legitimate. Like the retail stores, they also stand behind their products. The advantage to mail-order shopping is the competitive prices; you can find some real bargains. The disadvantages are that you have to pay for shipping and you can't actually "see" your modem before you buy it. However, if you've seen the product in a store and then find it for less through a mail-order company, by all means, order away!

Also, you may want to check out shops that sell used computer equipment. You may find a modem to get you by until you save up for a fast one—or at least find an inexpensive one you can practice with. These kinds of shops may also carry slower modems that are no longer popular with the state-of-the-art crowd.

Wherever you shop, be sure to ask questions when you have to. Even though you may suspect a lack of expertise, it never hurts to ask. Just to make you feel more confident, here's a list of questions that can help you:

- Is this the best modem available in its price range?
- Does it come with a manual and the appropriate cables?
- Does it have a warranty?
- What's the store's return policy like? What about exchanges?
- Does the store offer a repair service?
- Are you ripping me off? (Don't ask this unless the store frustrates you. And don't expect an honest answer either.)
- Where can I buy a bad toupee like yours? (Only ask this if the salesman has been rude to you.)

Money-Saving Tips

Sometimes it's really hard to be a good consumer—especially when you feel like you're out of your league. Shopping for computer goods can certainly take you out of your comfort zone, assuming that you're in one. It's not like picking out a new shirt or a ripe banana. You have to get in there and read the boxes, figure out what you're looking for, and then decide how much you're going to spend. To continue to help you through this difficult endeavor, here's additional information and some tips for buying a modem.

Free Software?

Look for free software with the modem. Remember, you can't use the thing without software. If you want to get started right away, you're going to need some software. Realize that it's not exactly free, either; nothing's free these days. Software packaged with a modem will make the modem's price go up. Also realize that it's probably not the best software for your needs. However, if you're looking for something to help you and your modem quickly get running, purchasing a modem that comes with a generic communications program is a good idea.

Ya Gotta Have a Manual

Whatever you do, never bring home a modem without a manual and an installation guide. For that matter, never bring home any electronic piece of equipment home without a manual. I don't have to tell you to save this item either, right? This written material is crucial—*crucial*, I tell you. You never know when you'll need it again, like when you have to reinstall or something. Of course, I realize a manual is difficult to read and incredibly confusing, not to mention boring. But hey—it will come in handy on occasion, so trust me on this one.

Watch Out for Warranties

Most computer manufacturers offer a five-year warranty on modems, and some even offer seven-year warranties. However, just stop a minute and ask yourself a couple of questions before you head up to the checkout counter. Are you going to use this product for five to seven years? Are you willing to pay extra for this warranty? This technology stuff is changing fast, and you may want a higher speed modem next year. Besides that, if there's something defective about your modem, it's going to show up right away, not five years from now.

What I'm trying to say is this: if it costs extra to have a warranty, don't bother. If the warranty is already part of the terrific price, great. And good grief, don't fall for that extended warranty scam. Many credit cards you use to purchase big-ticket items, such as a modem, offer warranties as well.

Does It Include an Online Service Hookup?

Most modems today come with offers for signing up with popular online services, such as CompuServe and PRODIGY. Sometimes these online services and their software come with modems for one low price. Whichever the case, check it out. It may be a good value if you stumble across it. On the other hand, you can easily hook up to these services the conventional way.

Brand Names to Look For

We've talked about prices, features, and where to shop. I've yet to mention specific brand names. Name brands are usually the safest to buy. There are many reputable manufacturers to choose from. Here are five top brands I like:

- Hayes
- Practical Peripherals
- Intel
- U.S. Robotics
- Supra

There are more than this. Consult a computer magazine and see who's on the top-ten lists. Many of the major computer publications do quarterly product testing and ranking, so find the appropriate issue and see who ranks where.

Make a Shopping List

This is it—you're armed and dangerous now. There's no stopping you and your quest for a modem. Just in case you have short-term memory, maybe you'd better make a shopping list to take along. I've whipped up a generic one that you can easily build on. Take a look at this:

- Internal or external? _____
- Price range? _____
- Modem speed? _____
- Specific modem standards?
  Hayes compatibility? _____
  V-series versions (which speeds do you want to communicate with)?
  _____
  Error correction and data compression? _____
- Speaker? _____
- Specific fax attributes? _____

Shopping for Software

By now, you're probably thinking that all your modem needs to start communicating is a good swift kick in the pants. Ah, if only that were so. What it really needs is software. Your software is the key to making contact with other modem people and computers.

It should come with some basic features to help you make those online connections, such as the capability to transfer files, terminal emulation, script language, and a few other basics.

For starters, you need to be aware of the different kinds of communications software. There are many software programs to choose from, most of which focus around two categories: general-purpose and service-specific. You can use general-purpose software, such as Qmodem or ZTerm, to communicate with other modem users, BBSs, and online services. Basically, general-purpose software is a generic program designed to meet a variety of modem needs. You need service-specific software for use with a particular online service. For example, to use America Online, you have to install its service-specific software or you'll never be able to connect. Of course, you can only use America Online's software with America Online, and not with any of the other online services.

Ask yourself what kind of software you need. Are you only going to use your modem to communicate with one online service all the time? Are you going to use your modem to connect to many different types of online opportunities? Are you just going to "talk" back and forth with your friend in Albuquerque? Your answers to these questions can help you determine what kind of software you need. Before you decide, read up about the various software features. This will help you determine exactly what you need. These features will focus on general-purpose software used with BBS chatting and some online services.

Software Features You Need to Know About

The following sections will describe the various software features that abound and what they can do for you. Remember that every communications program can perform some basic tasks. Also, more expensive programs can do more tasks or expand on the basic tasks.

Terminal Mode

One of the basics of any software program is *terminal emulation*. Terminal emulation is when you make your computer act like a plain old terminal. Why would you want to do that? When you use your modem to connect to another computer, you need to make your software program stay out of the way so you can tap into the other computer's power. For example, when you call up a big computer to look up a database, you need your computer to quit acting so smart and pretend to be an ordinary, powerless terminal. That way, you can send whatever you type directly to the computer you've dialed up, without letting your computer try to process the information itself. This is *terminal mode*.

> **It's Terminal**
>
> There are many different kinds of computers out there. Some are very powerful and some are just a simple monitor and keyboard. Online sites that you can dial up expect different kinds of computers to call. Some of these larger computers expect certain kinds of terminals to communicate with them. That's why your software program offers several basic terminal types to emulate, such as TTY, DEC VT52, and DEC VT100.
>
> The term *terminal* comes from early computer history when the only way of communicating to the giant mainframe computers of the '50s and '60s was through a keyboard and a simple monitor screen to show you what you typed.

Settings Mode

When you need to tell to your software program what to do, you need to use a *settings mode*. The settings mode lets you set up your software program to do what you want, without getting the modem involved yet. In settings mode, you can command the software, add phone numbers to your dialing directory, and adjust all of the modem's hardware settings. Simply put, settings mode lets you set the settings.

File Transfer

This is a major feature for all communications programs: the capability to transfer data files. File transfers are all about moving data back and forth along your communications link. For example, let's say you call up a BBS and there's an intriguing file on winter gardening (it's possible). You can copy that file onto your computer so you can read it. This process is *downloading*.

How about another scenario? Perhaps you've programmed a computer game and you want your friend in Buffalo to try it out. You can call him up with your modem and copy the files onto his computer. This process is *uploading*. When it comes to file transferring, uploading and downloading is the thing to do. You can upload and download files from online services, BBSs, and beyond. A file can be text, a graphic, a video clip (if you have a multimedia computer), a recipe, or a game, just to mention a few.

The Proper Protocols

There's one little catch to all of this uploading and downloading: *protocols*. A protocol is a set of rules that govern how two computers talk to each other with a modem. File protocols define how two computers send and receive data, and even which one sends first.

There are lots of protocols out there, and most communications software programs can support a good handful of them. It's safe to say this: the more protocols the software supports, the better.

In order for two computers to communicate, they must be using the same protocols. This is like visiting a foreign country where the people speak a different language. You may want to know where the nearest restroom is, but how are you going to ask someone without speaking their language? Unless you happen to have an translator with you, you're going to have a tough time. It's essential that two communicating computers speak the same language, or at least have a translator standing by.

I'll mention a few specific protocols. *Xmodem* is the name of an original binary file transfer protocol. It's kind of slow today, but it was used a lot in the '80s. Because of its widespread use, any communications software that you buy should support this protocol. *Zmodem* is the name of a fast file transfer protocol. Other protocols to look for on a software box are *Ymodem* and *Kermit* (not the frog).

It's Not in the Script

Another great feature found in communications software is *scripting*. Scripting lets you automate certain modem tasks you perform the most. For example, you can set up a script to log onto a BBS. The script could contain your name and password. Scripts can help you speed up the time you spend using a modem and software.

You can use scripts to make special menus, perform a function at the press of a single keyboard key, or retrieve your e-mail. Some programs even have "canned" scripts (premade) that will help you use a particular online service. If you want more productivity with your modem, look for scripting capabilities in the software that you purchase.

What's a Script?

Scripts are a lot like macros: recorded procedures for automating tasks you perform with a software program. You'll find macro features in word processing, spreadsheet, and database programs. To automate a task, you record the keystrokes you press to carry out the task. Then, you assign the recorded task to a single keystroke or a combination of keystrokes. Writing a script is very similar to recording a macro.

Miscellaneous Features

Why don't I tell you about some other features to look for in communications software? Look for a help function or context-sensitive help. This feature allows you to access information pertaining to the task you're trying to perform, read explanations about commands, and offer instructions on what to do next. Help features are useful, and they're also very common among software programs today.

You may also want a software program that offers text capturing capability. This lets you make a "picture" of what's on your screen and save it as a file so you can see it again. Make sure the software supports your modem speed and model. Other interesting features are built-in virus checking, archiving tools, and mouse support.

What's Hot and What's Not in Communications Software

You'll find brand names galore in the stores and catalogs when shopping for communications programs. Look for such hot products as ProComm Plus, QmodemPro, WinComm PRO, Smartcom, Crosstalk, Carbon Copy, White Knight, and others. You'll find software for faxing, too, such as WinFax PRO. Notice that you often see the letters COM or COMM? Communications is very important; it even shows up in the product name! Check out the computer magazines to see who thinks what product works best. That's the perfect place to find out what's hot. To find out what's not hot, look in the clearance rack at your local retail store. If you have a techie friend who uses a modem, ask him for a recommendation. If you're really clever, you'll get your friend to come over and install your program, too.

What? You have no friends? You want me to recommend something? I was trying to stay impartial. I like *all* the communications programs. (Personally, if I were you, I'd stick with the hot products listed in the previous paragraphs. Those are pretty good bets.)

In the following paragraphs, I'll offer some practical tips for searching for communications software.

How to Read the Software Box

You need to learn how to read the software box, or those pesky salespeople will really start to bother you. Here are some things to look for on the box:

➤ First, determine if the software meets your system requirements, or vice versa. Don't accidentally buy a Windows program if you're using DOS. (Okay, that one was pretty obvious—I'm just seeing if you're paying attention.)

➤ Check to make sure it supports the protocols you need, such as Xmodem, Kermit, Ymodem, Zmodem, and so on.

- ➤ Does it offer automatic COM port detection and selection? That's a nice thing to have.

- ➤ Does it have an unlimited data phone list? You can keep every modem number you ever want to call in such a list.

- ➤ What size are the disks? Will they fit your disk drive? There's nothing worse than getting home with software only to find it's the wrong disk size. If you're using a Mac, you won't have to worry about this one.

- ➤ Does it support several kinds of terminal emulations?

- ➤ Does it offer scripting language (for coding time-saving shortcuts)?

Once you purchase the software, make sure it comes with a manual and a registration card. If you don't send in your registration card, you'll never receive the oodles of junk mail the software company is waiting to send to you.

Your Modem Came with Software?

How convenient. There's a lot to be said about the software that gets packaged with modems. Some of this software is good, some of it is bad, and some of it will get you by until you have time to go out and buy software to meet your needs. That last approach is probably the best.

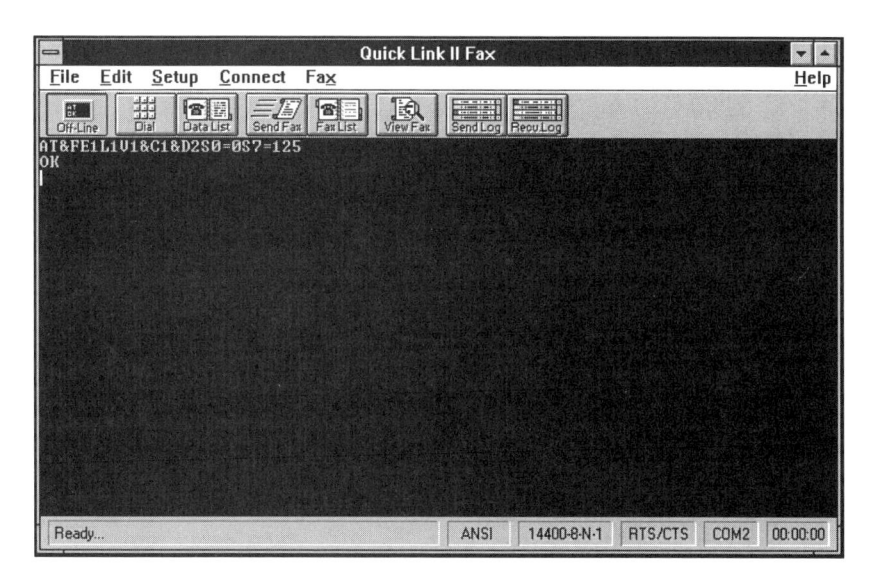

My Practical Peripherals modem came with Quick Link II software. You know what? I like it.

If software came with your modem, you may as well install it and see what it does. If you're a new modem user, you're probably anxious to get your modem up and running anyway, so installing the software will help. If you decide to install the software that came with your modem, be sure to keep the technical support number nearby—you're probably going to need it. Those software manuals leave a lot out.

If you decide that the free software isn't any good, go out and find an appropriate communications program to make you and your modem happy.

Searching for Software You Didn't Know You Had

Believe it or not, you may already have some communications software at your fingertips and not even know it. If you have any integrated software running on your computer system, such as Microsoft Works, Lotus Works, WordPerfect Works, or ClarisWorks, then you may have a communications program to get you online. Check your "Works" software box or manuals and see what's there and how to use it.

If you're using Microsoft Windows, you have a simple communications program called Terminal. You'll find it located in your Accessories group window. It's a little icon shaped like a phone and labeled "Terminal."

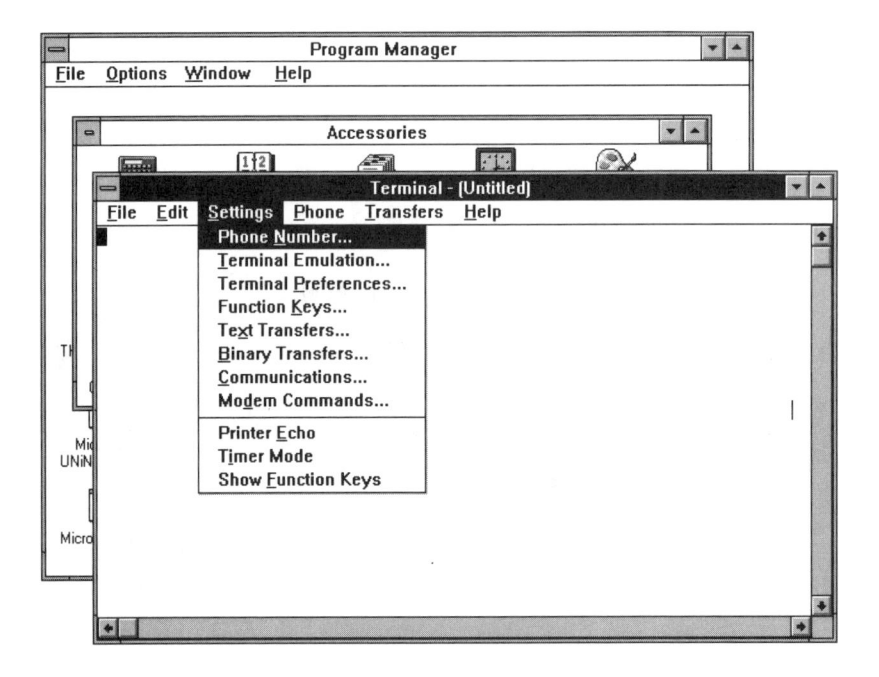

Windows Terminal program.

It's also a good idea to check your computer's hard drive for any directories or folders labeled COMM, Modem, or other words that look like communications stuff. A communications package may have been preloaded on your drive when you bought the computer.

Where to Shop for Software

Don't shop for communications software at your local gas station *yet*. Most likely, you'll find the hottest programs available at computer stores, office supply stores, and electronics stores. Mail-order catalogs are also an endless source of software. You can also look in the backs of computer magazines for a plethora of vendors and toll-free numbers. Just make sure you know what you're buying!

If you're looking for service-specific software, it's available in stores and catalogs, or from the online services themselves. There are many shareware programs you can try, so consult with your online buddies and see what they recommend.

Feeding and Caring for Your Modem

So, now that you're online chatting away via your modem, you're probably going to forget about taking care of the darn thing, right? Well, think again, pal. Your modem is an important part of your online communications, and you're going to need some helpful tips for taking care of the thing. For example, is there anything special you're supposed to do for it once you've installed it—like watering it twice a week? No, nothing like that. Your modem doesn't require a lot of high maintenance; however, you do need to take some steps in keeping it going—especially if you want it to last at least a few years before you decide to run out and buy the next fastest gadget on the technology horizon. The next few sections will give you some DOs and DON'Ts for the feeding and care of your modem.

These tips are mainly for external modem owners. If you're not one of those people, you can skip past all this stuff.

Spills, Chills, and Dust Pills

Your modem is a piece of electronic equipment, and therefore, susceptible to damage. (What isn't these days?) You wouldn't believe the accounts I've heard about modems that have been dropped, sat upon, mauled by a pit bull, shaken but not stirred, soaked with coffee, drooled on, thrown across a room, slept on by a cat, or baked at high temperatures. Of course, I don't have to tell you that most of these actions resulted in the demise of innocent modems.

It's a good idea to keep your modem out of the reach of small children, large dogs, and fat cats. I also caution you about having food and drinks near your modem—or near your computer for that matter. Do you know how many sad stories there are about naive computer newbies who inadvertently spill coke or coffee on their equipment in the middle of exciting online conversations and blow out fuses for blocks around? Liquids and electronics rarely go together well.

Another word of caution: although dust seems relatively harmless at first, it can make your modem malfunction if it gathers for too long. Too much dust is a bad thing with computers and computer components. (Of course, nobody likes to dust, including me. I used to tell everyone that the 1/4-inch of dust on my monitor screen was a glare filter. I've wised up since then, and you should heed my words.) Your external modem has a vent for keeping it cool. If that vent gets too clogged with dust, your modem can overheat. So, clean your modem off occasionally.

Be careful when you dust it, though. Try not to poke any dust into the vent holes; that could damage your modem's inner circuit board.

When you do actually clean off your modem, use a clean, slightly dampened cloth. Notice I didn't say dripping-wet cloth, but a slightly dampened one. You can use a spritz of cleaner on the cloth, if you want. Just don't try spraying it on your modem.

Also, you shouldn't stack anything on top of the modem vent. That cuts off its "air circulation," and it could overheat or faint from lack of oxygen.

The Surge Splurge

When you're dealing with electronics that you have to plug in, you have to worry about electrical surges. Why? Because they can wreak havoc on you and your computer. The havoc ranges from disconnecting you from the online chat you were conducting to completely frying your motherboard. To avoid such possibilities, invest in a quality power strip that has surge suppression.

A *power strip* is a long narrow box with several electrical outlets and an on/off switch. You can plug in your various computer components into the power strip, and then plug the power strip itself into your wall outlet. A power strip with surge suppression will protect the various components plugged into it from being affected by electrical surges. There are many brands and features to choose from. Look for one that specifically works to protect modems and fax modems. Whatever you do, get one; it's worth it.

Something else to note: any time an electrical storm sweeps through your area, you need to unplug all of your computer equipment, modem included. Ever heard of power spikes? Lightning can zap anything plugged into electrical sockets all over your house and really destroy electronic devices. This can damage computer stuff as well as VCRs, TVs, and stereos. So, pay attention to the weather reports and look out the window occasionally.

Going One-on-One, Modem-to-Modem

You don't have to sign up with an online service, join a BBS, or surf the Net to communicate using your modem. You can simply call up your friend who has a modem. Once you connect, you can exchange files, play games, or just chat—it's easy.

How Does It Work?

Modeming a friend is as simple as making a regular old phone call. In fact, you probably will have to make a regular old phone call to your modem friend to coordinate your connection. There are a couple of things you both need to establish before trying to connect. Let's go over these.

Host or Remote?

One of you has to decide if he's going to be the host or the remote user. The host sets up his computer to *host mode*, also called the *Answer mode*. This sets up your modem so that someone can call up your computer. Set your communications program to host mode. Other ways to set up host mode is to tell your software to issue an Auto-Answer command, or you can type in an AT command to do so; type in **ATS0=1** to reset your modem's S-register to Answer mode.

Host mode allows other modem callers to use the host's programs and access files (but not any files that have been locked and secured with a password). The remote caller can run the host's software programs, explore the host's computer, and even move files around. Naturally, you and your friend may want to establish some guidelines before committing to such activities. The host may not want all of his files moved around, you know.

If you have a fax modem, you're in Answer mode when you're receiving a fax. That's just a little tidbit I thought you'd like to know. Are those of you with speakers on your modems familiar with that shrieking noise that modems make when they connect? It turns out that the modem in the Answer mode generates the noise. So, when you set your own modem to Answer mode, it does the shrieking, and the calling modem responds with a detect signal that makes the connection complete. Isn't that the most fascinating thing you've ever heard of? Yeah, right.

Practical Parameters

The second thing you need to determine are the communications parameters. You and your friend must set both of the communicating computers to the same *parameters*. (Parameters define how the two computers will communicate.) If you don't, you'll never be able to communicate.

Most computers use the parameters 8-N-1, which translates to 8 data bits, parity set to None, and 1 stop bit. However, to be on the safe side, make sure your modem and your friend's modem are set to the same parameters, and decide what those parameters will be. Also, make sure you're both talking at the same speed. If your friend has a 2400 bps modem and you're using a 14,400 bps modem, you'll have to make your modem slow down and talk at 2400 bps, too. Most modems today have an auto-fallback mode that takes care of this for you.

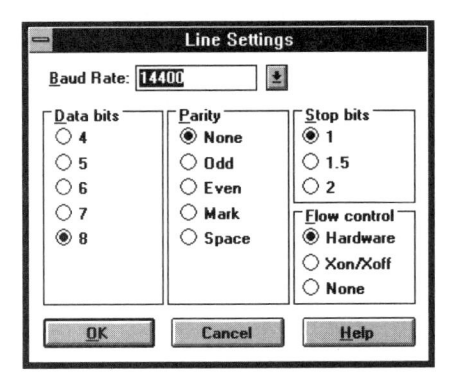

Typical communications parameter settings.

Making the Call

The final step in connecting is placing the call. Who did you decide was going to be the originator—the remote user? That person is the one who makes the call; he instructs his modem to call the host computer. Let's say you've volunteered to act as the remote user. Using either an ATDT command or your communications program dialing directory, dial up the other modem's number. Once you connect, you can easily begin communicating, transferring files, chatting, or whatever.

When Things Go Wrong

One of the problems you may encounter when communicating is the old double-character display. That's when every character you type appears twice on-screen, like you're stuttering. You can easily fix this by changing your modem's Echo or Duplex setting. Change your Duplex setting to Half Duplex or your Echo setting to Off (or On if that's the opposite of its current setting). You should be able to change your Duplex or Echo setting among your software's setting menus.

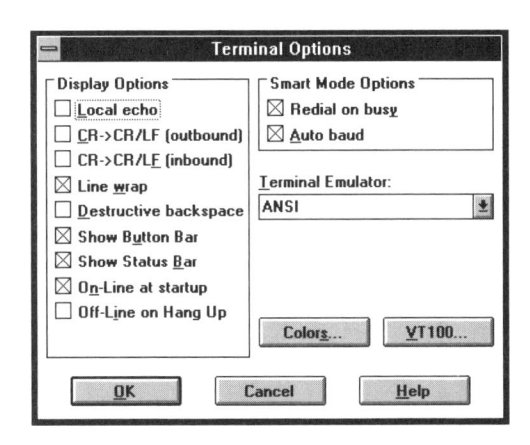

Look for your Echo or Duplex setting among your software's menus and dialog boxes.

Another problem you may face is a screen full of jumbled characters that make no sense whatsoever. When this happens, your communications parameters are not the same on both computers. You'll probably have to call each other with a regular old telephone call and coordinate your parameters again.

When you and your friend decide to exchange files, establish a file transfer protocol to use. You need to establish which protocols your respective modems can handle. After you've determined a common protocol, you need to know who's sending and who's receiving the file. If a file is being copied from the remote computer onto the host computer, that's uploading. If a file is being copied from the host computer to the remote computer, that's downloading. While the person on one end is initiating the downloading sequence, the person on the other end needs to initiate the uploading sequence.

That's just about all there is to going one-on-one. Some of it will involve a little trial and error before you get the hang of it. Once you do, you'll find great potential in being able to call up anyone with a modem and communicate.

Quit Reading This Book and Go Online

Okay... if this appendix hasn't equipped you to go online, I don't know what will. Get out there and chat, darn it. No more excuses. You have your modem, you have your software, and you know who you're going to call—so start dialing and quit hanging around these pages! (Unless you need help—then you can loiter as much as you want.)

Speak Like a Geek: The Complete Archive

America Online   A very popular online service. They call it AOL, for short. It offers a mix of features, from news to live chatting.

antivirus program   Checks the files you download for suspicious changes that may be caused by a virus. The antivirus program then alerts you to the danger, and assists in removing the virus from your system. See *virus*.

BBS   (1) British Broadcasting System (2) Short for Bulletin Board System. It's an electronic bulletin board that you can access through a modem. A BBS offers users a chance to communicate with other members (with e-mail, messages, and teleconferencing), to upload and download files, and to get help with computer problems.

bit   (1) Something you steer a horse with. (2) An abbreviation for **bi**nary digi**t**s. Each bit represents an electrical state, either ON or OFF. Eight bits combine to form a *byte*, representing a single character.

bps   Stands for **b**its **p**er **s**econd. Your computer measures modem speed by how many bits it can transfer during a single second. The higher the bps number, the faster the modem's speed.

byte   (1) Mosquitoes do this. (2) A byte is the equivalent of eight bits, such as 01000001, which represents the letter A. See *bit*.

COM port   Short for communications port. A special receptacle on the back of your computer for attaching communications hardware, such as a modem. Also called a serial port.

command   An instruction that tells the computer what to do.

Commercial online service   A service that offers you a variety of commercial features for your computer, such as news, sports, electronic shopping, stock reports, travel, and access to databases of information and files—all for a fee, of course. You can connect to an online service using your modem.

commercial software   A program you purchase through a store or catalog; it usually comes on disks you use to install the program onto your computer. There is usually a licensing agreement, as well as an identification number you enter when installing the software. When you use this software, you are saying you agree to all the terms in the license. Commercial software includes programs such as Microsoft Word, Lotus 1-2-3, or Aldus PageMaker.

communications software   A program that allows a computer to talk to its modem by communicating with other computers through the telephone lines.

CompuServe   One of the leading online services offering news, shopping, file transfers, and more.

cybersex   Simulated sex through your computer using words. (Like an erotic novel.)

dialing directory   A list of commonly called modem numbers that you can store in your communications program for easy usage.

download   To copy a file from another computer onto your computer.

duplex   A modem-software setting for controlling how your typed characters appear on-screen. The duplex setting can be half or full.

echo   (1) Something you listen to in a tunnel. (2) A modem-software setting for controlling how data appears on your monitor screen.

editor   (1) Someone who rewrites your text. (2) A very simple word processing feature found on BBSs and online services used for typing in messages.

e-mail   Stands for electronic mail. E-mail is any message sent to another online user.

emoticon   Special symbols typed in online chatting and messages that are used to convey emotions. :)

file transfer protocol   A protocol for checking the file data two communicating computers send and receive. You cannot transfer files unless the two computers are using the same protocols.

forum   An online special interest group or club where members with like interests can gather and exchange messages and information. Also called SIGs, RoundTables, clubs, bulletin boards, and newsgroups.

GEnie (1) Aladdin's friend. (2) General Electric's online service.

graphical user interface (GUI, pronounced "GOO-ey") A program interface that uses graphical elements, such as icons, dialog boxes, and pull-down menus. Mac and Windows use GUIs.

handshaking (1) What two business people do when they meet. (2) When two modems meet, they "shake hands" by settling on what protocols to use.

host mode When two or more computers are communicating, one usually serves in the role of host, like at a party. In most cases, the computer that you call ends up being the host. Some communications software programs let you turn your computer into a host so that friends can call you up and see all of your menus and screens.

icon (1) What that little train was always saying: "I think icon, I think icon." (2) A graphic image that represents a command, a program, or a feature.

Internet A vast network of many networks. Use it to access all kinds of data information around the world.

local access number A local phone number your modem can dial to hook up with an online service, without incurring long distance charges.

Log on/off To enter or exit a computer system.

modem An acronym for MOdulator/DEModulator. A modem lets a computer send and receive data through an ordinary telephone line.

network (1) How to find out what's *really* going on in the office. (2) Connecting several computers together for the purpose of sharing information.

newbie Someone who's just a beginner online or new to a service.

online To connect to another computer or network of computers.

online service Large commercial online services are places you can connect to with your modem to access news, databases, games, files, and more.

parameter A communications parameter defines a modem's settings, such as data bits, parity, and stop bits. In order for two computers to communicate, their parameters must match.

parity A communications parameter for controlling how your modem checks for errors when you send and receive files.

PRODIGY A popular online service that offers news, e-mail, message boards, shopping, and more.

protocol   Rules that determine how two computers will communicate and exchange data.

real-time   Actual time taking place now, even as you read this.

serial port   A port in the back of your computer used to attach printers, mice, and modems. Also called a COM port.

service provider   An organization that provides access to the Internet, usually for a fee.

service-specific software   A program created just for use with a particular online service.

shareware   Programs written by programmers for sharing among computer users on a trial basis. If you like it and decide to use the program, you send the programmer a registration fee to purchase it.

sysop   Short for **systems operator**, someone who oversees a BBS or an online area. They make sure everything is in order, especially uploaded files. They also monitor online activities and make sure everything is on the up-and-up. New users will find sysops very helpful in finding their way around a new online service or BBS. They answer questions and help out with problems, too.

teleconferencing   Live online chatting on a BBS or on the Internet.

terminal mode   A mode on your communications program that allows your computer to behave like a terminal to connect to large mainframes and minicomputers.

UNIX   An advanced, command-driven system used predominantly on the Internet.

upload   To copy a file from your computer onto another computer.

virus   (1) Something you can catch by touching doorknobs. (2) A program that vandalizes your computer system. The worst viruses destroy data and render your computer helpless. Others display strange messages, but do no damage. A virus can enter your system through an infected floppy disk or an infected file that you have downloaded. An *antivirus program* monitors changes to your files and alerts you to the presence of a virus.

Index

A

a2i Communications service provider, 234
abbreviations, 114-117
accounts
   bills, 207-208
   GEnie, 63
   online services, 22, 37-38
acronyms, 114-117
addiction (chatting), 204-206
advertising, 99
   business, 179-180
   e-mail, 181
age/sex check, 165
America Online, *see* AOL
ANSI graphics (BBSs), 89
ANSRemote service provider, 235
Answer modes, modems, 255
antivirus programs, 259
AOL (America Online), 52-57, 259
   chat rooms, 55-57
   logging on, 54
   phone number, 231
   rates, 57
   rating, 220
Apple (eWorld), 67
ARPANET, 70

B

BAARNet service provider, 234
BBSs (Bulletin Board Systems), 3, 11, 22-28, 84-88
   Boardwatch Magazine, 25
   callback verification, 89-90
   chatting, 90-92
   Computer Shopper, 25
   connecting, 24-25, 38
   directory, 235-237
   editor, 260
   graphics (ANSI), 89

handles, 90
hobbies, 127
logging on, 88-89
membership procedure, 89-90
phone numbers, 86-88
private messages, 161
software, 85-86
sysop (systems operator), 84, 262
technical support, 24
BCnet (British Columbia) service provider, 234
Bell Laboratories modem standards, 238
bills, 207-208
    accounts, 207
    credit cards, 39-40
bits, 259
Boardwatch Magazine (BBSs magazine), 25
bps (bits per second), 194, 259
brackets [ ], UNIX commands, 228
browsing, 126-127
business, 176-181
    advertising, 99, 179-181
    chat lines, 182-183
    e-mail, 181
    education, 183-184
    job-seeking, 182
    newsgroups, 176-178
        FAQs (Frequently Asked Questions), 179
        networking, 181
        online surveys, 181
bytes, 259

C

callback verification (BBSs), 89-90
capital letters (shouting), 99
CB Simulator (CompuServe), 50-52, 230
celebrity group discussions, 138
CERFnet—General Atomics/CERFnet service provider, 235
channels
    children, 167-172
    teenagers, 170-172
characters (troubleshooting), 196
chatting, 8-10
    addiction, 204-206
    AOL (America Online), 55-57
    BBSs, 90-92
    business, 182-183
    children, 164-167
    chitchat, 122-124
    CompuServe (CB Simulator), 50-52
    costs, 14-15
    ending conversations, 225
    flirting, 129-130
    GEnie, 64-65
    humor, 214-218
    lurking, 212
    online services (ratings), 220-221
    peak times, 213-218
    personas, 134-136
    pick-up lines, 224
    PRODIGY, 59-61

Index

ratings
   best, 221-222
   worst, 222
real-time, 9
rejection, 215
rudeness, 216-218
checking age/sex, 165
children, 164-167
   age/sex check, 165-166
   crime, 188
   pedophiles, 188
   personas, 171
   rooms, 167-171
   safety, 171-172
CICNet, Inc. service provider, 234
CIM (CompuServe Information Manager), 48-49
classes (business education), 183-184
coliseums (group discussions), 138
Colorado Supernet, service provider, 234
COM ports, 259
command-line operating system, 25
commands, 259
   IRC (Internet Relay Chat), 229
   UNIX, 227-229
commercial online services, 10, 20-22, 260
   see also, online services
commercial software, 260
communications software, 36, 260

CompuServe, 46-52
   CB Simulator, 50-52, 230
   CIM (CompuServe Information Manager), 48-49
   connecting, 47-48
   local access numbers, 47-48
   logging on, 48-49
   modems, 47
   phone number, 230
   rates, 52
   rating, 220
Computer Shopper (BBSs), 25
computers (help), 128
CONCERT service provider, 234
connecting
   BBSs, 24-25, 38
   CompuServe, 47-48
   Internet
      dial-in direct, 39
      dial-in terminal, 39
      service providers, 39, 71-75
   online services, 37-38
   permanent connections, 71
Consultive Committee on International Telegraphy, modem standards, 239
costs, 14-15
   bills, 39-40
   online services, 21
   saving money, 223
   see also rates
crackers, 189
credit cards

bills, 39-40
online services, 37-38
crime, 186
    children, 188
    crackers, 189
    free offers, 187
    hackers, 189
    harrassment, 189
    passwords, 186
    pedophiles, 188
    software distribution, 187-188
    viruses, 188
    see also safety
CSUnet service provider, 234
cybermanners, 96-98
cybersex, 131-134
    private messages, 217
    rejection, 215
cyberspace, 8, 260

D

dedicated connections, 71
DELPHI, 66
Demon Internet Limited (UK) service provider, 234
dial-in direct (Internet), 39
dial-in terminal (Internet), 39
dialing directory, 260
disconnects (troubleshooting), 193-194
downloading, 260
Duplex (troubleshooting modems), 195-196, 257, 260

E

e-mail, 9, 161-162, 215, 260
    advertising, 181
Echo (troubleshooting modems), 195-196, 257, 260
editors (BBS), 260
education (business), 183-184
ellipsis (...), UNIX commands, 228
emoticons, 106-110, 260
employment (job-seeking), 182
ending conversations, 225
Esc key (troubleshooting), 193
eWorld (Macintosh), 67, 221
external modems, 35

F

FAQs (Frequently Asked Questions), 102-103
    newsgroups, 179
faxing capabilities (modems), 242
female
    gender concerns, 147-151
    pick-up lines, 224
file transfer protocol, 260
files
    downloading, 260
    uploading, 262
flaming, 100, 137-138, 225-226

Index

flirting, 129-130
forums, 9, 260
free offers (crime), 187
freeware, 188
freezes (troubleshooting), 192-193

G

games (ImagiNation Network), 66-67
Gateway to the World service provider, 235
gender, 142
   female, 147-151
   male, 144-147
   neither, 151
GEnie, 61-62
   accounts, 63
   chatting, 64-65
   logging on, 64
   phone number, 233
   rates, 65
   rating, 221
graphics on BBSs (ANSI), 89
group discussions, 138
GUI (Graphical User Interface), 28-29, 261
   Macintosh computers, 30
   Windows, 30
guidelines (online behavior), 98

H

hackers, 97, 189
handles, 40-43
   BBSs, 90
   female, 147-151
   genderless, 151-152
   male, 144-147
handshaking (modems), 261
hanging
   troubleshooting, 192-193
harrassment, 103-104, 189
Hayes AT command set (modems), 242
Hayes Microcomputer Products Company, 242
help, 197-199
   computers, 128
history (Internet), 70
hobbies, 127-128
host mode, 255, 261
hotchat, 131-134
humor, 214-218

I

ICNet/Innovative Concepts service provider, 235
icons, 261
ImagiNation Network, 66-67

267

IMs (instant messages), 154-158
  see also private messages
interfaces (GUIs), 28-30
internal modems, 35
Internet, 11, 27-28
  ARPANET, 70
  connecting
    dial-in direct, 39
    dial-in terminal, 39
    permanent connections, 71
    service providers, 71-75
  history, 70
  NSF (National Science Foundation), 70
  service providers, 26, 71-75
    connecting, 39
    phone numbers, 234-235
  UNIX, command-line operating system, 25
InterNIC Information Services service provider, 235
IRC (Internet Relay Chat), 158-160, 229

J-K-L

job-seeking, 182

JVNCnet service provider, 234

killing messages (software), 103-104

language (netiquette), 216

light (troubleshooting modems), 196

local access numbers, 261
  CompuServe, 47-48
  online services, 22
logging off (automatic), 194, 261
logging on, 261
  AOL (America Online), 54
  BBSs, 88-89
  CompuServe, 48-49
  females, 147-151
  genderless, 151-152
  GEnie, 64
  males, 144-147
  PRODIGY, 58-59
lurking, 212
  browsing, 126-127

M

Macintosh
  eWorld, 67
  GUI (Graphical User Interface), 30
mail, see e-mail
males (gender), 144-147
  pick-up lines, 224
MBnet service provider, 234
membership procedure (BBSs), 89-90
message boards, 9
messages (private), 103, 154-158, 217
  BBSs, 161
  IRC (Internet Relay Chat), 158-160
  online services, 160
MichNet service provider, 234

Index

Microcom Networking Protocol, 238-239
Microsoft Network, 221
MIDnet service provider, 234
modems, 34-36, 261
   Answer modes, 255
   bps (bits per second), 194
   brand names, 246
   communications software, 36
   CompuServe, 47
   dialing directories, 260
   duplex, 260
   external, 35
   faxing capabilities, 242
   handshaking, 261
   Hayes compatibility, 242
   host mode, 255
   internal, 35
   local access numbers, 261
   maintenence, 253-255
   parameters, 261
   purchasing, 237-246
   speed, 36, 194, 240
   standards, 238-240
   TDD communications capabilities, 243
   troubleshooting
     light, 196
     phone lists, 195
     settings, 195-196
MSEN, Incorporated service provider, 234

N

National Science Foundation (NSF), 70
NETCOM service provider, 235
NetILLINOIS service provider, 234
netiquette, 96-98
   FAQs (Frequently Asked Questions), 102-103
   flaming, 100
   guidelines, 98
   harrassment, 103-104
   language, 216
   personas, 98
   punctuation, 100
   rudeness, 216-218
   shouting, 99
networking (business newsgroups), 181
networks, 261
newbies, 102-103, 261
newsgroups, 9
   business, 176-178
     advertising, 179-180
     networking, 181
   FAQs (Frequently Asked Questions), 179
   spamming, 180
nicknames, 40-43
   see also handles
NSF (National Science Foundation), 70

269

O

OARnet service provider, 234
online services, 10, 20-22, 27-28
    accounts, 22, 37-38
    AOL (America Online), 52-57, 259
        chatting, 55-57
        logging on, 54
        phone number, 231
        rates, 57
    commercial, 260
    CompuServe, 46-52, 260
        CB Simulator, 50-52
        CIM (CompuServe Information Manager), 48-49
        connecting, 47-48
        local access numbers, 47-48
        logging on, 48-49
        phone number, 230
        rates, 52
    connecting, 37-38
    credit cards, 37-38
    DELPHI, 66
    eWorld, 67
    GEnie, 61-65
        accounts, 63
        chatting, 64-65
        logging on, 64
        phone number, 233
        rates, 65
    ImagiNation Network, 66-67
    local access numbers, 22
    phone numbers, 229-233
    private messages, 160
    PRODIGY, 57
        chatting, 59-61
        logging on, 58-59
        phone number, 232
        rates, 61
    rates, 21
    ratings, 220-221
    service providers, 262
    software, 22
online surveys (business), 181

P

parameters, 261
parity, 261
passwords, 186
peak times, 213-218
pedophiles, 188
permanent connections, 71
personas, 98, 134-136
    children, 171
    gender, 142
        female, 147-151
        male, 144-147
        neither, 151
    profiles, 142-144
phone lists, 195
phone numbers
    BBSs, 86-88, 235-237
    Internet service provders, 234-235

Index

local access numbers, 22
   online service providers, 229-233
pick-up lines, 224
Portal service provider, 235
ports
COM, 259
   serial, 262
   privacy, 97-98
power strips, 254-255
private messages, 103, 154-158, 217
   BBSs, 161
   IRC (Internet Relay Chat), 158-160
   online services, 160
   responses, 226
   see also IMs (Instant Messages)
PRODIGY, 57
   chatting, 59-61
   logging on, 58-59
   phone number, 232
   rates, 61
   rating, 220
profanity, 99
profiles, 142-144
protocols, 260, 262
PSInternet service provider, 234
punctuation, 100
   expressing emotion, 110-112

R

rates, 14-15
   AOL (America Online), 57
   bills, 39-40
   CompuServe, 52
   GEnie, 65
   online services, 21
      credit cards, 37-38
   PRODIGY, 61
   saving money, 223
   see also costs
rating chatting, 220
   best, 221-222
   worst, 222
real-time chatting, 9, 262
rejection, 215
relationships, 130-131
responding to private messages, 226
rooms
   AOL chatting, 55-57
   browsing, 126-127
   children, 167-172
   teenagers, 170-172
rudeness, 216-218

S

safety (children), 171-172
   see also crime
saving money, 223
scripts software, 249

security
    passwords, 186
    virus protection, 188
sending private messages
    BBSs, 161
        IRC (Internet Relay Chat), 158-160
        online services, 160
sends (private messages), 154
serial ports, 262
service providers, 26
    connecting, 39
    Internet, 71-75
    phone numbers, 234-235
service-specific software, 262
SESQUINET service provider, 235
sex, 131-134
    see also, cybersex
shareware, 188, 262
shouting, 99
smileys, 106-110
software
    antivirus, 259
    BBSs (Bulletin Board Systems), 85-86
    commercial, 260
    communications, 36, 250-253, 260
    crime, 187-188
    file transfer capabilities, 248
    freeware, 188
    killing messages, 103-104
    online services, 22
    protocols, 248
    purchasing, 246-253

scripting capabilities, 249
service-specific, 262
settings modes, 248
shareware, 188, 262
terminal emulation, 247-248
terminology, 250
sound cards, 217
sound waves (private messages), 217
spamming (newsgroups), 180
specific interests, 127
speed (modems), 36, 194
standards (modems), 238-246
support service (help), 197-199
SURAnet service provider, 235
surveys (business), 181
symbols (smileys), 106-107
sysops (system operators), 84, 97, 262
    automatic logging off, 194

T

taglines, 110
TDD communications (modems), 243
technical support BBSs, 24
teenagers, 164-167
    age/sex check, 165-166
    channels, 170-171
    rooms, 167-171
    safety, 171-172
teleconferencing, 262

272

terminal emulation software, 247-248
Terminal mode (troubleshooting modems), 195-196, 262
text (troubleshooting), 197
troubleshooting, 192
    characters, 196
    disconnects, 193-194
    freezes, 192-193
    help, 197-199
    modems, 195
        light, 196
        phone lists, 195
        settings, 195-196
        speed, 194
    text, 197

U-Z

UNIX, 25
    commands, 227-229

uploading, 262

UUNET service provider, 234

viruses, 188, 262

warranties (modems), 245

Windows (GUI), 30

World dot Net service provider, 234

World service provider, 235

WVNET service provider, 234

GET CONNECTED
to the ultimate source of computer information!

The MCP Forum on CompuServe

Go online with the world's leading computer book publisher! Macmillan Computer Publishing offers everything you need for computer success!

Find the books that are right for you!
A complete online catalog, plus sample chapters and tables of contents give you an in-depth look at all our books. The best way to shop or browse!

➤ Get fast answers and technical support for MCP books and software

➤ Join discussion groups on major computer subjects

➤ Interact with our expert authors via e-mail and conferences

➤ Download software from our immense library:
  ▷ Source code from books
  ▷ Demos of hot software
  ▷ The best shareware and freeware
  ▷ Graphics files

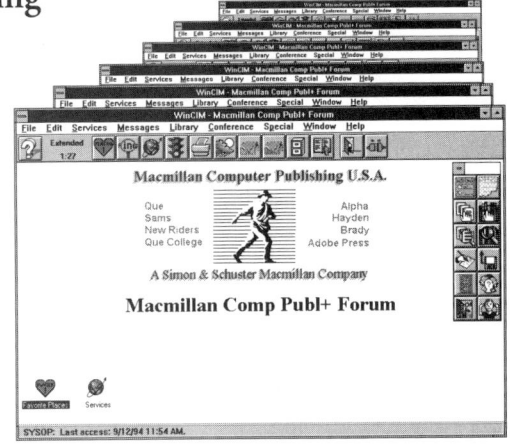

Join now and get a free CompuServe Starter Kit!

To receive your free CompuServe Introductory Membership, call **1-800-848-8199** and ask for representative #597.

The Starter Kit includes:
➤ Personal ID number and password
➤ $15 credit on the system
➤ Subscription to *CompuServe Magazine*

Once on the CompuServe System, type:

GO MACMILLAN

for the most computer information anywhere!

MACMILLAN COMPUTER PUBLISHING

CompuServe

PLUG YOURSELF INTO...

The Macmillan Information SuperLibrary™

Free information and vast computer resources from the world's leading computer book publisher—online!

FIND THE BOOKS THAT ARE RIGHT FOR YOU!
A complete online catalog, plus sample chapters and tables of contents give you an in-depth look at *all* of our books, including hard-to-find titles. It's the best way to find the books you need!

- **STAY INFORMED** with the latest computer industry news through our online newsletter, press releases, and customized Information SuperLibrary Reports.
- **GET FAST ANSWERS** to your questions about MCP books and software.
- **VISIT** our online bookstore for the latest information and editions!
- **COMMUNICATE** with our expert authors through e-mail and conferences.
- **DOWNLOAD SOFTWARE** from the immense MCP library:
    - Source code and files from MCP books
    - The best shareware, freeware, and demos
- **DISCOVER HOT SPOTS** on other parts of the Internet.
- **WIN BOOKS** in ongoing contests and giveaways!

TO PLUG INTO MCP:

GOPHER: gopher.mcp.com
FTP: ftp.mcp.com

WORLD WIDE WEB: http://www.mcp.com

The Complete Idiot's Guides to Computer Topics

More Fun Learning from Alpha Books!

If you liked this *Complete Idiot's Guide*, check out these other completely helpful books!

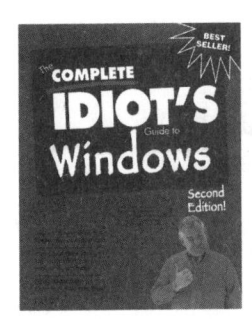

The Complete Idiot's Guide to Windows, Second Edition
ISBN: 1-56761-546-5
$16.95 USA

The Complete Idiot's Guide to PCs, New Edition
ISBN: 1-56761-459-0
$16.95 USA

The Complete Idiot's Guide to DOS, Second Edition
ISBN: 1-56761-496-5
$16.95 USA

The Complete Idiot's Guide to the Internet, Second Edition
ISBN: 1-56761-535-X
$19.95 USA

Look for these books at your favorite computer book retailer, or call 1-800-428-5331 for more information!

Okay, so you finished this book and now you can do all the basic stuff that gets you through the day. Congrats!

But what about those other cool features you never get to use? Welcome to the perfect follow-up to *The Complete Idiot's Guide!*

The Complete Idiot's Next Step!

Ready to move to the next step?!

The *Next Step* books begin where *The Complete Idiot's Guides* leave off. You learn how to use all those powerful features that make life easier. And it all comes in the same lighthearted, beginner-style format that the *Idiot's Guides* are famous for!

Plus, the *Next Step* books come with a free disk full of software to make your work even more impressive! Get full-powered results without all the work!

NOW AVAILABLE ➤

The Complete Idiot's Next Step with Windows
ISBN: 1-56761-525-2,
$19.95 USA

The Complete Idiot's Next Step with the Internet
ISBN: 1-56761-524-4,
$19.95 USA

You too can do things like an expert—without actually being one!

Who Cares What *YOU* Think?

WE DO!

We're not complete idiots. We take our readers' opinions very personally. After all, you're the reason we publish these books! Without you, we'd be pretty bored.

So please! Drop us a note or fax us a fax! We'd love to hear what you think about this book or others. A real person—not a computer—reads every letter we get, and makes sure your comments get relayed to the appropriate people.

Not sure what to say? Here's some stuff we'd like to know:

- Who are you (age, occupation, hobbies, etc.)?
- Which book did you buy and where did you get it?
- Why did you pick this book instead of another one?
- What do you like best about this book?
- What could we have done better?
- What's your overall opinion of the book?
- What other topics would you like to purchase a book on?

Mail, e-mail, or fax your brilliant opinions to:

Product Development Manager
Que
201 West 103rd Street
Indianapolis, IN 46290
FAX: (317) 581-4669

CompuServe: 75430,174
Internet: 75430.174@compuserve.com